Owner.

Nicholas Cortys.

2 Abbey Place,
Wexford Soon.

TEL → 21548.

THE IRISH TIMES
SPORTING YEAR
2001

Edited by
MALACHY LOGAN

Gill & Macmillan

Gill & Macmillan Ltd
Hume Avenue
Park West
Dublin 12
with associated companies throughout the world
www.gillmacmillan.ie

© 2001 *The Irish Times*
0 7171 3337 0
Design by Identikit Design Consultants, Dublin
Print origination by Carole Lynch
Printed by Butler & Tanner Ltd, Frome, Somerset

*The paper used in this book is made from the wood pulp
of managed forests. For every tree felled, at least one tree
is planted, thereby renewing natural resources.*

A catalogue record is available for this book
from the British Library.

1 3 5 4 2

C O N T E N T S

INTRODUCTION

To see a book through from conception to publication requires almost as large a squad as an average GAA or rugby panel. For a volume like *The Irish Times Sporting Year 2001* this figure can safely be doubled.

Throughout the year *Irish Times* sports writers have covered the whole spectrum of national and international sport and this book relives many of the moments from 2001 that will be argued over and treasured for years to come.

The sporting journey through 2001 has been never less than fascinating. Every month threw up its controversies, its triumphs and its failures. Heroes and villains disappeared almost as quickly as they emerged. But the sublime moments that caught the breath and warmed the heart will live for a long time.

Who will forget the adventures of the Republic of Ireland soccer team and their heroic victory over Holland in September, or the wizardry of Brian O'Driscoll for Ireland and the Lions, or the captivating performances of Galway and Tipperary in winning the All-Ireland Football and Hurling championships?

Compiling and editing *The Irish Times Sporting Year 2001* has been as challenging as it has been enjoyable. While reports on all of the major events of the year are chronicled in detail, the book also includes the background stories and analysis on the issues that framed the sporting year and will continue to set headlines in 2002 and beyond.

Complementing these reports are the offbeat stories and quotes that gave the sporting year many of its lighter and more amusing moments.

I would like to express my gratitude to countless colleagues and friends who helped in the production of this book, the Editor of *The Irish Times*, Conor Brady, who gave it the green light and the Commercial Director, Maeve Donovan, who tied up all the loose ends in the initial stages.

I would also like to record my particular appreciation to Breda Keating of *The Irish Times* for helping in so many ways and for keeping the project on track at all times. Other *Irish Times* sports department colleagues who assisted in a multitude of ways were Tom Humphries, Liam Ryan,

Eddie Longworth, Damian Cullen and Carol Kirwan. The photographic department also offered unswerving co-operation and enthusiasm. Imaging Editor Dermot O'Shea, Photographic Editor Peter Thursfield and his team at the picture desk, Paul Hayden, Terry Thorpe, Mark McGrath and Derek Grant are owed a special thank you. The advice, patience and encouragement of Fergal Tobin and Deirdre Greenan at Gill & Macmillan also proved invaluable in bringing it all together, as did the kindness and understanding of Mary, Jack, Ailbhe and Ben.

I hope that readers derive as much pleasure and entertainment from this book as sport has given us throughout 2001.

Malachy Logan
Sports Editor
The Irish Times
October 2001

THE VALUE
OF SPORT

Well, a year's worth of sport in a time when some would say that sport isn't worth what it used to be. We have no index for these things, no handy conversion chart. The 24-hour market in sports doesn't produce those type of results. Sport just goes on, sport just gives us its harmless simulacrums of triumph and disaster in the face of war, hysteria, wealth, poverty, famine, pestilence and the Beckham family.

We have no ready reckoners for measuring the value of sport in bad times as opposed to good times. We have hokey theories about perspective and creaky notions that sport and politics don't mix. Or that they are forever inseparable. Who knows anymore?

We know that this was a year of unrelenting bad times though. No doubt about it. From the biblical darkness which descended on these islands when the sheep began to get sick in early spring, to the epochal images we were left with when a bright September morning in lovely Manhattan turned into a heap of charnel house memories.

It was a year when people without imagination decided that sport ought to know its place. There is a ghoulish pleasure taken by those who don't understand sport in chastising those who set their daydreams to sports seasons. It seems that it is never indecent to count the loss of money which disaster brings, to fret openly about stocks and shares, to wonder when the greasy till will be open for fumbling in again.

The joy of sport is to be shelved however. Mere romance and distraction saps the will of ordinary people when stern men in suits are convincing them that here is a policy or a god worth dying for.

Well they are wrong. If we are going to go in a great fireball of indignant self-immolation I'm for being in a stadium watching somebody do what they do best as I go. I'm for the sense of community, the sense of sharedness which sport brings. I'm for defiantly enjoying that as we say goodbye.

What else brings us together, what else provides us with such a harmless valve for letting off our energies? There are two things which bring the world together in its sitting-room, watching the same pictures and thinking the same thoughts. Great sporting moments and war. When CNN blithely released its viewing statistics for its comprehensively numbing coverage of the World Trade Centre attack, it was framed somewhat poignantly by the figures for past Superbowls.

I'm for teaching the mullahs the harmless joy of the Mexican wave, I'm for getting George W. to spend a few afternoons at the baseball park with some beer in one hand and some crackerjack in the other. Sport should be mandatory for world leaders. Not just as an electoral touchstone but as a duty. Get out and coach some little league, go and watch some girls' camogie, take a group of ten-year olds to Old Trafford for the first time. Then come back and let's talk about perspective.

So pass the iodine tablets Joe Jacobs, we're going to a game. The year just past was never billed as a vintage one for sport and it was bookended by disasters but, hey, we enjoyed it anyway. Are you going to sue us?

We loved the unlikely, bloody-minded rise of the Irish soccer team. There is a mendacity in their relations with press and public which does them no good but, somehow, even the most callow among the squad rise to a certain heroism in the green jersey. All through their freakish World Cup campaign we have watched the antics of our defence with our hands over our faces peeping through the crack between our fingers screaming that we can't look, we can't look.

Yet Richard Dunne has somehow unicycled across the tightrope. Ian Harte's aversion to tackling has been kept a secret. Steve Staunton's return from mothballs has been a success. And the fact that the strikers still hang onto their job title has more to do with a superstitious belief in footie feng-sui – for serenity you should always arrange your furniture with two items at the front – than any goals they might have scored? Well who cares? Just recite the names. Overmars, Stam, Zenden, Davids, Kluivert, Van Nistelrooy etc. NOT going to the World Cup!

And what of the longest Gaelic football season ever? A success surely. Small boats were floated on the great tide of matches which swept over us. Westmeath were perhaps the team of the year. Sligo and Carlow had novel summers. Even Wicklow had an afternoon wherein they set out the good china and crispest linen and entertained Galway in Aughrim.

It was wonderful. The Dubs and Kerry in Thurles twice. The piquancy of Maurice Fitzgerald's famous sideline kick. The saga of Meath's progress which seemed settled when they blew Kerry away in a mesmerising game in Croke Park. And the healing that went on within the Galway camp. The team, which more than any other in recent memory has been a band of (many sets of) brothers, seemed to be splintered and sundered in May. Yet they looked like a different team in September as Padhraic Joyce scored ten and Declan Meehan ignored speeding restrictions and Kevin Walsh defied the ageing process.

Hurling had a good if not epic summer. If the clearest chime of the year was Galway's defeat of Kilkenny, well, Tipperary still deserved their All-Ireland, not just for their patient orchestration of a young team, but for hitting more high notes than anyone else. They played the best and they beat the best. The lesson for hurling lies in football's success. More radical change than what is proposed for next year is needed. Round robin series of games, more and more matches. The game can only grow.

Rugby stood in a state of suspended animation for much of the summer. The Triple Crown was anticipated in months when it should have been but a memory. Then Autumn came and that was what it became. A memory. But there was good stuff to recall too – Irishmen in Lions' jerseys, the national fascination with the European Cup, a sense of optimism long missing from the domestic game.

So it went elsewhere. Golf was to be eaten by Tiger Woods, but ended up providing a major for Retief Goosen. The Ryder Cup, perhaps the event in sport which actually needed perspective was postponed for a year. Perhaps when it comes around it will have some of the lightness of former times restored to it.

And on and on. We could delve into detail in a hundred sports, thousands of events, millions of names. No need. It is enough to think of all the names out there – competing and practising and cheering – and be sustained by the commonality of what they do.

In bad times what unites us is more important than what divides us. That might not be the spirit which inspired all the words in this collection, but it is the thought best taken from them. So that's it. Sport, memories and words, a little souvenir of an otherwise terrible year.

Tom Humphries
The Irish Times
September 2001

Rare fall . . . Champion hurdler Istabraq and Charlie Swan crash at the last flight in the AIB December Festival Hurdle at Leopardstown. The race was won by the Barry Geraghty-ridden Moscow Flyer (centre). Photograph: Matt Kavanagh.

JANUARY

2001

HIGHLIGHTS

1 Jan: New Year's Day and the Premiership title race is already over. Boring, boring Manchester United extend their lead to 11 points after a 3–1 win over West Ham. Owner JP McManus purchases Cheltenham Gold Cup favourite First Gold and Stayers' Hurdle favourite Baracouda for a price in the region of £750,000.

2 Jan: Martin O'Neill's Celtic beat Kilmarnock 6–0 and go into the Scottish season's winter break with an 11-point cushion over the unlikely lads of Hibernian.

3 Jan: Irish rugby stalwart Sir Ewart Bell dies, aged 76.

5 Jan: Businessman Richard Burrows goes public with his challenge to Olympic Council president Pat Hickey.

8 Jan: Shay Given, out of favour at Newcastle, submits a transfer request. Eight days later, the Newcastle board turn it down and tell Given to get on with it.

9 Jan: England manager-elect Sven Goran Eriksson steps down as manager of Lazio, hastening the arrival of a Swede at Lancaster Gate.

13 Jan: Down 15–0, Munster do another Lazarus act at Newport, winning 39–24 and ensuring their place in the European Cup quarter-finals.

15 Jan: The Fennelly brothers may forever be associated with Kilkenny hurling, but Kevin shows that it isn't all glamour by taking on the Dublin manager's job.

16 Jan: Track and field great Heike Drechsler admits she took part in the infamous East German doping programme.

21 Jan: Istabraq bounces back after his New Year's Eve fall with a win in the AIG Champion Hurdle at Leopardstown. Rally great Bertie Fisher and two of his children die after his helicopter crashes in Fermanagh.

22 Jan: FAI board of management meeting hears the cost of the proposed Eircom Park will be £130 million, £56 million more than original estimates. Chief executive Bernard O'Byrne remains steadfast in his belief that it will be built.

23 Jan: After 20 years in the maroon of Galway, Joe Cooney hangs up his inter-county hurley.

27 Jan: Jennifer Capriati, the teenage prodigy who fell from grace with drugs and shoplifting problems, completes her return from the edge with victory at the Australian Open.

28 Jan: With the help of three Anthony Foley tries, Munster qualify for the European Cup semi-final with a 38–29 win over Biarritz at Thomond Park.

2 JANUARY 2001

Lockerroom: All the Dope on the Year Gone By

Tom Humphries

2000? How was it for you? Tiger Woods set the tone did he not? All Tiger Woods, all the time. Enough for everybody. Except Tiger. Tiger won everywhere with a majesty which was unprecedented but he sang dumb on Nike employment practices in the Third World and then scabbed on striking actors to make a car ad in Canada before rounding off the year by letting it be known his unimaginable income is, frankly, insufficient. Tiger would like a bigger slice of that TV pie please.

Eurotrash caught the mood. Richard 'I Am Absolutely Innocent' Virenque, who denied for two years he had permitted anything stronger than an Anadin to pass his lips, cheerfully admitted to a courtroom that, well, he was gobbling the gear just the same as all the other boys. Quelle surprise! Willy Voets, whom Virenque had coldly sold down the Swannee River, stood and embraced Virenque.

By year's end we had a new word to add to the lexicon of cheating: Actovegin. 'I am absolutely innocent,' said Lance Armstrong as authorities investigated why his team car had so much Actovegin in the glove compartment.

Respect, too, to CJ Hunter, trundling around Europe in the grand style. Hey, if it's Tuesday, I must be testing positive in Oslo. What a touch to come to an Olympic press conference and weep before the media low-lifes. And bravo to his lovely wife, Marion Jones, who had the chutzpah to launch her 'drive for five' and then entertain us by suggesting she never noticed anything different about her bad-tempered, souped-up chappie. He's just a big ole testosterone bear ...

Merlene Ottey was forcibly inserted on to the Jamaican track team. Ouch! You know, once upon a time we found Merlene inspiring.

Robbie Keane, without a full season of Premiership football under his belt, was whisked away to Internazionale. All's well that ends well. He finally found a decent home and we must wait to see how being transferred for more than £30 million before you are 21 years-old affects him. Hopefully he will be untouched.

In Lisbon one night, Luis Figo, the most expensive footballer in the world, spent more time talking with Irish journalists than did the Irish team collectively. And that was on a good night. Genetic scientists are said to be reaching the breakthrough stage in their work on the first non-surly Irish player of the post-Charlton era. Wasn't there a time when to be young, gifted and rich meant being happy as well?

At home, the Gaelic Players' Association became the first people ever to attempt to gatecrash the GAA Congress, therein to sample the pious grooves. Relations between top players and the media became so distant and joyless a hack would have a better chance of interviewing Lord Lucan between the months of July and October.

Speaking of the disappeared, that odd woman from the Sindo made it a touchstone of all virtue here in the land of the saints and scholars to announce piously that all paralympians are a great wee bunch altogether; which is a pity, because any event that includes an entirely phoney Spanish basketball team, 10 juiced weightlifters and athletes tying piano wire around their scrotums or clamping their catheters in order to get their central nervous system illegally kick-started deserves closer examination than a quick pat on the head allows.

Kevin Keegan spat his dummy out. Ronnie Delany and Michelle Smith schmoozed with Marion Finucane, shiny, happy, champions all. Inge de Bruijn metamorphosed.

Ian Thorpe felt obliged to offer to have his blood frozen for future examination. When we heard that we didn't even know what Actovegin was, but it seemed like a good idea anyway. The

Silver lining in Sydney . . . Sonia O'Sullivan en route to second place in the Olympic 5,000 metres final in the magnificent Olympic Stadium in Sydney, one of the most heart-warming stories from 2000. Photograph: Eric Luke.

Irish Olympic effort dissolved into all-out civil war. Watch this space for news of the tribunal.

The FAI deployed blue smoke and mirrors to convince itself it needed a big stadium with a roof and an oppressive mortgage over it more than it needed life itself. In a moving humanitarian gesture, An Taoiseach, The People's Champion, Wearer of Anoraks and Drinker of Bass, The Little Flower of Drumcondra, insisted he would be building his BertieBowl even if only to stage three rugby games a year. Give us your huddled, prawn sandwich-eating masses ...

Mike Tyson announced that he would like to eat Lennox Lewis's children. Paul Ingle almost left us. Wayne McCullough sped through the warning lights. The NBA airbrushed the jewellery and tattoos from the picture of a black player gracing the cover of its official magazine; the same player, Allen Iverson, released a record apparently endorsing hate crimes against gays.

What else? The US Olympic Committee's former anti-doping head, Wade Exum, launched a legal action against the USOC alleging consistent attempts to suppress positive tests ... the Irish Amateur Boxing Association refused to release the name of one of its members who tested positive for drugs ... two NFL stars were charged with separate murders ... NHL star Marty McSorley received a record ban after assaulting Chris Brashear on the ice; McSorley said that his axeman's swing

From Tallaght to San Siro . . . Robbie Keane in an Inter Milan shirt after his early-season move from Leeds United.

at Brashear was merely intended to provoke a fight …

Cricket was blown apart by a match-fixing scandal. The rivalry between southside rugby schools in Dublin spilled over into something more ugly than songs about bestiality … Dianne Modahl lost her case, alleging that she had been treated unfairly by a British athletics federation disciplinary hearing … Marie Jo Perec fled the Olympics claiming intimidation …

There was more, lots more, but my head isn't right this morning and this is just a scoop from the top of it. 2001? Well sure, here's to sport retaining its lovely, uncomplicated innocence in these crazy times.

5 JANUARY 2001

United Way Suits Young Contender

Emmet Malone talks to a young man in the foothills of what may be a remarkable career

If you're blessed with a name like Jedd Gaff, then you've got to be good to survive in the often wonderful but sometimes desperately cruel world of professional football. But Gaff, a young centre half who had a spell in the Manchester United youth team, wasn't quite good enough, and two years ago Alex Ferguson took him aside to tell him the bad news.

While it must have seemed like the end of the world for Gaff, aspiring professionals come and go every day of the week at clubs like United and the comings and goings tend to be linked – indeed Gaff was being released to make way for another, younger, and more promising centre-half.

United had beaten off competition from a string of big clubs to land the new boy and here he was, newly-arrived from Waterford.

Enter John O'Shea, fresh-faced but well used to being much sought after. The young Irishman was thinking only of success when he arrived to start his new life at Old Trafford, but before he had really settled, Gaff's departure was to teach him something about failure in his chosen career. 'It was hard,' O'Shea recalls now, 'because they moved me into his digs so I was taking his home as well as his place in the team.'

Gaff's career path has seen him quit football and he is soon to join the Royal Air Force. O'Shea has taken a different road and this week he has started a three-month spell at Royal Antwerp, the result of a loan deal between the clubs that will keep the 19-year-old in Belgium for at least three months.

'The manager told me that he thought the move would be the making of me in terms of getting into the first team here at Old Trafford, and anybody who has been there already has loved every minute so I'm looking forward to it,' says the amiable teenager. It's not O'Shea's first spell away from United. Last season he went to Bournemouth for a couple of months and reckons he came back much wiser. He learned a bit about the realities of genuinely competitive football, what it's like to play with men whose families notice the difference when dad brings home a win bonus.

'It was an eye opener for me in that I learned to "keep my elbows up" as they say,' he recalls,

laughing. 'This time I'd be playing at the highest level in Belgium, against good players with different styles and I'd hope to learn as much again.'

Then, the plan goes, he'll return to Old Trafford to begin in earnest the long campaign to make an impact at the world's wealthiest club.

O'Shea admits that he has a great deal still to learn before he can count on having a long-term future at United. All the signs, an extended contract last year and increasing involvement with the first-team panel, would suggest that Ferguson rates him. Still, he wouldn't be the first to make a handful of appearances at a big club, only to be discarded.

Few of those showed the sort of maturity he displays on and off the pitch and as he talks about the need to make sacrifices to succeed you get the feeling that it's more than just a young pro's patter.

And his attitude has already brought its rewards on the international front where he made the step up from Youths to under-21 level last year.

The Toulon tournament in June was not a great one for Don Givens or his team, but while several players were discarded afterwards O'Shea was one of the few success stories and, in part thanks to some good fortune, ended up on the bench for the senior international against Finland.

The year wasn't entirely without setbacks for O'Shea and he recalls, in particular, the recent English League Cup match against Sunderland as one of the best and worst nights of his career so far.

Having generally played well, he gave away the injury-time penalty that cost United the game when he wrapped himself around Kevin Phillips after the striker had got the wrong side of him and appeared to be bearing down on goal.

'At the time I was devastated,' says O'Shea, 'but the way I look at it now, it's just another one of those things that I have to learn from.'

He was heartened by the fact that Ferguson, while pointing out his error, insisted that the penalty had been harsh. In reality few were in any doubt that the referee had been correct, but O'Shea is slightly vague regarding his own opinion on the matter.

Pressed for an answer he pauses for a moment. 'Well,' he finally replies, 'he made the most of it.'

Ah yes, he might still have a lot to learn but the time he has spent around the senior pros certainly has not been wasted.

5 JANUARY 2001

O'Gara Leads Munster Revival

Gerry Thornley

Newport – 24, Munster – 39

The Fat Lady could have bought her evening gown, tried it on, applied her make-up, recited a few words and then cleared her throat as the curtains rose, but you still would not count out this Munster team.

Declan Kidney observed afterwards it would have taken an exceptional side to have lived with Newport in the first quarter. True, and not even Munster could as they fell 15–0 behind. Ultimately, though, it took an exceptional side to beat Newport.

Cue the pitch invasion and an away match had become a home match. The Fat Lady was elbowed aside for the usual renditions, first Munster Branch honorary secretary Dermot Kelly grabbing the microphone and leading a hearty 'Fields of Athenry' (which happens to be in Connacht, but never mind) and then the squad went into their customary dressing-room circle for the Brian O'Brien-inspired 'Stand Up and Fight' anthem of the last three seasons.

To outscore an inspired Newport in their near impregnable Rodney Parade fortress (one defeat in the preceding 20 matches and 14 months) by 29–3 in the second half may have been a bit misleading, and certainly outrageous, but it says volumes for

this team's mental strength. You may call it character or spirit; Kidney calls it honesty.

It was a privilege to be there. They never fail to provide a tonic. Everything it seemed had conspired against them. Leinster and Ulster had been caught cold the night before (and both would assuredly have been beaten long before the finish here), raising the real fear Munster too would be crippled by the enforced 10-week break and relative inactivity of December. Shred that theory.

Even so, the early skirmishes added to the sense of foreboding. Newport's cosmopolitan array of stars set the tempo with Shane Howarth's beautifully mixed running game – varying his flatness and depth, his eye for the break kept the close-in defence honest and his deft handling kept the black and amber waves in full flow – the rapier like intrusions of Matt Pini and finishing of Matt Mostyn ensured they were full value for their 15-point lead.

Even the bounce of the ball was going cruelly against Munster, as were the balance of the officials' decisions. About the only consoling thoughts at this point were that Munster had hardly touched the ball and that such opening flurries by the home side are the norm in the European Cup.

They needed a break and got it with Mostyn's sinbinning for dangerously taking out an airborne Anthony Horgan – foolish rather than malicious – but whereas others might have taken an opportunity to catch their breath, Munster applied their own quick tempo and patterns.

As ever, it was a complete team performance in which no one played poorly, most played very well and some were outstanding. First and foremost, as we had said beforehand, for the comeback to be realised it needed big displays from Ronan O'Gara and John Langford.

Some things change but the importance of goalkicking and set-pieces is still pretty much cast in stone. Whereas Shane Howarth missed four from eight (including one from his own half), O'Gara was unerring in his seven kicks, tagging on

Munster on the move . . . Anthony Foley in action for Munster. Photograph: Frank Miller.

a couple of drop goals and a try. One could nitpick about the turnover in contact which led to Pini's try, or a couple of sliced line-kicks, but O'Gara was majestic. Clearly benefitting from speed work, he took it on the gain-line at pace and has rarely looked more threatening.

Langford nicked three Newport throws, and debilitatingly for Newport these included a couple close to the Munster line after the home side had opted for penalties to touch – and there was also a crooked throw by James Richards. By comparison, there was a 100 per cent return off Frankie Sheahan's darts. Credit to him, to Langford, to the supreme lifting of John Hayes, to their organisation, and to Niall O'Donovan's work on the training ground.

The scrum too wreaked important damage, beyond the first of O'Gara's four uplifting three-pointers in the third quarter as the tide began turning irrevocably Munster's way. With Rome also in mind, no less than Peter Stringer and O'Gara, Peter Clohessy and Hayes had timely big games. Hayes was a colossus, particularly his thunderous brick-wall defending.

The back row became more and more influential, but when the going had been at its toughest, no one had been going stronger than the indestructible, indefatigable David Wallace. It was he as much as anyone who had lit the torch with the first gallop when Newport finally turned over the ball after 22 minutes and it was he who had brilliantly retrieved Stringer's loose pass to regenerate the momentum for O'Gara's opening try.

The game was still finely poised at 24–22 moving into the denouement when the awesome Fijian lock Simon Raiwalui was harshly adjudged not to have taken his mark correctly.

Aware of the try count and scoreline, Mick Galwey, who had a strong, strong game, signalled to O'Gara to have a drop goal (with a back-row move as plan B if the scrum was solid) and in putting Munster ahead for the first time undoubtedly it was a pivotal moment also. But they would probably have won anyway. Playing for territory and stealthily taking scores with almost every visit, tactically they had mastered Newport in the second period.

Where others we could name would assuredly have panicked and, say, kicked the leather off the ball, Munster kept it. Mike Mullins applied the *coup de grâce* with his storming, stirring outside break (anyone out there still think he isn't quick?) and Anthony Horgan's intercept probably gave the scoreline a misleading gloss.

Even so, astounding escapologists though they are, they're pretty good front-runners too. It would all be quite extraordinary except that the quite extraordinary is almost the norm for this lot.

SCORING SEQUENCE: 13 mins: Mostyn try, Howarth con 7–0; 17 mins: Howarth pen 10–0; 20 mins: Pini try 15–0; 26 mins: P O'Gara try and con 15–7; 36 mins: O'Gara pen 15–10; 39 mins: Howarth drop goal 18–10; 40 mins: Howarth pen 21–10; 49 mins: O'Gara pen 21–13; O'Gara drop goal 21–16; 54 mins: Howarth pen 24–16; 56 mins: O'Gara pen 24–19; 59 mins: O'Gara pen 24–22; 75 mins: O'Gara drop goal 24–25; 77 mins: Mullins try, O'Gara con 24–32; 85 mins: Horgan try, O'Gara con 24–39.

NEWPORT: M. Pini; M. Mostyn, J. Jones-Hughes, A. Marinos, M. Llewellyn; S. Howarth, D. Edwards; C. Jones, J. Richards, R. Snow, S. Raiwalui, I. Gough, A. Popham, G. Teichmann (capt), J. Foster. Replacements: J. Pritchard for Marinos (45 mins), J. Powell (74 mins).

MUNSTER: D. Crotty; J. O'Neill, J. Kelly, K. Keane, A. Horgan; R. O'Gara, P. Stringer; P. Clohessy, F. Sheahan, J. Hayes, M. Galwey, J. Langford, A. Quinlan, A. Foley, D. Wallace.

REPLACEMENTS: M. Mullins for Keane (58 mins).
REFEREE: Joel Jutge (France).

6 JANUARY 2001

January is Simply a Load of Old Bull

Mary Hannigan

JANUARY, eh? I know, I know: it's grim. A nothing, gloomy, dull, dreary, dismal, miserable excuse for a month, stuck in the calendar purely so that we don't complain about the other 11 months as much. Some would say it's why Mikael Silvestre is still in the Manchester United starting line-up, so that the crowd will get off Gary Neville's back. I've heard worse analogies.

They even wrote songs about January's direness. Dire songs too. Remember 'January, sick and tired, you've been hanging on me, you make me sad with your eyes, you're telling me lies, don't go, don't goooOOO'? Like me, did you often wonder why they didn't want it to go when it made them sick and tired? Maybe they were being sardonic or a tad ironic, although I don't think irony was big in your average mid-seventies Hit Parade smash tune. Maybe they meant 'shag off January, you've a face like a heifer's rear end', but worried that the song would be banned and, thus, they'd never see Pan's People do their funky thang to it. Who knows. It's too late to ask now because they're probably all dead.

Anyway, January. It's when they should stage the football World Cup, or the All-Ireland finals, or the Olympics or any sparkly sporty event, anything to cheer us up and give us a good enough reason to get out of bed in the morning. But, in the first half of this godforsaken month, what do we get? The Darts World Championships. That's as exhilarating as January gets, in a sporty sense. So, at that point, your honour, I rest my case. Did you watch it? Me too. Well, as Victoria Wood once put it: 'Jogging is for people who aren't intelligent enough to watch Breakfast TV.'

Mortified for John Part, the lad annihilated 7–0 in the final at the Circus Tavern in Purfleet, darts' Croke Park, Madison Square Garden and Nou Camp rolled into one. Phil 'The Power' Taylor did the damage, leaving Part to describe his mauling as 'a totally oppressive experience'.

'John Blown A Part', I confidently predicted the headlines would say, and, spookily enough, they did.

Two colours blue . . . UCD again beat Trinity in the annual colours match at Belfield with Ronan Kelly out in front of Trinity opponent Ciaran Quinn. Photograph: Frank Miller.

I read a report on the final and it went something like this: 'Taylor was a man on a mission, and the mission was to take the game to the most elevated heights in its history.' Ah lads, steady. The ship is listing. And during the final I learnt that Phil 'The Power' was in rattling good form because he'd locked himself away for a two-week practice session in a secret hideaway on the outskirts of Durham.

Now, one of my New Year resolutions was not to be bitchy about darts, Mikael Silvestre, showjumping or Eurosport ever again, but why was it a secret hideaway? Did Phil 'The Power' truly believe that the paparazzi would scuttle south, faster than the speed of sound, from the scene of Madonna's wedding in Scotland so that they could hide in the bushes of a garden of a house on the outskirts of Durham and use their telephoto lenses to take pictures through the bedroom window of him practising his 'one 'undred and 'ay tees'?

And then follow him to the corner shop to surreptitiously snap pics of him purchasing 800 John Player blues and a dozen cans of Scrumpy Jack? 'Where do you want to go today?' Microsoft always ask the paparazzi when they turn on their computers, and never once have they said 'the bushes of a garden of a house on the outskirts of Durham to photograph a dart chucker.'

Trust me, they haven't. Secret hideaway my … howarya Jim Royle.

And what is it about English women and dart chuckers? Why is the Circus Tavern packed to the rafters every January with Hildas and Veras swooning at the mere sight of a dart chucker steadying himself on the oche? I guarantee you, if a naked Brad Pitt obscured their view of the stage while serving them their brews they'd holler 'Moooove Chuck, Phil The Power's limbering up.' I don't see the attraction myself, but clearly polyester smocks (with 'The Power' embroidered on the back) and beards that stretch from the belly button to the cheek bones are a turn-on for your average

Hilda and Vera. But, each to their own, that's what I say.

What we probably all have in common with Hilda and Vera, though, is that we've all devoted a little spell of our lives to dart chucking because it seemed like the easiest way to earn a quick, big buck.

'So, what area do you want to work in when you're released from here?' our Career Guidance teachers asked all of us when we were 18 and which one of us didn't reply, 'Darts'? And which one of us didn't end up with a bedroom wall covered in circles of pin-pricks, revealed when we moved our dart boards to another room once we'd discovered a smidgeon too late that the water pipes were housed behind the wall, four feet to the left of the bull's eye? Eh?

Never once, though, was I on a mission to take the game to the most elevated heights in its history. All I wanted was an easy way to make a living. All I wanted was something to help me forget it was January, like a trip to the Circus Tavern in Purfleet. It wasn't to be, though, and now there's nothing for it but to wait for January to go. 'Cos, tell you something, it's making me sick and tired, it's been hanging on me, and it has a face like a heifer's rear end.

8 JANUARY 2001

Burrows Won't Get Helm Off Hickey

Tom Humphries

What's eating Richard Burrows? Does he not enjoy living? Can he not leave a blue sky unclouded, a smooth pond of contentment unrippled? Is there something lacking in his life that would make him consider taking up arms against Pat Hickey? People ask why it is that in horror movies pretty girls always dander into haunted houses, and I say, well, in real life rich guys keep going after Pat Hickey. Same thing.

Listen up. Hickey has nice yachties like Richard Burrows for breakfast. Hickey doesn't just live in the war zone; he is the lord mayor. Look behind him. Great and many have been the little Balbirnies who have picked up the sword and set off to slay the ogre. Quiet and unmarked are the graves.

You think nobody else wanted that IOC seat? You think nobody opposed Hickey as he rose through the ranks of the IOC? You think the Dublin International Sports Council needs to hire the Point Depot for its Christmas parties? You think Hickey ever saw a fight he didn't like the look of? Oh boys, boys, boys. Hush! When the wind is right you can hear him licking his lips, sharpening his knife and fork. Eerie.

I first met Hickey eight years ago. We were in Monte Carlo covering the bid campaign which ended with Sydney winning the 2000 Games. Three of us wound up at a restaurant table – two journalists and Hickey. Posh French restaurant. Three Northsiders. Hickey looked around with boyish glee and pointed a finger at us in turn, then at himself. Kilbarrack! Finglas! Phibsboro! And here we all are!

Since then he has been the best show in Irish sport. Yup, he has done many things I can't begin to defend him for. He is suing or has sued most of the people I call friends; he gave accreditation in 1996 to a banned athlete and, like a lot of others, he kept his trap firmly shut when the Michelle de Bruin raft sailed clean over the falls; he has cultivated a Zelig-like ability to be wherever there is a sniff of Irish success, culminating in his triumphant RTÉ cameo as Sonia O'Sullivan's au pair on the morning after the silver was secured in Sydney.

He and I have more bones to pick than a couple of vultures hovering over a mass grave. Yet something about that glee in being a northsider who made it big still makes him compulsive viewing and good company.

He is the original of the species in terms of much being said about him but little being proved. Sometimes the whispering campaigns against him could deafen you. He gave Eve the apple to pass to Adam and it's been downhill since. Yet nothing has ever firmed up. Could it be that he's just a guy who gets things done?

What's the story here? Last week the mullahs of canoeing, swimming and athletics announced they were going to Lausanne to complain about Pat Hickey. Swimming and athletics!!! These guys are our Neighbourhood Watch all of a sudden? Beautiful!!! If you wanted to keep your butter unmelted, the first place you'd look to put it would be in the mouth of an Irish swimming or athletics official.

What else have we? Was it my imagination, or did not Petty Officer McDaid and John Treacy publicly demob Hickey and assume complete control of Irish sport some years back? All aspects of Irish sport – except the blame – apparently.

They're both too dumbstruck to tell Bertie what a monstrous mistake the BertieBowl is, but, having assumed control, the Irish Sports Council is now stridently surveying athletes to find out what the OCI did wrong in Sydney.

Myles na gCopaleen, where are you in our time of need?

What else? The IOC bribes scandals. Be honest. Hickey-watchers tipped forward their seats the better to hear the wireless breaking the news. Could it be our boy has done something rash? Not a whistle, not a murmur. Hickey gets mentioned passingly in a dispatch about being a guest at a golf match before he was an IOC member. Given that Dublin journalists systematically put the arm on golf clubs for free use of their facilities every day of the week, there was some quiet coughing and everyone went back to their desks and imagined Hickey cutting a swathe down a fairway.

Later, a 10-year-old letter from Hickey to Tom Welch in Salt Lake City is uncovered. Hickey

The best show in Irish sport ... Pat Hickey embracing Sonia O'Sullivan when he presented her with the silver medal she won in the Women's 5000m final at the 2000 Olympic Games, in Sydney. Photograph: Eric Luke.

is warning Welch about bribes being paid by other campaigns. Drat!

Go watch Hickey work a room at IOC level. He's smooth and genial and has the ear of those more powerful than himself. He laid down a marker in Sydney during the elections for the IOC executive and would have finished stronger had Samaranch not intervened to insist that two seats be reserved, one for an athlete and one for a woman. Come next summer in Moscow, Hickey will almost certainly be elected to the IOC executive level. That takes savvy and ability.

This column went on an advance trip to Sydney last summer to sample the preparations, and at every port of call Hickey's name was cited as an example of how to get things done. Like it or not, he is our most powerful sports administrator and will continue to be so even if Richard Burrows drops him off the starboard side.

That's the thing. Hickey won this battle long ago when he was elected to the IOC. He's got the power. The wise thing is to get on with him and harness his ability in a collective push for Irish sport.

Right now most of those standing ready to throw their pebbles are living in houses made of glass and urging another pretty girl to go into the big scary house. Drop the cudgels lads, and go do something more constructive. And Pat, you go watch Ireland's smartest sports administrator, Liam

Mulvihill, and see how mountains can be moved without the use of noisy machinery.

10 JANUARY 2001

Eriksson's Pit-Stop Conversion

Paddy Agnew

It was on the road to Formello yesterday morning that Sven-Goran Eriksson finally saw the light. The England manager-elect stopped just up the road from Lazio's training ground north of Rome for petrol. As the pump

It's always a battle in Aughrim . . . Dublin forward Vinnie Murphy struggles with Mark Coffey of Wicklow in the O'Byrne Cup match in Aughrim. Photograph: Bryan O'Brien.

whizzed, he made up his mind to resign as coach of the Italian champions.

In hindsight, there is an apparent inevitability about Eriksson's resignation. On the day, however, the Swede took everyone by surprise, as not only football commentators but Lazio club officials alike had concluded that, having survived a meeting with club owner Sergio Cragnotti on Monday, Eriksson would stay in place – at least until the next Lazio defeat.

Eriksson's resignation thus ends a troubled two months that started on the day last October he accepted the England job, to begin in July. Since then, every slip by Lazio (and there have been many) has been reassessed in the light of his coming employment.

British media speculation has been unremitting. Has he taken his eye off the ball? Has he lost the players' respect? Do Lazio now want rid of him? Until last weekend and a 2–1 home loss to Napoli, 98 per cent of this speculation was merely wishful (English) thinking.

Last weekend's defeat, however, was one too many for Cragnotti. On Monday, the Lazio boss tried in vain to persuade Eriksson to resign. Typically, the Swede refused, arguing that he and the side with which he won last season's Italian championship still had some long way to go together.

At the petrol station yesterday morning, something snapped. In an uncharacteristic gesture, Eriksson bowed to the combined pressures of his employer's wishes and recent results. Yesterday, as he sat alongside Cragnotti at a hastily convened news conference in Formello, Eriksson looked dignified but disappointed:

'The results are not what I had hoped they would be. I'm in charge of the team. I'm the one who is responsible. I don't particularly like what I did but I think and hope it is better for the club.'

Speaking to *The Irish Times* afterwards, Eriksson developed his thoughts.

'Look, it is just boring, I mean, boring to wake up every morning after a defeat and find people asking if the fact that I am about to become England manager can explain our loss. Okay, now I have taken that alibi, that excuse, away from the players …'

Eriksson thus ends a three-and-a-half-year spell at Lazio during which he won not only last season's Scudetto but also the 1999 Cup Winner's Cup and two Italian Cups. Until Eriksson's arrival, Lazio had won nothing of significance for 26 years. His role in converting perennial losers into winners, albeit with the help of generous funding from Cragnotti, clearly convinced the English FA.

His winning role in Lazio history was the main reason Cragnotti simply refused to sack him, and hoped rather that Eriksson would finally leave of his own accord. In other circumstances, Champions League defeats by Arsenal, Anderlecht and Leeds, not to mention Serie A losses to Verona, Parma and Roma, would have been enough to see Eriksson sent packing a long time ago.

Eriksson now heads off to the England job, leaving Lazio in the hands of club vice-president Dino Zoff, the man who coached Italy to within 20 seconds of winning Euro 2000 last summer. Four years ago, in similar circumstances, Zoff stepped down from the Lazio board to replace sacked Czech coach Zdenek Zeman. On that occasion, Zoff did well, taking the club on an unbeaten run to the end of the season which ended with a fourth place finish in Serie A.

On this occasion, he faces an arguably more difficult task. Lazio's problems this season did not start with Eriksson, but rather with a midsummer transfer campaign which saw the club sell vital elements such as Portuguese midfielder Sergio Conceicao and Argentinian midfielder Matias Almeyda, and replace them with expensive Argentinian purchases, strikers Hernan Crespo and Claudio Lopez. While Conceicao and Almeyda have done well at Parma, neither Crespo nor

Lopez have contributed much, through injury and loss of form.

Furthermore, Eriksson and Lazio have paid a high price for remaining loyal to Yugoslav defender Sinisa Mihajlovic, whose brilliance with free-kicks does not compensate for manifest defensive shortcomings. Zoff, who will sign a contract through to June 2002, acknowledged the difficult task facing him.

'This side has, above all, failed to understand how difficult it is to repeat yourself. What you did last year doesn't count this year. We simply haven't given as much, tried as hard, as we did last year.'

Intriguingly, Zoff did seem to acknowledge that Eriksson's decision to take the England job had affected the club's performances.

'In theory, something like that shouldn't affect anything. But we [footballers] live in a very special world where people create doubts, even if the reality of the situation is entirely different, and this is something that produces problems.'

Too many problems for Sven Goran Eriksson, it seems. Lancaster Gate, here he comes.

13 JANUARY 2001

Sent To Coventry

Like him or loathe him, Eddie Irvine is king of the quotable quote. Mary Hannigan went to Coventry for the launch of Jaguar's new car

Attend the launch of Jaguar's new Formula One car? Yes please, we could all do with a bit of glamour in our lives. So, what exotic hot spot are we off to, eh? The Seychelles, Kuala Lumpur, Goa? Close: an industrial estate in Whitley, a suburb of Coventry. Lovely!

Last year Jaguar had their launch at Lord's Cricket Ground, a glitzy, ritzy affair by all accounts, all trumpets and flashing lights. But then they had what their new boss, American Bobby Rahal, describes as a 'disappointing' season (i.e. humiliating,

with only the pointless Minardi and Prost teams finishing behind them in the constructors' championship). This time around the unveiling of their car is done in a near diffident fashion, with not a trumpet to be heard. Modest expectations, modest surroundings, it seems.

So, here we are, on an icy January morning in Jaguar's design and engineering centre, located in a place our Birmingham Airport taxi driver wasn't aware existed. We're two and a half hours early, just enough time for the F1 press pack to outline their travel plans for March to October: 'Australia, Malaysia, Brazil, San Marino, Spain, Austria, Monaco, Canada, France, England, Germany, Hungary, Belgium, Italy, the USA and Japan. Yourself?' 'Oooh, Kinnegad in March, God willing.'

'But it's not as glamorous as it sounds, you know,' they insist. 'Bla, bla, bla … all hotels and airports and airports and hotels … bla, bla, bla … we work very hard, you know … bla, bla, bla … we're talking blood, sweat and tears here … bla, bla, bla.' Jeez lads, ye sound like Westlife.

Only Peter Collins, RTÉ's Formula One commentator and self-confessed Shirley Bassey fan, gets any sympathy after his experience in a Magny Cours (the least popular F1 venue, by common consent) hotel last year. 'I was just drifting off to sleep when I felt something tickling my foot,' he says. 'I jumped up, saw a mouse in the bed, freaked, kicked it 10 feet into the air. It landed on the floor and scurried in to the bathroom.' Waiter, smelling salts please.

'Problem was there was a big gap under the bathroom door so I blocked it with some T-shirts. Hardly slept. Got up, stared at the bathroom door and thought "I can do this." Stormed in, but there was no sign of him.' And you had to commentate that day? 'I did.' Heroic. Bet you Murray Walker never shared a bed with a mouse.

Someone suggests that Eddie Irvine probably had his foot tickled in a Magny-Cours hotel last year too but there was a fair chance the tickler

Eddie archives ... Eddie Irvine in the Jaguar R1 Cosworth.

wasn't a mouse. Where is Eddie anyway? 'He's on his way, I just saw him on the motorway – overtook him in my Punto,' giggles a just-arrived English member of the press pack. Cue jokes about Jaguar's clutch problems.

So, what's Irvine like, then? Consensus: it depends on his mood. He's either (a) a tiresomely insufferable, bad-mannered, pampered, spoilt, puerile smart ass who's never grown up and probably never will (when Jane Nottage wrote a book with him on his Ferrari years she concluded that 'at 33, he's probably just passing adolescence') or (b) an uproariously hilarious, entertaining charmer, one of the few drivers in Formula One to possess a personality and one who is capable of acts of big-hearted generosity, especially to up-and-coming

drivers. Usually one or the other, rarely anything in between.

Mention Irvine and the conversation, invariably, turns to models of the female rather than vehicular variety. And that's the problem for the F1 press pack: they want to talk rear suspensions with Irvine; the other half of the room want to talk 'babes'. They never have this problem with Michael Schumacher.

But Irvine obliges. You know you shouldn't laugh but sometimes it's hard not to. The Eddie archives?

Do you have any role models?

'Role models? No, but models? Oooh, I've had hundreds of them.'

Liz Hurley says she thinks you're sexy.

'Well, she's only human.'

Who's that pretty Italian woman walking around your yacht?

'She's the torso in the Benetton black and white ads.'

He probably didn't actually know her name, but then this is the guy who went out with a Brazilian supermodel who didn't speak English, the same guy who when asked 'Is there any truth in the rumour that you are seeing a supermodel?' replied, 'Does a bear ★★★★ in the woods?'

'I have to admit that I'm pretty shallow when it comes to women,' he said in an interview with *Superbike* magazine last March (on being asked – no kiddin' – 'Wouldn't you fancy bedding some 20 stone, hairy-armpitted, ugly old boiler with halitosis for a change?'). True, in comparison, Benny Hill's relationships with women were cavernously deep.

But, as a rule, you don't fund Irvine's class of lifestyle doing a paper round so, now that the new season is less than two months away, it's time for him to put away his toys and start earning his annual salary of £6 million from Jaguar. Today we get to see the car in which he will attempt to do it in the 2001 season.

Bobby Rahal, a legend in Indycar and CART racing, opens proceedings by addressing the assembled press pack in what looks like half a basketball court. 'Tough decisions were made late last year regarding staff,' he tells us (F1 speak for 'a bunch of people were sacked') and refers to Jaguar's 'drive-ability issues' last season. Eh? 'F1 speak for when the engine doesn't start – and when it does it doesn't keep going,' I'm told.

Then Bobby introduces us to Rick (Mr Roscitt to you), president of American communications company AT&T who have just formed a relationship with Jaguar (you don't have sponsorship in F1; you have mutually beneficial 'relationships' or 'partnerships'). Rick assures us that he'd been driving a Jag even before AT&T started dating Jaguar and 'as the New Jersey state police will attest it's a very fast vehicle'. Bobby chuckles and Rick flashes a smile that you only ever see in toothpaste ads.

'Now, let's talk about the car,' says Bobby, and he tells us about the new longitudinally mounted magnesium-cased seven-speed gearbox and the AP Racing triple-plate pull-type clutch. Just as we're beginning to lose the will to live, the drivers are introduced.

Irvine evidently lost a bet during the off-season because his hair, once again, is peroxide blonde, only this time it looks like he bleached it himself in the sink at home (with one of those sachets that cost £2.99 at all good chemists). He and Jaguar's new number two driver, Brazilian Luciano Burti, whip the dust-sheet off the new car and, well, there's silence. If a pin had dropped at that moment we'd have been able to locate the exact spot it landed.

You're tempted to clap, out of the goodness of your heart, but you kind of reckon no clapping at all is better than one person clapping at the back of the room.

Psst. Press pack? Why is no one clapping? 'Well, they never do. You've seen one car you've seen 'em all, unless they've put the back wheels on the front, which in Jaguar's case is entirely …". Behave. (Is there one for everyone in the audience? 'No.')

Questions for Eddie? 'Do you think you can improve on last season?' 'It will be difficult to do that bad again – if we did then we would deserve a good kicking,' he says and Rick and Bobby beam. Nervously. Then the drivers mingle, answering questions from groups of four or five at a time.

'Do you think you can improve on last season, Eddie?' asks the first.

'Do you think you can improve on last season, Eddie?' asks the second.

'Do you think you can improve on last season, Eddie?' asks the third.

Irvine's new model . . . Eddie Irvine (right) at Jaguar's far from glamorous launch of their new Formula One car in Coventry, with fellow drivers Luciano Burti (centre) and Tomas Scheckter.

The fourth is more adventurous. 'Eddie, do you think you can improve on last season?'

The queues to speak to Burti are, at a guess, a twelfth the length of Irvine's. But then Irvine is the king of the quotable quotes and even if it took him three minutes to get from nought to 60 he'd never be short of interview requests from the press pack. 'There is a constipation about Formula One, because many are frightened to speak out in case they upset one or two people,' Jackie Stewart once said. The 'many' doesn't include Irvine who has a penchant for upsetting people and will never be in need of a verbal laxative.

Looking on, like a couple of wide-eyed kids in a toy shop, are 19-year-old German Andre Lotterer and 20-year-old Australian James Courtney, who've just been signed up as drivers for Jaguar's new F3 team.

'I haven't stopped smiling since I found out – I think my jaw is going to snap off,' says Courtney, who wouldn't look out of place on the set of 'Home and Away'. 'Yes, I'm very happy,' says Lotterer, who looks like a chemistry student. Where are you both living?

'Milton Keynes,' says the Sydney native. Hmm. 'It's very nice,' insists Lotterer. Courtney bursts out laughing. Lotterer shrugs. Schumacher and Irvine? Fast forward. Lotterer and Courtney? Mmm, maybe.

Meanwhile, Irvine's still answering questions. 'Do you think you can improve on last season, Eddie?' His eyes are beginning to glaze over but he's on his best behaviour today and has managed to avoid offending anyone, much to everyone else's disappointment. Give him time, though. The season's only just begun.

Then there's lunch, the cost of which, for Jaguar, would probably buy you the television rights to Premiership football (featuring parts of animals you didn't know were edible) and then the press pack bid adieu to each other, with cries of 'See you in Melbourne'. Well, you get a better view on telly and, any way, at least there's no danger of picking up deep vein thrombosis on a trip to Kinnegad.

13 JANUARY 2001

Little Room for Regret on Shoulders of Genial Giant

Keith Duggan talks to the former Irish Lion on the differences between his playing days and the modern professional game

Keane today . . . former Ireland rugby international Moss Keane. Photograph: Bryan O'Brien.

When Moss Keane laughs, the floor beneath shudders, as if a great juggernaut has rumbled past the door. The big man fills the room in a way that has little to do with the chiselled shoulders that stretch impossibly like great plains, or the wonderful hands that make his tea cup disappear every time he takes a drink.

Nor is it the facial expressions, vivid and hide-nothing and generous. Nor even the butter-rich, carefully preserved Castleisland brogue, baritone and lively and God given for late nights of story-telling.

No, Moss Keane's presence springs from the easy geniality that seems to have fallen away with the sports stars of a generation ago. Good nature seeps out of him, not in any holy-Joe way – he defines mischief with his grin – but through a carefree gait that can set a dead room humming.

Like so many Lions of yesteryear, Keane's rugby life seems less a dimming montage of tries and scars and silverware than a glowing series of tales and observations and, most chiefly, a succinct lack of regret. The best thing Keane got out of rugby was friendship and that, he says, was more than enough.

He is here because he has agreed to talk about Munster rugby. On the wall is a framed report from the *Cork Examiner* dating back to 1 November 1978, the day after 'that game' in Thomond Park.

Keane points to the report and photograph, his younger self staring fiercely back at him, an image incarnate of Hopkin's great phrase, 'big-boned and hardy handsome'.

'This a coincidence or something?' he enquires gruffly, almost embarrassed by the tribute to the province's win over the All Blacks. 'I suppose that is the day all right. I mean if we played them 100 times we probably wouldn't have done it again.

'But then, Munster always had a very good record against touring sides and there was something magical about that day. I can't quite put my finger on it. There was an unwritten obligation, almost, to go out and do something more that day.

'And the All Blacks were kind of set up for it. In September, we played Middlesex in a warm-up game and were beaten by 28 points. The All Blacks had played the best of London counties and won 37–6. So they probably weren't expecting much from us. People said the All Blacks were arrogant.

'But they weren't arrogant, just hard players. Defeat was not in their milieu. They were very upset afterwards. To be honest I got a bit of pleasure out of seeing their feckin' agony. Andy Haden was crying afterwards and I went up to him and said: "We're used to this losing, Andy. You're not". Sure we could write a feckin' thesis on it.'

Although Keane enjoys the occasional nostalgia trip, he has never hankered after what's gone before. He fell into rugby in his own happy-go-lucky way, starting in UCC after winning three Sigerson medals with the football team. He was raw and got burned for it. 'Jumping in the scrums and pushing in the line-outs,' he laughs.

He began playing at university level around 1972 and, by the summer of 1977, he was playing second row for the Lions. That was a three-and-a-half-month tour and work holidays only covered a few weeks of that.

So he took unpaid leave for two months and toured with the Lions. A year later, he spent a month touring with Ireland and had to take a further two weeks pay-less leave to go on honeymoon after he returned.

'Sure, what harm was it? Over time, all those sort of things disintegrate. They don't matter. Travel was the bonus then and it was a different thing to what it is now. Today teams travel to a game the night before and leave straight away after.

'We'd go on the morning of a match and stay that evening. Game, bar, home the next day. Today every game seems of fierce importance and the next morning, lads are hanging out of the rafters in gyms again. We'd take 'till about the following Wednesday getting back into it.'

Moss Keane lifted weights. Once. He abandoned the practice after 10 minutes, culled by boredom. He reckons he stands at about 6 ft 4 in, but has never measured himself. The tallest player he ever encountered was David Gray, who stood at 6 ft 8 in, but the Scot was of gentle disposition and didn't bother Keane unduly. But the physiques that dictate the modern game never cease to amaze him.

'They are all built up and, you know, it's not from mother's cooking. I think it's got to the stage where the field is too small now. If it was the right size in our day, then it can't be right now.

'Players of great flair are always being closed down, teams employ this bloody blanket defence and the midfield gets crowded. I think they should reduce it to 13-a-side. The modern game needs more space.'

Not that Keane is stuck in any time warp, maudlin for the days of Gareth Edwards. He remains an avid follower of rugby and today will find him in Newport.

The current Munster players are achieving, he believes, what he and his contemporaries attempted at amateur level. Like the rest of the province, he became captivated by last year's wonderful odyssey and is happy to speak of himself as a fan.

'The thing is, I see a horrible parallel between this Newport game and last year against Northampton. Newport had two tough games recently, against Edinburgh and Cardiff, and even though they lost both, they know where they are.

'Munster are after a long break and they go out into the dark, in a sense. I'm not being pessimistic, but I honestly think they will do extremely well to get anything from the game. That said, they revel in these high-pressure encounters and they have the players to do it.'

Although he doesn't state it, it is apparent that Keane has a soft spot for the elder warriors of the pack, Clohessy and Mick Galwey, now among the lone survivors from the amateur era.

Keane yesterday . . . Moss Keane in his halcyon days.
Photograph: Peter Thursfield.

'Those lads are interesting all right. They crossed the Menin Road. Our generation, well, we were models designed for different courses. Could we have made the transition? Possibly, but when we were playing, we were adhering to an ethos that was around for what, 100 years.

'I'm sure the game is much better now in many respects, but it's possible that something has been lost also. I don't know. You could measure it in the dressing rooms. Dressing rooms used to be great fun. I'd imagine the talk is more about bonuses now than anything.'

Keane is indifferent to the recent torrent of

cash that has transformed the game. When he was a Lion, the players got an allowance of £2 a day. Food and drink were all laid on so he used to have a flutter on the local ponies.

'And it worked.'

The pocket money was amusing, but he believes, in retrospect, that the fact the Lions weren't given a cut of the massive gate tolls was 'morally and ethically wrong'. But finance was for accountancy firms back then. No one even thought to mention it.

When Keane retired in 1985, at the age of 37, it was becoming apparent that monetary issues were going to play an increasing role in the game. In his last years, he worked hardest on his fitness, doing a solitary evening as well as the two regular sessions with Lansdowne.

'No, we did work at it. It would be untrue to say there was this totally cavalier attitude towards fitness or whatever. We did put hours in. Thing is, how hard were we pushing ourselves? Nothing like today I'm sure.'

This afternoon in Newport, Moss Keane will watch a sport that is, in essence, a different game to the one he played – still enjoyable, but different. But Munster is still Munster.

'There is a spirit there that was probably born back in the '50s or '60s. And it's hard to put into words, but it's very real. It's a unifying thing.'

Last summer, he was walking one evening when he took a call from a producer who had interviewed him for a documentary on Mick Galwey. The producer was in London and happened to be with Richard Harris.

'He asked me if I'd like a word with him and I said I might as bloody well. I'd never met him. So he asked me if I was still playing. I'd played a game the year before but said I was getting a bit old now. And Harris said to me, "Ara, you're still feckin' young. I'm 70 today."'

Moss Keane throws back his head and guffaws. The actor was right.

Kinsale Put Price on Head

Dermot Gilleece

At £190 per round, the Old Head of Kinsale will be providing the most expensive golf in Ireland this coming season. And individual bookings will have to be fully guaranteed financially, while a 25 per cent credit card deposit will be required from tour operators.

'We're in pursuit of excellence and excellence costs money,' said John O'Connor, joint owner of the facility with his brother Patrick. 'Our objective is to provide a standard the like of which may not be found elsewhere in Europe.'

In that context, O'Connor is convinced his clientele will not be concerned at having to pay a green fee which is £15 dearer than the next highest in this country – the £175 at the K Club. After that, it is quite a drop down to the £125 weekend rate at Portmarnock (£100 on weekdays) and the Sterling £90 at Royal Co. Down and Royal Portrush.

Prices at leading courses in the south-west are: Waterville (£100 any day); Ballybunion, Adare, Lahinch and Tralee (£75); Killarney (£50). Other selected venues with weekday and weekend prices are: Mount Juliet (£85/£100), Druids Glen (£85), Royal Dublin (£75/£85), Portmarnock Links (£75), Portstewart (Stg£55/Stg£75), The Island (£70), Luttrellstown Castle (£60/£65), Fota Island (£55/£65), Mount Wolseley (£35/£40).

Meanwhile, when he refers to the emphasis on quality at the Old Head, O'Connor can highlight an investment of £1 million in the course during the last 12 months alone. Perhaps the most significant of all his marketing decisions, however, was to reduce the number of rounds this season from 26,000 to 18,000.

Those of you proficient at mental arithmetic will already have worked out from those figures that the green fee income at the Old Head this year will be in the region of £3.4 million – even with reduced traffic. 'We had far too many six-hour rounds last year for my liking,' said the owner. 'We have now decided on 15-minute intervals between fourballs for the coming year and we'll also be limiting visitors' time to five hours on the tee, with three hours for our members and guests.' He added: 'As for the booking guarantees: that is essentially a response to the fact that we had far too many phantom bookings last year.'

The Old Head is an international members' club where the 300 members paid an entrance fee of $50,000 and an annual subscription of $2,000. As the currency would indicate, the majority of its members are from the US, but O'Connor is anxious to increase the current complement of about 30 from this country.

Since its official opening in June 1997, green fees at the Old Head have increased from £50 to £90, to £120 and now £190. O'Connor explained: 'When we started here, I knew it would never work as a conventional golf club. A small, local population could not hope to repay the high level of investment.

'So my options were to produce conveyer-belt golf, like you will experience at certain American clubs and in Spain and Portugal, or to aim for excellence, at a price. I chose the latter option and those who would criticise our rates should note that apart from casual, seasonal labour, there are 70 people on our payroll. And our customers make a huge contribution to the local economy in and around Kinsale.'

Meanwhile, O'Connor can point to the fact that the increased rate has not had a negative impact on bookings. 'We are selling a unique, golfing experience at the Old Head', he said, 'so, strictly speaking, we don't need to depend on repeat business.

But making money is only a part of his long-term objective. 'By the time I'm finished here, I want people to be comparing the Old Head with Pine Valley as a course of the highest quality,' he said. 'That's my objective.'

Istabraq Silences the Doubters

Brian O'Connor

The doubters were silenced, the champ reigns supreme and the road to history is wide open. Everything in the world of Istabraq is as it should be.

Bookmaker reaction to the great horse's majestic victory at Leopardstown yesterday was to go as low as 2 to 5 on him recording a fourth successive Smurfit Champion Hurdle win at Cheltenham on 13 March. Public reaction verged on idolatry.

The signs of their worship were everywhere. The crowds around the pre-parade ring where Istabraq was saddled were at least four deep. The depth of the crowd around the parade ring could nearly be measured in fathoms.

Among them were fans wielding 'Istabraq' scarves, just a fraction of the five busloads who had travelled from the South Liberties GAA club in Limerick, and who turned the number one spot into a mini Kop.

Aidan O'Brien seemed to sense the idolatry too and he tried desperately to inject some caution into the wildly euphoric scenes in the winner's enclosure.

'I think it must be next to impossible for a horse to get to Cheltenham in one piece for five years in a row,' the trainer warned, although nobody appeared to listen. No trace of doubt was permitted, and such was Istabraq's brilliant bounce back to form it was hard to blame anyone. Istabraq started a 4 to 11 favourite and waltzed home from Mantles Prince with the 50 to 1 outsider Penny Rich in third. The result caused mayhem among the 11,190 attendance.

Everyone successfully forgot how the pre-race rumour mill had been fanned into such an inferno that earlier in the day few would have been surprised if the horse had been accompanied by someone ringing a bell and shouting 'unclean'.

'The rumours were obviously wrong,' grinned rider Charlie Swan, 33 on Saturday, who confessed to some irritation with the rumour train. 'The phone never stopped ringing but the horse and the trainer did the talking.'

Istabraq's owner J. P. McManus was showered with congratulations in a thronged parade ring and said: 'I'm very pleased and very relieved. I don't know where these rumours start but Aidan wasn't worried and that's who I listened to.'

O'Brien, for his part, tried to joke them away and said: 'Rumours don't mean a lot to me. But I hope there are plenty of them when we get to Cheltenham!'

And all things being equal, Cheltenham looks a date with history for the remarkable Istabraq. Never before has a horse won four Champion Hurdles. Istabraq's festival record also takes in the 1997 SunAlliance Hurdle, and he will travel to England on the back of a fourth successive AIG Europe Champion Hurdle.

Throw in how yesterday's £66,500 first prize takes the nine-year old well past the £1 million mark in career earnings and the huge Leopardstown crowd could assure themselves they were watching something special.

There was certainly no hint of the fatigue that led to Istabraq's dramatic last-flight fall over the course and distance on New Year's Eve, and those rumour mongers who helped the Paddy Power firm offer an overnight 11 to 10 price on Istabraq for Cheltenham might wish to steer clear of their offices for a while.

Only 1 to 2 is now generally available for the March festival, with the nearest rival in the

Normal service resumed . . . Istabraq and Charlie Swan are in sync again as they clear the last hurdle and win the AIG Europe Champion Hurdle at Leopardstown. Photograph: Alan Betson.

Cheltenham ante-post market, Geos, as long as 9 to 1. The worrying thing for all rivals is the note of bullishness that even O'Brien couldn't prevent escaping from his lips.

'The time off we've given him seems to have made him even stronger and he's probably better than he's ever been. We've trained him very cautiously this season because we want him to peak at the right time,' O'Brien said.

'He's heavier than he's ever been. He only lost four kilos from his last race whereas other runners we had that day lost almost 20. But Charlie had been very happy with how he went up until the fall. If Charlie had got negative vibes from the run I would have been worried,' he added.

J. P. McManus confessed to always suffering from anxiety when his star runs but added: 'Istabraq is just that little bit different to every other horse. He's special.'

25 JANUARY 2001

A Legal Way to Gain an Edge

Ian O'Riordan, who took creatine while running competitively, on his own feelings about it

It was early 1994 when I first saw an advertisement for creatine in a popular athletics magazine. At the time I was in the final year of a running scholarship in the US and eager for any possible edge.

The promise of increased energy, stamina and power certainly seemed attractive, although it wasn't the first food supplement to make such claims. Carnitine and chromium were also causing a buzz at the time.

Word got around that a lot of top international athletes were starting to take creatine on a regular basis. A number of them were even endorsing it. And as a food supplement, it was perfectly legal.

It didn't come cheap (about $50 for a month's supply) but along with a few members of the track team, I decided to try it out. It wasn't discussed with any of the coaches but the theory was simple. Increased energy supply meant better training. No different really to carbohydrate loading.

The instructions were straightforward. For seven days you went on a loading phase of about eight grams. It was half that dose a day from then on. The creatine powder was dissolved in warm water and could be mixed with orange juice, milk, or whatever. Of course there was the temptation to spill in a few extra doses but I always followed the instructions on the label. For the next month the training remained intensive.

There were no immediate effects. Like any food supplement, it is difficult to assess whether or not there is any benefit. The placebo effect may have played some role, and there were days when training did seem to come easier than usual. Some days I felt better than ever. But there is no way of knowing for sure whether this had anything to do with the creatine.

Some of the sprinters on the team were sure that their power in the weight room had increased from the time they started taking the supplement. Most of the apparent benefits from creatine do seem to favour power sports, and as I ran longer distances I was probably in the wrong event to gain any advantage. Some takers also complained of weight gain, but I didn't notice any side-effects.

That summer I returned home to race. I had stopped taking the supplement for about a week when the form dropped very quickly. Once again there is no way of knowing if the lack of creatine had anything to do with it.

The use of creatine in sport has increased dramatically over the last couple of years. Fears that it may not be safe are generally dismissed by examination of what it actually does.

A compound of three amino acids – arginine, glycine and methionine – creatine is found in meat and fish. It plays a crucial role in the ATP cycle of energy in the muscle. And with increased creatine stored in the muscle, there is the potential for increased power.

Details of a possible link between creatine and cancer have yet to be backed up with long-term studies. Until then, creatine will remain a popular supplement, whether it works or not.

THE FINAL WHISTLE

Tongue-tied

Planet Football has had a soft spot for former Aston Villa midfielder Mark Draper ever since he uttered the immortal line 'I'd like to play for an Italian club, like Barcelona'.

We loved him even more last year on hearing of his difficulties learning Spanish after he joined Rayo Vallecano. 'Permiso, permiso,' he confidently shouted at his team mates, which he had been reliably informed meant 'pass, pass'. Not so. He was, in fact, shouting 'driving licence, driving licence'.

Come home Mark.

2 JANUARY 2001

From Mary Hannigan's Planet Football

Toilet Papers

Be assured this column has no intention of descending into toilet humour, but two fascinating items of news caught my attention this week. The first concerned the installation of television advertising screens over the urinals at the Hammersmith Palais, and the other had to do with the lavatory cubicles at Prestwick GC.

You may be interested to learn that following on the experiment among male theatre-goers at the Palais, it is envisaged 1,000 such screens will be installed at 100 locations in Britain over the next 12 months. But at Prestwick, the objective is no more ambitious than to provide the comforts of home for the readers of broadsheet newspapers. (It seems unthinkable that members might be tabloid readers, even in the WC.)

Prestwick, as devotees of the Royal and Ancient game will be aware, was founded in 1851 and played host to the first British Open nine years later. It was also the scene of Christy O'Connor's first Dunlop Masters triumph in 1956.

Anyway, the fact that the club is playing host to the British Amateur Championship this year as part of its 150th anniversary celebrations focused attention on some refurbishment. A club memo advised that the lavatory cubicles should be dimensioned 'so that a broadsheet newspaper may be read in comfort'. It went on: 'While the importance of this characteristic to some members is recognised, it is not at this stage planned to supply reading material.'

Meanwhile, the club chairman, Colin MacGregor, commented: 'Some of the members are quite large and a number of them said that, when we did the refurbishment, they wanted plenty of room.'

There is no suggestion, however, of matching the dimensions of the massive Cardinal bunker, which characterises Prestwick's famous third.

6 JANUARY 2001
From Dermot Gilleece's Golfing Log

Another Hockey Light Goes Out

Fiona Ruttle died on Monday at home. She was due to move into a hospice in Raheny but decided before the ambulance arrived that she would leave us peacefully when at home. Single minded to the end.

It was too premature for the rest of us, for those who played hockey with her in Trinity and Pembroke, knocked golf balls around Howth Golf Club with her, or failed to beat her at tennis.

In sport, Fiona was the player who would play for the duff team rather than the firsts because her friends were there. She loved sport but her interests encompassed too broad a sweep for her to place it at the centre of her universe.

Her considerable talent as a hockey player far outweighed her ambition to collect baubles or seek acclaim. It was a frustrating exercise for those with less talent to watch someone so acutely self-aware but apparently unable to see what gifts she had at her own disposal. Of course, Fiona saw everything. But with her psychology degree and a career in law, she looked at it through a different prism.

At her removal in Sutton on Tuesday, Irene Johnston, an Irish Hockey Association stalwart, arrived to St Fintan's Church somewhat perturbed and spoke privately about what many people had been already thinking. She drew Fiona and another young hockey player, Jacqui Potter, who died just before Christmas, into the same circle. In that light hockey has indeed been winded.

Who knows what Fiona would have made of the funeral fuss? Certainly, she'd have been uncomfortable at being the centre of attention.

13 JANUARY 2001
From Johnny Watterson's Sidelines

O'Leary's Overview

Ever wondered about the real story behind Jack Charlton's reluctance to include David O'Leary in his plans during the Olé Olé years, or why he preferred playing Mark Lawrenson and Paul McGrath at full-back or in midfield, even though they were born and bred centre-halves? Over to you David O'Leary. 'The bottom line with Jack is that he hates any centre-half who passes the ball. End of story,' he told the *London Independent* at the weekend. 'It was all about putting the ball, and the player if necessary, into the stand. Basic as that. He told me that if I passed the ball to my other centre-half, he'd have me off the pitch. Jack used to look at me, Paul McGrath and Mark Lawrenson as poofy centre-halves. His cure for Paul McGrath was to put him into midfield.'

There you are. O'Leary's comments were prompted by Charlton's questioning of Rio Ferdinand's qualities. Young Rio's main weakness, according to Jack? He's 'good on the ball'. Crikey.

22 JANUARY 2001
From Mary Hannigan's Planet Football

The video try . . . the key moment — brilliantly captured — in Ireland's great win over France at Lansdowne Road as Brian O'Driscoll seems to touch down the ball for a try which was awarded by the video referee after long deliberation. Photograph: Bryan O'Brien.

FEBRUARY

2 0 0 1

HIGHLIGHTS

1 Feb: Irish rugby squad have papal audience ahead of Six Nations game in Rome.

2 Feb: Bookies decide to pay out on Fulham winning first division title three and a half months before season ends.

3 Feb: Darren Clarke shoots a course record 63 in Sun City Pro-Am in South Africa.

4 Feb: Early jitters but Ireland win 41–22 against Italy on opening weekend of Six Nations rugby championship.

5 Feb: Florida Pearl completes Hennessy Gold Cup treble at Leopardstown.

6 Feb: Consultants recommend sweeping changes to sports policy after poor performances at Sydney Olympics.

7 Feb: Tempers nicely set for weekend league meeting after Celtic stroll past Rangers in League Cup semi-final.

9 Feb: Fergal O'Brien wins Irish snooker showdown against Ken Doherty to move into semi-finals of British Masters.

11 Feb: Celtic stretch lead in Scottish Premier League with second victory in a week over Rangers.

13 Feb: Leeds' march on Europe is kept alive by Lee Bowyer with late goal which secures 2–1 win over Anderlecht.

15 Feb: Olympic Council of Ireland president Pat Hickey sees off challenge from businessman Richard Burrows for OCI presidency after heated political battle.

17 Feb: Controversial Brian O'Driscoll try gives Ireland first win over France at Lansdowne Road since 1983.

18 Feb: Vijay Singh beats Padraig Harrington in a play-off for Malaysian Open.

19 Feb: New Celtic League in rugby given green light.

21 Feb: 15 Irish players named in preliminary Lions squad for summer tour to Australia.

22 Feb: Members of the Island Golf Club reject £15.6 million offer to buy course from anonymous consortium.

25 Feb: Man Utd drive home total Premiership supremacy with crushing 6-1 win over Arsenal at Old Trafford.

26 Feb: Horse racing and Six Nations game between Ireland and Wales called off as foot and mouth crisis intensifies.

1 FEBRUARY 2001

Pope is Spared a Rendition of 'Ireland's Call'

Paddy Agnew

You might have missed them – until they stood up. Almost lost among the 4,000 pilgrims who packed out Pope John Paul II's weekly audience in the Paul VI hall in the Vatican yesterday, the Irish rugby squad became suddenly and impressively visible as their presence was announced.

Needless to say, this was a historic first for the IRFU which had never previously been received in a papal audience. Not, mind you, that they had the limelight to themselves, since they joined schoolchildren, teachers and assorted pilgrims from Brussels, Copenhagen, Santiago de Chile, Detroit, Minneapolis, Arlington and Warsaw, as well as a group of religious and lay people working with Vietnamese exiles.

Throughout the traditionally multi-lingual audience, the Irish players sat in respectful silence near the front row, looking the essence of sobriety in their dark team blazers. At the end of the audience, they took their place in the queue, behind the sick and the disabled and after the newly weds, before being presented to the Pope up on the hall stage, where they also posed for a group photograph.

Often on these occasions, sportsmen present the Pope with a team shirt. Yesterday, however, the IRFU chose to offer a tasteful piece of Waterford crystal, complete with IRFU logo.

Speaking after the audience, IRFU president Eddie Coleman summed up the significance of the day for Irish rugby: 'This was a great privilege for us. We came out here early, specifically to be at this audience. We would probably have travelled out a day later, but this was a marvellous opportunity, one we couldn't possibly miss.'

'This was simply an incredible experience and the guys are just thrilled to bits with it. They're absolutely gobsmacked. The Pope was very interested in us, asked us where we came from and wished us good luck in the game.'

Captain Keith Wood said: 'I had never been to a papal audience before, even though I did see the Pope in 1979 when I crawled through the mud in Limerick, but that's a long, long way away. It's a great experience and a great privilege for us.'

As the Irish team mingled in St Peter's Square alongside their team bus, second row Jeremy Davidson, a Protestant, put the perfect seal on an ecumenical morning: 'That was wonderful. We were very, very lucky to meet the Pope and I can tell you a lot of people here are very happy.'

Perhaps the only anxious moment had come when the team's presence was announced during the audience. Traditionally, the pilgrims just announced stand up and sing a hymn or psalm for the Pope. Indeed, yesterday five different choirs and a large group of especially enthusiastic Polish pilgrims honoured that tradition. Fortunately, when it came to their turn, the Irish rugby men remained soberly tight lipped.

Despite his customary slow progress as he walks to centre-stage, John Paul II was looking good yesterday, as fledgling Vaticanologist, Wood, pointed out with one of the understatements of the pontificate: 'He's pretty sharp, too, isn't he?'

5 FEBRUARY 2001

Few Complaints After Italian Job

Gerry Thornley

Veni, vidi, vici. Three games, three wins, 22 tries, 172 points scored and 12,000 Irish supporters savouring a historic Roman holiday in possibly the most beautiful city on the planet. Great junket and a

Henderson hat-trick . . . No dispute here as Rob Henderson dives over the line for the first of his three tries against Italy in the Six Nations game in Rome. Photograph: Eric Luke.

good first weekend in the championship too. There may be malcontents back home but there were few out here.

No harm in hindsight, perhaps, that Ireland had this one first-up. A better team than the Italians, or even the Italians with Diego Dominguez, would assuredly have punished Ireland's looseness in the opening period. Ireland won handsomely in the end, but no harm in hindsight either that they didn't record a third 60-pointer in Italy over the weekend, for some tempered Irish optimism, before the French come calling, may be no bad thing.

Cobwebs were dusted off and for sure there'll be a tighter, more focused performance against the French. There'll be a restful week for the majority of the players and none of the 13 home-based players will play for their clubs next weekend. The Munstermen, especially, need a break. With Brian O'Driscoll and perhaps Denis Hickie also back on board, there'll be plenty for them to work on when they come together in a week's time.

The rucking for one, the scrum for another, even the line-outs have been slicker, not to mention the missed first-up tackles and the flawed decision-making by the ball carrier. To pass or not to pass; it befuddled them continuously in that unnerving first period.

'I have to say I thought some of us didn't play too well,' admitted Keith Wood. 'I hold my own hand up – in the first half I was pretty poor. I thought a few of our guys didn't bring ourselves up to the standard we could have done. And I think, in the second half, we upped our level considerably.'

That Ireland are in classical, one-game-at-a-time mode was also made clear by Wood. 'France is going to be a serious match. I haven't really put any thought into it. Actually if you asked me two weeks ago I wouldn't have known. But this was a nervous match. It's a horrible feeling because everybody expects you to win and if you don't win you're the greatest losers ever and if you do win, nobody's going to get terribly excited.

'I think they'll have had a great weekend in Rome. It was quite Irish. "The Fields of Athenry" at the start was a little bit funny. I'm going to have to tell the championship new guys that this doesn't happen every time we play away from home.'

Wood also revealed that during the interval 'we got the proverbial bollocking and deserved it. After that we just maybe committed a few more people to rucks and started playing into the areas of the pitch we needed to be playing. And once we did that, we found ourselves in a more enviable position.

'There was one try, Shane Horgan's into the corner, that was a brilliant try. We had that ball for 10/15 phases. I'm looking up seeing that going on and thinking "We've held on to the ball and done so well in the last 60 seconds, this deserves a score". But we threw away the ball too much in the first-half.'

Compared to other winning post-match dressing rooms, this one was tired but happy, if not ecstatic. 'I thought Italy were quite cynical and in the nature of that they mightn't win too many matches, but they'll stop people playing. And it's very annoying. But if that is the manner people are going to play against us, in future we need to have ways of counteracting that.'

There were still quite a few garlands to be thrown around, David Wallace leading from the front when the going was toughest with some trademark dynamic ball carries. What odds the brothers Wallace providing a third Lion? And, of course, there was Rob Henderson, the buffalo on stampede, yet again, and maybe silencing those critics who label him a one-trick pony.

It was not, Wood maintained, a question of him filling Brian O'Driscoll's boots. 'Rob has been on fire all season, and all last season. It's not a question of him stepping up because he's oft over-looked and I'm happy he played well. But I also have to say Girvan had a good game; I thought Wally had a good game. Quinny did a lot of good work, and I thought Mick Galwey was one of the few guys who did play well in the first half.

'I was happy for Tyrone Howe in his first championship game. I was happy for Emmet Byrne when he came on. We've blooded a few more new guys today. There are so many things we have to tidy up in our game we can't be happy with certain things, but at the end of it you have to take it as a Six Nations win. I don't give a damn who it's against or where it is.'

It's said that if you throw a coin into the Trevi fountain and make a wish, you'll come back. So there were about 12,000 extra coins in the Fontana di Trevi then. *Ciao Roma.*

6 FEBRUARY 2001

Late-Night Activity Leaves Players With Red Faces

Paddy Agnew

'Players are regular clients, they're the sort of people who come looking for our services, even if they don't do it directly themselves … They want you, to talk to you, to drink together, to have a laugh and then, logically, you usually end up the night in bed with them. That's what they pay $1,500 for.

'Mind you, footballers are not my preferred type. They're often arrogant and then, in a group, they get even worse. They're vain and always worrying about their physique. They're rich and good looking and they let you know it.'

The above speaker is 'Monica', a woman whose 'services', until recently, were featured on an Internet site called metropolitan.it, which advertised the names of men and women (complete with photographs and phone numbers) offering sex for money.

Monica and her colleagues made the sports pages last week when it emerged that police investigators, carrying out surveillance on metropolitan.it, had discovered that a group of players from Inter Milan were among the clientele. A few weeks ago Inter players and team officials came together for a night out at a well-known Milanese restaurant. The mood in the team camp was light-hearted and relaxed. Inter had picked up five points in their previous three Serie A games against Atalanta (1–0), AC Milan (2–2) and Parma (1–1). By the standards of this season's Inter, that was a good run.

After the meal, most of the players headed for home. However five, plus one team employee, opted for a little late night activity.

Phone calls were made and, soon enough, some attractive young women appeared on the scene. The players and the women then headed off to the apartment of the team employee, when each of the six man team managed to 'score'.

Nothing especially unusual about this, a cynic might argue. Indeed, not. Young and wealthy professional footballers are not monks, nor have

they taken vows of chastity. There was a problem, however: one of the women was being tailed by Milan police within the ambit of the investigation into metropolitan.it.

The site has since been closed down and the two men who ran it have been accused of aiding and abetting prostitution. The players, however, face no charges as they have committed no offence.

According to investigators, the Inter players had 'hired' their company for the night via the site.

There has been more amusement than indignation among the public. At Inter's training ground one set of fans greeted the players with a chorus of: 'Next Time, Bring Us Along Too'.

Even coach Marco Tardelli played down the whole incident, telling reporters that if it happened, 'it was only a superficial thing'.

'Mind you, if you do things like this and then get caught, it just goes to show that you're not used to doing certain things … In my time, I never got caught.'

One person who was less amused was Inter owner, petrol millionaire Massimo Moratti. He

Level with the playing field . . . Kevin Hunt of Bohemians tumbles in a challenge with Ciaran Kavanagh (UCD) in the National League game at Belfield. Photograph: David Sleator.

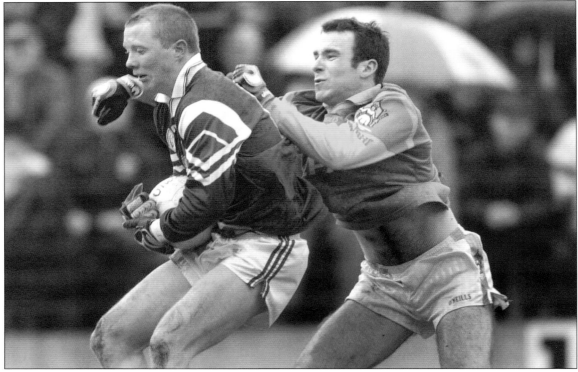

Personal Traynor . . . Jason Reilly of Cavan gets some close attention from Meath defender Hank Traynor in the National League game at Breffni Park. Photograph: Matt Kavanagh.

confessed last week that the latest saga at the troubled club had prompted him to think of selling his majority shareholding.

He added that the players involved would be subject to unspecified disciplinary action.

10 FEBRUARY 2001

Dundalk Man's Putting Invention a Hit with Kite at Orlando Show

Dermot Gilleece

It could be described as a field of dreams for inventors of golf gadgets. The annual PGA of America Merchandising Show in Orlando, Florida, has opened and closed its doors for another year, bringing wild hopes of riches to some exhibitors and bitter rejection to others.

The Irish were there, on both sides of the counter. And Dundalk's Martin Smith had the satisfaction of selling his putting invention 'The Gimme' to none other than former US Open champion Tom Kite, who now plies his craft in the senior ranks. Though the product retails at $50, Smith gave Kite a generous discount, naturally.

'It's been a tough slog since I started working on my invention five years ago and there were times when quitting looked to be very attractive,' he said. 'But after investing £200,000 of my own money, it looks as if I will finally make a go of it.' Which is more than can be said for countless fellow travellers.

USGA officials find themselves at the sharp end of the rejection process, when inventions don't conform. As in the case of the man who developed a putter design which had a little bubble in the clubhead itself. On having it rejected by the USGA, he insisted: 'You know, I spent so much time and money on this. Do you understand?' They did understand, but it was still non-conforming.

He went on: 'I conceived of this idea in a fox-hole in Korea. I was there defending my country when I came up with the concept for this design.' After about four phone calls, technical director Frank Thomas felt obliged to tell firmly, that the product still didn't conform.

Thomas takes up the story: 'Next I heard from him he said: "I've had a divorce from my wife over this. I've spent so much money on it. And I would really like you to reconsider it." But I replied: "I'm sorry about that." The final one I got, he was writing from his hospital bed.

'He said: "I've had a heart attack, I divorced my wife, I thought about this in a foxhole and would you please reconsider it? I really need it. It's going to be the make-or-break thing of my life." What do you do in a case like that?'

It was the last the USGA official heard of that particular inventor. And as he put it: 'Telling them their product is non-conforming is almost like telling somebody they've got cancer.'

For my own part, I've lost count of the calls I've received about Irish golf inventions over the years, 99 per cent of which were doomed to failure. Many ideas are prompted by a growing demand for corporate gifts at golf outings. But according to Smith: 'Suppliers won't buy those gifts unless they're endorsed by a leading personality. So there's no easy route into the market.'

Yet the situation is not without hope. During

Tilting at windmills . . . Dublin's James Gahan and Wexford's Robert Mageean (front) get their arms in a flap in the Leinster Under-21 Football Championship game in Parnell Park. Photograph: Alan Betson.

a recent game at Royal Dublin with Albert Lee, chairman of the Leinster Branch GUI, a chilling wind drew me towards an ingenious item on the handle of his electric golf trolley. It was a simple, fleece-lined sleeve which covered his hand while he guided the trolley along. Would it conform to requirements? Absolutely.

14 FEBRUARY 2001

Dissection Is Uniquely Capital Punishment

Sean Moran argues Tom Carr's critics have their timing all wrong

When Dublin manager Tom Carr protested mildly that Saturday's defeat by Roscommon shouldn't be taken out of context, he probably knew he was on a loser. With the national media parked on their doorstep, Dublin's teams come under disproportionate scrutiny.

Consequently – or subsequently – the Dublin public is less patient about their team's performances than the public in any other county. Carr's predecessor Mickey Whelan was hounded out of the job after losing a league match to an Offaly side that had just won the Leinster Championship.

Over the past 25 years, Dublin's real status in the game has been much misunderstood. Since the 1920s, the county has only averaged one All-Ireland a decade. There was a period of dominance in the 1970s, but the rise of Kerry put a stop to that.

Yet, expectations have been on the rampage since and created ridiculous pressures for county managers. The huge population disguises the struggle for the hearts and minds of a catchment area with plenty of other things to occupy it.

Over the past 10 years, the championships have become far more competitive and Dublin have discovered that winning Leinster no longer guarantees a serious shot at an All-Ireland and there

aren't anything like the number of handy matches in Leinster that there used to be.

Last summer, Kildare were simply better. They failed to challenge in the first half and gifted Dublin the space to build a six-point lead, but once Dublin came under pressure in the second half, they folded.

Maybe Carr's initial instinct was correct. 'I don't know what we have left to offer,' he said afterwards. 'We have put an awful lot of work in over the past three years and we have scoured the county to build this team.' But a good deal of reflection at county board level resulted in his being given another crack at it.

Regardless of whether this was the right thing to do, such a decision shouldn't come up for review because three league matches are lost.

The problem is a championship problem, and league performances have no bearing on it. As Carr himself pointed out, last season Dublin pulled impressive wins out of the hat against Galway and Kerry. He didn't finish the point but we can. This springtime steel didn't offer any accurate reflection of how they would react under pressure in the summer.

For nine years from 1986, Dublin qualified for all the league play-offs – winning three titles – and each summer suffered sickening championship disappointments. As soon as the sequence was abruptly halted with relegation in 1995, they won the All-Ireland.

It can be argued that this isn't a fair comparison as, in 1995, Dublin had a settled team and didn't need anything out of the league, other than the strong evidence that Jason Sherlock would make a big difference.

Look back at 1989 and the manner in which a wretched league final defeat by Cork followed a demoralising 1988 Leinster final defeat by Meath (when Charlie Redmond missed an injury-time penalty to draw the match). The team still managed to overturn Meath and win Leinster 10 weeks later.

The one thing Carr needs is a consistent team selection throughout the league. Teams which are in development as Dublin are can't afford the chopping and changing which is commonplace in the NFL.

Two years ago, Cork built an outstanding defence by keeping it together as a unit throughout the campaign. By contrast, Dublin have used 29 players in their three league matches to date.

Injury, unavailability and club commitments all contributed to that. When Carr has had the opportunity to field his best team in the championship, then is the time to judge. But, in the meantime, Carr's fiercest critics should calm down and concentrate on the club championships like the rest of us.

16 FEBRUARY 2001

Emphatic Victory for Hickey

Johnny Watterson

All the talk, all the swagger, all the original confidence transpired to be well-founded yesterday in Jury's Hotel, Dublin, when Pat Hickey launched his Olympic presidency into an unprecedented fourth term.

Hickey, who had predicted a landslide victory at the beginning of his campaign against sailing's Richard Burrows, finally finished where he had begun. It was a landslide. Hickey polled 27 votes to Burrows' 10 from the 37 votes on offer.

Much had been written about the 10-vote bloc of the executive committee, but even without that base, the incumbent president would still have won. The sports federations, deciding not to heed the wishes of the new Athletes Commission and the pleas of former Olympians Michael Carruth, Eamonn Coghlan and Mick Dowling to support Burrows, went overwhelmingly with Hickey.

'I'm absolutely overwhelmed,' said Hickey. 'It appears that amongst the federations I got 17 votes,

even if you assume that I got the 10 block executive vote, which you can't because it is secret.

'I want to thank those who supported me and for those who didn't support me,' he added. 'I hope that I can earn their respect over the next four years as we lead an Irish team into the Olympic Games in Athens. I would also want to thank my family.

'I'm very much aware of my election manifesto and I give an undertaking to deliver on every one of them. My first port of call next week will be to the Minister and John Treacy of the Sports Council,' he said.

It was an emotional moment for the former judo competitor. But as he had done four years ago, when there was a threat to his power base, Hickey was the best in the house at crunching the numbers.

Burrows, who had urged federations to change the way things had been done for the good of the athletes, was disappointed but stoic. 'While I am disappointed at the result, I am not surprised,' he said. 'I have been greatly heartened by the support I received from so many athletes and from the federations who voted for me. They also voted for badly needed change, which I now hope will be speedily implemented in the best interests of Irish Olympians.

'Finally, I wish all our athletes well in the Winter Olympics in 2002 and in Athens in 2004. I wish Pat Hickey well and hope the need for focus on the athletes and on supporting them throughout their training and international competition phases is now well understood.'

The Irish Sports Council (ISC), with whom Hickey has not enjoyed a good relationship over the past four years, also noted Hickey's significant win.

'The Irish Sports Council congratulates Pat Hickey on his re-election as OCI president,' a spokesman said. 'The council notes that Mr Hickey campaigned on the basis of ending all conflicts involving the OCI and operating in collaboration and co-operation on all fronts. The council looks forward to Mr Hickey implementing his campaign promises.'

At the fag end of the affair, the meeting adopted a resolution to review the memorandum and articles of association of the company, taking cognisance of the Olympic Charter and Irish Companies Acts. That decision appeared to address what many of Hickey's detractors had been complaining about for some time, namely, that there are anomalies in the articles. In that, at least, everyone seemed to agree.

Along with Hickey, the entire board were re-elected. Football's Louis Kilcoyne easily defended his first vice-president position, while Shay

McDonald from gymnastics held his second vice-president place. General secretary Dermot Sherlock and treasurer Peader Casey were also returned with large margins.

The ordinary members of the executive elected were: Mary Baneham (basketball), Bobby Begley (athletics), Dermot Henihan (rowing), Billy Kennedy (cycling), John Mcloy (hockey) and William O'Brien (archery).

One obstacle over, Hickey's next manoeuvre may take him to Moscow, in July, where he is likely to run against some of the most important sports administrators in the world for one of the positions on the élite International Olympic

Before the count . . . Richard Burrows waits for the OCI a.g.m. to start at Jurys Hotel in Dublin as Pat Hickey enters the room. Photograph: Cyril Byrne.

Committee executive. Don't count him out of that one either.

Owen Delivers Striking Blows for Liverpool

Paddy Agnew

Roma – 0, Liverpool – 2

The English football renaissance continues. Liverpool struck another mighty blow for English soccer in Rome last night against current Serie A league leaders, AS Roma. Seventeen years after Joe Fagan's Liverpool defeated Roma in the Champions Cup final, the men in red struck again, this time winning in an arguably much more emphatic manner. England striker Michael Owen, a surprise starter, was the hero of the night scoring both goals.

For the third time this season, a Premiership side has come, seen and, if not conquered, at least done very well at the Olympic Stadium. Reigning Italian champions Lazio have already been held to a 1–1 draw by Arsenal and beaten 1–0 by Leeds in Champions League games here this season. Last night, Liverpool did arguably better, making the most of a surprisingly tame Roma performance in which the home side complicated things for themselves by gifting a soft goal early in the second half. When Liverpool's French coach, Gerard Houllier, suggested last weekend that the English Premiership is the most competitive league in the world, you had better believe him.

Both opening line-ups had contained an element of surprise. Whilst it had been widely expected that Roma coach Fabio Capello would rest his Argentine ace, Gabriel Batistuta, it came as a mild surprise to find that the club doctor had also ruled out captain Francesco Totti.

Japanese midfielder Hidetoshi Nakata, a player perhaps headed for the English Premiership next season, replaced Totti in an otherwise familiar formation in which Marco Delvecchio moved into the Batistuta role, partnered by Vincenzo Montella. As a replacement for Totti, however, despite some good first-half passing, Nakata proved disappointing.

Liverpool's Houllier also sprang a few surprises, opting for German Christian Ziege rather than Czech Republic midfielder Vladimir Smicer and, more surprisingly, going for a front line comprising Michael Owen and Robbie Fowler.

By half-time, the visitors already had every reason to be pleased. Not only had they held Roma scoreless but, more significantly, they had done so in a 45-minute period in which their Dutch goalkeeper Sander Westerveld had not had to make anything resembling a serious save.

For all that Roma inevitably made the running, the home side had to wait until the 42nd minute before creating their first real chance. That came when Brazilian Cafu and reserve defender Alessandro Rinaldi combined well on the right, with Rinaldi knocking in a fine cross that Delvecchio headed just over from close range.

If the first half had proved satisfactory for Liverpool, the second half began on a postively perfect note, when the normally reliable Roma defence gave away a soft goal in the first minute. In a moment of distraction, Rinaldi broke every rule in the defender's code when delivering a square pass across his penalty area.

Owen gratefully accepted the gift and danced past Amedeo Mangone before slotting home a brilliantly taken goal out of reach of the blameless Roma goalkeeper, Francesco Antonioli.

That goal inevitably dropped the Roma fat in the fire but, for all that, the home side upped their rhythm and tempo, they had only one fiercely driven drive from Brazilian substitute Assuncao to show for their efforts. Twenty-five minutes from the end, Capello had little option but to throw Batistuta into the fray.

The big Argentine had hardly had time to warm himself up, however, before little Owen struck again for a splendid 71st-minute second goal that, in itself, has probably put Liverpool into the quarter-finals.

From out on the right, Ziege hit a powerful free-kick that was parried by Antonioli. The rebound fell to Finn Sami Hyppia, who combined neatly with Ziege to send the German to the bye-line, from where he delivered a wickedly fast and low pass which Owen read brilliantly, getting in to head home from a narrow angle at the near post.

A jubilant Houllier hailed Liverpool's performance but said: 'We mustn't get carried away, there's still the second leg. Roma are an outstanding side, a great team but we managed to keep them quiet and nullified them. But the second game will be very difficult.'

ROMA: Antonioli; Rinaldi, Samuel, Mangone; Cafu, Emerson, Tommasi, Candela; Nakata; Delvecchio, Montella. Subs: Assuncao for Nakata (51 mins); Batistuta for Tommasi (66 mins); Gigou for Delvecchio (82 mins).

LIVERPOOL: Westerveld; Babbel, Henchoz, Hyppia, Carragher; Barmby, McAllister, Hamann, Ziege; Owen, Fowler. Subs: Smicer for Ziege (74 mins); Litmanen for Owen (80 mins).

REFEREE: M. Merk (Ger).

19 FEBRUARY 2001

Multiple Choice for Olympic Failure

Tom Humphries

LockerRoom has been shown a copy of the Olympics post-mortem questionnaire distributed to Irish athletes recently. Here is a sample.

Since 1984 Ireland has won one track and field medal. This is the fault of:

A. Pat Hickey. B. Patrick J. Hickey. C. Hickeys everywhere. D. Other countries.

For much of the time since 1996 Irish swimming has been unfunded due to a child abuse scandal. In your view who/what is to blame then for the poor performance of Irish swimmers in Sydney.

A. Pat Hickey. B. The OCI. C. The deep end. D. Piranhas.

An Irish boxer steps into the ring at the Olympics and discovers, to his surprise, that he is fighting a southpaw. This is an example of:

A. How cunning Pat Hickey is. B. OCI dirty tricks. C. Bloody foreigners. D. Bad luck.

An Irish badminton player draws the silver medallist from the previous Olympics in the first round of the Games. This proves that …

A. Pat Hickey is a pox-bottle. B. Juan Antonio Samaranch has it in for us. C. Badminton players get great tans. D. We need the BertieBowl.

Irish rowers do far worse than expected. This is the responsibility of:

A. Blazers. B. Journalists. C. Hickey. D. The uphill course.

The ideal person to lead the Irish Olympic movement should:

A. Be alive and well and living in Paris. B. Have dated Anne Doyle. C. Have created this questionnaire. D. Be rich.

The best thing about being an Irish Olympian is:

A. Going on the big aeroplane. B. The free food. C. Fit looking chicks/guys. D. The infighting.

Of 34 Irish track athletes with the A standard qualification only one reached a final in Sydney. The solution to this is:

A. To send athletes with the slower B standard. B. Have 30 people per final. C. Blame Pat Hickey. D. No change in Athletics Ireland.

Of the £4,067,592 in Olympic year grants given by the Irish Sports Council in January 2000, athletics (£400,949), sailing (£281,889), tennis (£221,889), boxing ((£215,536), canoeing (£198,163), swimming (£164,243) and cycling (£143,243) accounted for £1.62 million or 45 per cent of the funds. Each will vote for Richard Burrows.

The remaining money was divided between 52 other organisations. These figures suggest that these seven sports:

A. Know which side their bread is buttered on. B. Have little to be complaining about. C. Should have brought home lots of medals. D. Are more important than other sports.

By permitting only recent Olympians to join its ranks the Athletes Commission:

A. Perpetuates the very system it purports to criticise. B. Keeps things cosy. C. Ensures that track

and field will dominate. D. Marginalises itself.

The opinions and views of elite athletes are:

A. Very, very important. B. Of tantamount importance. C. Infallible. D. All that matters.

The opinions of ordinary athletes are:

A. Insufferable. B. Plain embarrassing. C. Not to be found in newspapers. D. Drug free.

Successful Irish track athletes have always:

A. Been to college in America. B. Owed everything to The Artists Formerly Known as BLE. C. Been deemed unsuitable to run athletics in Ireland. D. Been few and far between.

During the Sydney Games it was said of

Colleges football . . . Colaiste Eoin's Manus MacGabhan (right) gets to the ball ahead of Luke Naughton (Marist) in the Leinster Colleges Football Championship game at Silverpark, Leopardstown. Photograph: Eric Luke.

Athletics Ireland that it wasn't 'an athlete friendly situation', 'that we in Athletics Ireland need to get more professional' (Patsey McGonagle Irish athletics team manager) and 'it has gone beyond the time for change. That's not just my view but the view of the vast majority of people inside and outside Irish athletics' (Eamonn Coghlan). This suggests that:

A. Pat Hickey runs Athletics Ireland. B. Pat Hickey wasn't wrong in the gear row but it would have been helpful had he been. C. People in glass houses are throwing stones. D. Eamonn never misses a bun-fight.

Getting rid of Pat Hickey will:

A. Make up for not having a series of trained full-time sports executives in place. B. Make up for the absence of a long-term fully funded sports strategy. C. Make up for all that lottery money which is supposed to go to sport but doesn't. D. Make the IOC give extra accreditations to Sports Ministers.

At the last Olympics he attended, Michael Carruth won a gold medal and had no complaints. Since then the Irish Amateur Boxing Association has torn itself apart internally and imperilled its funding by declining to name a drugs cheat, while Michael has gone on to be a professional in what is the most perfectly administered sport in the world. This implies that:

A. Something is bugging Michael. B. Michael sees the big picture. C. Eaten bread is soon forgotten. D. Boxers should wear head gear.

The Irish public expects:

A. More infighting. B. More scandals. C. Another gear row. D. That the Minister can bring his entire constituency to the next Olympics.

(This questionnaire is confidential and has been commissioned by the Irish Sports Council. The final report, a distillation of the views of 40 very disappointed athletes, will be released during the internal elections of another sports body. Fingers crossed!)

You'll Get No Babble from Psycho

Michael Walker

Longevity is an underrated virtue – often confused with time-serving, people working their ticket. Age has withered its reputation. Longevity has a stoop.

But on the steep banks of the River Wear on Saturday, longevity had a different demeanour and appearance altogether. Muscular, upright, committed, aggressive and fit as a boxer, longevity was personified by Stuart Pearce in Sunderland. He will be 39 in two months.

Eighteen years on from his debut for Coventry City, which he joined from Wealdstone, where he worked as a bricklayer, Pearce almost mocked the frenzy surrounding the younger generation at West Ham United with a performance that was, in Harry Redknapp's estimation, the definition of professional. Not promising, not tempting, just professional. Redknapp was right.

Pearce was named man of the match by the television organisation that forced the game to kick off at noon. Had the vote gone to the crowd, Pearce, despite his recent Newcastle United attachment, would have been a unanimous choice. Not often at the Stadium of Light do they see Niall Quinn and Kevin Phillips outjumped and frustrated with such gusto. But they did on Saturday.

The evening highlights may have shown Pearce's athletic second-half clearance from Quinn from under his crossbar, and his perfectly timed tackle on John Oster soon after that. But what Redknapp, Peter Reid and Quinn himself appreciated equally, was the manner in which Pearce played throughout. Getting to the ball first is football's golden rule and Pearce did that more than anybody. At 38, the sheer desire within Pearce remains fierce. He has a young heart beneath old shoulders.

Even among those put off Pearce by his British bulldog personality – his autobiography's title followed his nickname, Psycho – it was easy to understand Redknapp's post-match description of Pearce as 'special'. Redknapp used the word twice.

'He's fit as a fiddle,' Redknapp said. 'He'll be in on Monday. He'll be in a five-a-side or nine-a-side. And he'll want to win. He always wants to win. He kicks them up in the air in training. It's that will to win he's got that is special. Stuart Pearce is just so special.

'He was the best left-back in the world in his prime. Some say Paolo Maldini, but I know which one I'd rather play against. People talk about coaching, but the game is about players. That's why I said Arsene Wenger had the easiest job in football when he came to Arsenal because he had Tony Adams in the dressing room.

'So you don't need to be a great coach. You just say to the kids: "Watch Pearcey play." He doesn't stand three yards off people and let them get their crosses in. He's up their arse, kicking them, tackling them, frightening them. You just tell the kids to watch him work, watch him head the ball, watch the commitment he plays with. Half the kids who come into the game now have got no appetite, they don't want to work.

'He broke his leg twice last season. Twice in one season! How do you come back from that? How do you come back at 38 years of age from two broken legs in one season?

'He trained all through the summer, came back as white as a sheet. I don't think he'd seen any sun. Hadn't had a holiday. He said: "Just give me monthly contracts." After six weeks, I said: "You look great. Let's sign through to the end of the year." He said: "Nah, I'll stick on the monthlies. If I do get an injury I won't be a problem to you. I'll just drift off." That's how he is.'

Reid simply said 'outstanding', while Quinn said: 'I'm 35 and there aren't many people whom I look up to, but Stuart Pearce is one of them.'

Pearce has signed a longer deal now and shows no sign of wanting to spend more time with his family. He has lost two FA Cup finals with Nottingham Forest and Newcastle and would be a popular candidate to win at the third attempt should West Ham make it to Cardiff.

Not that he revels in it all: at Old Trafford and the Stadium of Light he was first off the pitch while his colleagues cavorted in front of their fans. There is something brilliant about his refusal to want to be among celebrity squares.

In the tunnel he gave one brief interview in which he said: 'I enjoy playing. The day I stop enjoying it is the day I stop. It was enjoyable to come here and win. Especially with a clean sheet – I'm a defender.' Then he was off, first on the bus.

Not raging against the dying of the light. The light isn't dying. Longevity rules.

19 FEBRUARY 2001

Ireland Make their Own Luck

Gerry Thornley

Ireland – 22, France – 15

In the dressing room after the game, Warren Gatland approached David Wallace and good-naturedly warned him never to kick the ball away like he had done in that nerve-jangling finale. Wallace admitted he knew he'd messed up as soon as he'd done it. All part of the learning curve. If you don't make mistakes, you don't make progress.

Ireland deserved this massive, hard-earned win for being the more positive side over the 80 minutes, for adhering to a running game, and also for generally keeping their heads better and being notably more disciplined.

For sure, Peter Stringer and Ronan O'Gara pulled the strings deftly while Brian O'Driscoll was

Crossing the gain line . . . Brian O'Driscoll causes France more heartbreak as he accelerates past Xavier Garbajosa in the Six Nations game at Lansdowne Road. Photograph: Eric Luke.

the ace in the hole, but it was always going to be as important that the pack fronted up and they assuredly did. The match statistics confirm Ireland's dominance of the leather and the territory.

This, after all, was a French pack that steamrolled both the All Blacks and the Scots up front in their last two outings. It helped that the set-pieces provided the platform. The scrum, apart from two exceptions, was rock solid and allayed the fears of many.

Afterwards, Peter Clohessy acknowledged the two aberrations. 'We had our legs too far up underneath us. Scrummaging against a French team, you need to stay low and long.'

Clohessy and the mighty Bull, John Hayes, rumbled and also put in the big hits, with Keith Wood getting through a mountain of work. His darts hit the bull's eye regularly, and Ireland's two-to-one ratio in the line-out (where Malcolm

O'Kelly reigned supreme, with Mick Galwey and Alan Quinlan providing assured alternatives) contributed significantly to the scoreboard. Just as significantly, the Irish pack didn't roll over for the French juggernaut.

A key moment in the match was the early double-hit by O'Kelly and Hayes when David Auradou came rumbling around the side of a ruck. As resolute as a brick wall, first they held them up and then Ireland drove France back to earn a penalty. In that moment Ireland drew a line in the sand. You wanna bosh it up close-in? Fine, we're not going anywhere.

From the ensuing field position Ireland went ahead and territorially dominated the game. A 9–3 interval lead was hard earned to put it mildly. The French put in some ferocious tackles and Irish ball carriers were forced to perform acrobatics in presenting the ball back.

With their heavy tackling and good organisation, France rarely had to commit too many men to rucks and so Ireland were regularly outnumbered across the pitch, even when probing off good recycled ball. It is an enduring memory of the match, Irish ball carriers searching for near non-existent gaps amidst a thicket of blue. No one succeeded better than O'Driscoll, whose ability to duck and weave through the most heavily guarded areas of the pitch, even off static ball, was single-handedly responsible for Ireland's field position and the second O'Gara penalty to regain the lead.

He was a remarkably persistent threat, though as the match progressed, he got some notable assistance, most obviously from his able foil Rob Henderson and the increasingly influential Wallace, while the oft under-appreciated Anthony Foley was second in the ball-carrying stakes (with 13) behind O'Gara (27) and ahead of O'Driscoll (10).

On a good day at the office for the Irish management, a subtle change of tactics and a refocused energy had seen Ireland hit the ground running on the resumption. A brilliant lineout steal by O'Kelly and some pick-and-go rumbles from O'Kelly and Hayes were clearly the product of the Irish management's interval pep talk.

They also began probing the blind side more. France had done their homework and packed midfield but when Ireland began relocating the points of attack to pick and go up the middle or down the narrow side, half-gaps began to appear. With French hands indiscriminately loose on the deck at ruck time, O'Gara was also able to land two more penalties from three attempts, and at 22–3, Ireland had produced as fine a third quarter as has been seen by the home side in a long, long time at the venue.

True, O'Driscoll didn't appear to ground the ball for his try, but them's the breaks. An incident leading up to the first French try was just as debatable. When O'Gara was obliged to step inside Christophe Lamaison and was collared by Olivier

Magne, Lamaison was literally yards offside but this somehow went undetected. Were the touch judges communicating with referee Scott Young regarding offsides across the gain-line? It didn't seem so. From the ensuing scrum and close-range penalty, Richard Dourthe was mauled over the line. Had Lamaison been properly penalised, who knows how it might have panned out from there?

For all the inquisitions, the debate about the try that wasn't but was, Ireland and France each got what they deserved. Ireland the two points for playing the more positive, disciplined and controlled rugby over the 80-plus minutes, France zero points and food for thought because they didn't start playing until the final quarter. It served them right really.

No doubt the guillotine will drop. Dourthe and Magne, to name but two, surprisingly seemed relative soft touches in the wider midfield area whenever Henderson, Wallace and O'Driscoll (fittingly the incisor, link and poacher respectively of Ireland's try) went galloping.

Indeed, the French back row made a negligent impact but then that in part was down to their tactics.

Until beyond the hour mark France hardly set up any worthwhile forward momentum for their back row, concentrating (as we expected) on bashing away around the fringes or else kicking for territory.

They kicked far too much ball in the first half and only kept it in the hand when faced with a 22–3 deficit and impending defeat. It was as if they were fearfully locked in Bernard Laporte's straitjacket.

As Ireland showed when stemming the tide and plotting a course for victory in the denouement, the game is about keeping the ball in hand. Forget about the rub of the green. Fortune favoured the brave.

SCORING SEQUENCE: 5 mins: O'Gara pen, 3–0; 19 mins: Lamaison pen, 3–3; 29 mins: O'Gara pen, 6–3; 40 mins: O'Gara pen, 9–3; Half-time:

That man again, that try again . . . Another view of Brian O'Driscoll's try against France — the crowd in that corner seemed to think it was okay. Photograph: Eric Luke.

9–3; 44 mins: O'Gara pen 12–3; 51 mins: O'Driscoll try, O'Gara con, 19–3; 55 mins: O'Gara pen, 22–3; 62 mins: Pelous try, Lamaison con, 22–10; 72 mins: Bernat-Salles try 22–15.

IRELAND: G. Dempsey (Terenure College and Leinster); D. Hickie (St Mary's College and Leinster), B. O'Driscoll (Blackrock and Leinster), R. Henderson (Wasps), T. Howe (Dungannon and Ulster); R. O'Gara (Cork Con and Munster), P. Stringer (Shannon and Munster); P. Clohessy (Young Munster and Munster), K. Wood (Harlequins, capt), J. Hayes (Shannon and Munster); M. Galwey (Shannon and Munster), M. O'Kelly (St Mary's College and Leinster); A. Quinlan (Shannon and Munster), A. Foley (Shannon and Munster), D. Wallace (Garryowen and Munster). Replacements: E. Byrne (St Mary's College and Leinster) for Clohessy, G. Longwell (Ballymena) for Galwey, A. Ward (Ballynahinch) for Quinlan (all 73 mins), K. Maggs (Bath) for Henderson (75 mins).

FRANCE: X. Garbajosa (Toulouse); P. Bernat-Salles (Biarritz), F. Comba (Stade Français), R. Dourthe (Beziers), D. Bory (Montferrand); C. Lamaison (Agen), P. Carbonneau (Pau); S. Marconnet (Stade Français), R. Ibanez (Castres), P. de Villiers (Stade Français); D. Auradou (Stade Français), F. Pelous (Toulouse, capt); C. Moni (Stade Français), C. Juillet (Stade Français), O. Magne (Montferrand). Replacements: C. Califano (Toulouse) for Marconnet (63 mins), A. Benazzi (Agen) for Auradou (16–24 mins and 63 mins), S. Betsen (Biarritz) for Moni (70 mins), C. Dominici (Stade Français) for Bory (70 mins).

REFEREE: Scott Young (Australia).

Clongowes Are Simply Swept Aside

John O'Sullivan

Terenure – 36, Clongowes Wood – 7

It had been billed as the confrontation in this season's Leinster Schools' Senior Cup, the defending champions against the tournament's second favourites, a potential classic and certainly a contest to savour. This match did not fulfil the pre-match hype, but it would be churlish to downgrade the quality of Terenure College's performance at Donnybrook yesterday.

The team collectively and in several individual contributions produced a stunning display, their rugby the epitome of the modern game, where a premium is placed on ball players and utilising the width of the pitch.

Terenure mixed the power of their pack with strong running from midfield and the back three, and when the occasion demanded, turned to the prodigious boot of excellent out-half David McAllister.

They played with pace, offloaded the ball in the tackle and mixed up their game plan beautifully to stretch their opponents remorselessly. They scored five tries to one and yet wouldn't have been flattered had they added more.

The bravery and determination of Clongowes were insufficient as Terenure dominated up front. Roy McDonnell and flanker Conor McGinn were a constant source of ball out of touch, and in what was a superb performance from the Terenure pack, the back row of Donal Dunlop, McGinn and Jonathan Barretto was outstanding.

Paul Coleman was an excellent link at scrum-half while McAllister, a few wayward passes notwithstanding, bossed the game intelligently. Killian Coleman's strength in the centre gave his forwards a platform while the back three all enjoyed fine individual moments.

Clongowes demonstrated their customary character, but with the exception of the set scrum and number eight Ronan Farrell's couple of breaks, were second best up front. Behind the scrum only right wing Paddy Berkery offered discomfort to the Terenure defence.

Terenure were 10–0 up in as many minutes, McAllister's penalty followed by a beautifully worked try for right wing Oliver Pugh, who came off the blindside wing, raced on to Killian O'Toole's exquisitely-timed pass and crossed under the posts.

McAllister converted as he would do so again on 26 minutes. A great break by left wing James Donnelly took play into the Clongowes 22 and two rucks later prop John Anthony Lee forced his way over.

Killian Coleman grabbed his side's third try, this time unconverted, in first-half injury time after good work by Dunlop and full-back David Cabazon. The centre grabbed a second eight minutes into the second half, using his strength to force his way over. McAllister converted.

Clongowes had reduced the deficit just after half-time when Farrell's run culminated in James O'Reilly racing 40 metres for the try. Connellan posted a fine conversion.

However, Terenure finished the stronger and centre Killian O'Toole scored his side's fifth try six minutes from the finish. McAllister converted.

SCORING SEQUENCE: 2 mins: McAllister pen, 3–0; 9 mins: Pugh try, McAllister con, 10–0; 26 mins: Lee try, McAllister con, 17–0; 37 mins: K. Coleman try, 22–0. Half-time: 22–0. 43 mins: O'Reilly try, Connellan con, 22–7; 48 mins: K. Coleman try, McAllister con, 29–7; 64 mins: O'Toole try, McAllister con, 36–7.

TERENURE COLLEGE: D. Cabazon; O. Pugh, K. O'Toole, K. Coleman, J. Donnelly; D. McAllister, P. Coleman; J.A. Lee, G. Doyle, F. Cronin, E. Wallace, R. McDonnell, J. Barretto, D. Dunlop (capt), C. McGinn. Replacements: S.

Schools' rugby . . . Though knocked out by Terenure in the Leinster Schools' Senior Cup, Clongowes showed their mettle in an earlier round against Belvedere at Donnybrook when Paddy Berkery raced through for a try. Photograph: Eric Luke.

Healy for Donnelly (52 mins); S. Jenkinson for P. Coleman (59 mins); K. Molloy for Cronin (65 mins); L. Comer for K. Coleman (65 mins); A. Dunlop for R. McDonnell (66 mins); R. Hegarty for Doyle (66 mins).

CLONGOWES WOOD COLLEGE: G. Hayes; P. Berkery, D. Sharkey, R. Jenkinson, J. O'Reilly; B. Culliton, D. Connellan; S. Dunne, C. Klinkenberg, J. Moran, B. Carlos, A. Houlihan, D. Brides, R. Farrell, R. O'Toole (capt). Replacements: S. Meagher for Connellan (49 mins); R. Sharkey for Brides (50 mins); G. Murphy for Farrell (51 mins); D. Campbell for Dunne (57 mins).

REFEREE: D. Courtney (Leinster).

26 FEBRUARY 2001

McEnroe Sees Off the Young Guy

Johnny Watterson

Maybe he'd said enough this week anyway. The last sighting of John McEnroe after he'd beaten Guy Forget in the final of the KPMG Challenge was of him jogging out the side door of the Point, a minder in pursuit with shoes, watch and sundry items of clothing draped over his arm. A suitable image. The New Yorker chasing a plane to London, to get to New York, creating chaos from order.

McEnroe generally had it all his own way in Dublin since Thursday, with his contests against John Lloyd, Michael Pernfors and Bjorn Borg coming perilously close to mismatches. But this final was regularly in doubt, McEnroe winning the two setter with tie breaks and neither player once dropping his serve.

The closest anyone came to a service break was when McEnroe threatened Forget's serve in the ninth game of the second set and held two break points. Forget responded with two aces to ultimately haul the game into the tie break. There it simply hinged on a couple of points.

'Sometimes it's funny to see John out on court. Winning is sometimes like a matter of life and death to him. We are all competitive but he is the most competitive. That's just the way he is,' said 36-year-old Forget, a Wimbledon quarter-finalist as recently as 1994.

'It doesn't hurt to lose to someone six years older than me. If I was playing all the tournaments and practising three hours a day I'd get a little upset. But I think it could have gone either way today. It was one or two points in each set.'

Although the crowd clearly enjoyed the match, the questions over what sort of life span the event has are still there. It hinges on McEnroe, who still plays great tennis, a brand that nobody else has been able to match. Never having relied on power, the years have been kind to his game, although the stage-managed histrionics are occasionally absurd enough to take the game closer to panto than he or anyone else would wish.

Borg too is a draw, although he doesn't want to play any more, which makes it increasingly obvious that players such as former Wimbledon champions Stefan Edberg, Michael Stich and most importantly of all, Boris Becker, will have to come through in order to keep it alive.

The event is scheduled to run next year, with the Dublin and London events the two most suc-

Still serious . . . John McEnroe in action at the Point against Guy Forget whom he beat to win the Seniors Challenge event.

cessful on the calendar. 'I hope to be back next year,' said McEnroe when receiving his trophy on court. That alone means that it is highly likely to be an event next year, one that over 2,000 people wanted to see yesterday in Dublin.

1st-2nd: J. McEnroe bt G. Forget 7–6, 7–6 3rd-4th: P. Cash bt M. Pernfors 6–1, 6–4

Schools' rugby . . . Castleknock number eight Simon Crawford is held by Mark Shanley of Monkstown in the Leinster Schools' Senior Cup match at Donnybrook. Photograph: Cyril Byrne.

THE FINAL WHISTLE

A Fool and His Money

Could you do with a few extra bob? Well, last week the *Star* had a story that seemed to us to be a sure-fire, no-small-print-honest, get-rich-quick scheme that should solve all your fiscal troubles. Just get on a cheap flight to Liverpool, get the bus to the English Rose pub in Halewood and ask the bloke at the pool table for his autograph.

And ask him again and again and again. Eh? Landlady Jayne Scroggie told the *Star* that none other than Paul Gascoigne has been spending all his time playing pool in her pub since picking up a thigh injury in November (drinking pints of orange squash, she insists) and whenever anyone asks him for an autograph he whips out a £10 note, scribbles his name on it and hands it over.

In five afternoons last week he paid out ... £900. The bulk of which went to a coach load of kids and their parents who arrived from London. 'He is the most generous bloke I've seen in ages,' marvelled Jayne. Orange squash, eh?

5 FEBRUARY 2001

Mary Hannigan

Old Heads Still Draw Top Dollar

Tiger Woods will collect $54.6 million from endorsement deals this year. And it will surprise no one that this is three times what the second-placed player will receive. But the really interesting thing is that the second-placed player happens to be none other than Arnold Palmer, who will be 72 next September.

According to *Golf World* in the US, Pennzoil, Cooper Times and Office Depot are among 20 endorsements which will earn Palmer $18 million this year. In fact he is the only golfer who can match Woods' appeal to non-golfers.

Also fascinating is that the third man on the list happens to be another player some way past his prime. Greg Norman, who was 46 last Saturday, will earn $16 million through endorsements with 15 companies, including Titleist, Reebok and Chevy Trucks.

The others in the top-10 are: Phil Mickelson ($7 million); Davis Love and David Duval ($6 million each); Jack Nicklaus, Colin Montgomerie, Tom Watson and Jumbo Ozaki ($5 million each). Montgomerie's earnings would be appreciably higher, however, were all of his European endorsements included.

Meanwhile, it is estimated that a player finishing around 80th on the USPGA Tour money list this year will be guaranteed overall earnings of $1 million – $650,000 from prize funds and the remainder from endorsements.

17 FEBRUARY 2001

Dermot Gilleece

Referee's Match Strip

Wacky goings-on in Portugal last week where, allegedly, the referee in the second division clash of Academica and Imortal lost the run of himself after the final whistle. Two policewomen, known only as 'Fatima' and 'Paula', were guarding the changing-room of referee Bruno Paixao after the game when, they allege, he appeared naked at the door, exposed himself 'four or five times' and invited them inside. Bruno was charged with indecent exposure – but is none too happy about it.

'I didn't offend anybody. I'm 26, educated and attending a university degree course,' he protested, failing to explain quite what that had to do with anything. 'It wouldn't enter my head to defame anybody, much less police officials.

'If the policewomen lodge a complaint, I'll reply with one of my own – that of defamation – as I have a family.' The Portuguese FA are saying nothing but Bruno is desperately hoping that 'Fatima' and 'Paula' don't present them with video evidence. As are the linesmen who, as usual, hadn't a clear view of the incident.

26 FEBRUARY 2001

Mary Hannigan

That old white magic . . . Jimmy White, still able to mesmerise an audience, in action at the Citywest Hotel, the new venue for the Irish Masters. Photograph: Dara Mac Dónaill.

MARCH

2 0 0 1

HIGHLIGHTS

1 March: Sonia O'Sullivan wins 3,000 metres in Melbourne Track Classic.

4 March: Padraig Harrington and Tiger Woods share second place behind Thomas Bjorn in the Dubai Desert Classic. Teams call for better safety measures as race marshal dies at Australian Grand Prix. Evander Holyfield loses his World Boxing Association version of world heavyweight title in Las Vegas to John Ruiz.

5 March: Padraig Harrington moves to a career best – 19th place in the official world rankings.

6 March: The World Cross Country Championships move from Dublin to Brussels because of the foot and mouth epidemic. The GAA declines to comment on the Government package worth £45 million on offer to the FAI.

7 March: IRFU accept Department of Agriculture recommendations and postpone internationals against England and Scotland. Punchestown postponed. Stan Collymore calls time on his career.

8 March: C.J. Hunter, husband of US athlete Marion Jones, officially retires following two-year suspension for positive dope test.

9 March: Eircom Park formally consigned to history as FAI decide to become tenants of Stadium Ireland.

11 March: Sonia O'Sullivan's ambitious attempt on double gold at the World Indoor Championships in Lisbon backfires.

12 March: British Horse Racing Board Chairman Peter Savill defends the decision to carry on racing in the face of the foot and mouth crisis.

13 March: Manchester United beat Sturm Graz 3–0 to reach quarter-finals of UEFA Champions League. Each member of Special Olympics Team Ireland wins a medal in last day of Alpine skiing at the 2001 Special Olympics World Winter Games in Alaska.

14 March: GAA director general Liam Mulvihill is set for discussion with the Government about further funding for Croke Park. The Irish Football Association announces a code of conduct aimed at clearing Windsor Park's terraces of bigots.

15 March: Liverpool on course to win all three cups they have entered by reaching semi-finals of the UEFA Cup.

18 March: Celtic beat Kilmarnock 3-0 to lift the first trophy of a possible treble. Des Smyth becomes the oldest winner on the European Tour by taking the Madeira Open.

21 March: Leinster Council scraps round-robin section of provincial hurling championship.

25 March: Republic of Ireland beat Cyprus 4-0 in World Cup qualifier. All goes wrong for Sonia O'Sullivan at World Cross Country Championships while Paula Radcliffe takes home gold and silver medals.

26 March: Tiger Woods claims the 'fifth major' at the Players' Championship at Sawgrass.

27 March: Tables released by Irish Sports Council show that Irish athletes are no better or worse than those from other nations when it comes to cheating in sport.

28 March: Republic of Ireland beat Andorra 3-0 to share the top of Group Two World Cup with Portugal.

29 March: Glen Hoddle unveiled as new Tottenham Hotspur manager.

3 MARCH 2001

No Way Back for Tipperary and Kilkenny

Seán Moran

Some people in Tipperary remember it quite vividly. Seamus J. King, the hurling historian and broadcaster, says that he was talking to such a person. 'He remembers it well. What they did when slaughtering was dig a pit and there were no mechanical diggers then, it was all done by manual labour. They built a ramp into the pit and drove the cattle down into it. Then they shot them in the pit and covered the carcasses with lime and buried them. There was no burning.'

Viewed from our current tremulous perspective, the wonder about the 1941 epidemic of foot and mouth is that it left so few traces. According to King, local newspapers gave it comparatively scant coverage. Even now, it's hard to come across references in general history books to the eight-month outbreak and whereas there was a specific relevance to the GAA's championship, it looks extremely localised compared to the sense of national emergency this weekend.

First identified in February 1941, the disease was largely concentrated in south Leinster and Munster, leading to the slaughter of between 21,000 and 24,000 animals, and most seriously affected Kilkenny, Carlow and parts of Laois and Tipperary. This obviously threatened an important part of hurling's prime territory and, in the end, it was Kilkenny and Tipperary who suffered most – both being withdrawn before the championship ended.

Yet, earlier in the year, the games proceeded. On St Patrick's Day, Leinster beat Munster in the Railway Cup final. Kilkenny backboned the winning Leinster team and Tipperary was represented on the Munster side. Tipp were even to play in the summer's championship, but never got to finish it.

Apart from Tipperary's withdrawal, the football championship was hardly affected at all.

Compared to today, there were obvious environmental factors helping contain the epidemic. War time travelling restrictions were in force and private motoring was virtually unknown. Buses, trains and taxis, where available, and bicycles were the primary means of transport and, as a result, there was no major movement of population and consequently the dangers of the disease spreading were much reduced.

Despite the obvious difficulties hanging over a county that had done little hurling since March, Tipperary were due to play neighbours Waterford on 1 June. Plans were, however, quickly thrown into disarray on all fronts. Tipperary secretary Johnny Leahy announced that there would be no trains to Thurles for the match because of war time fuel rationing. In the week before the fixture, there were 41 outbreaks of foot and mouth in Ballingarry in south Tipperary. The Waterford match was postponed until the end of July and won comfortably by Tipperary.

'The disruption was more in the south of the county than in the north,' according to King. 'This also helps explain why the Tipperary footballers conceded a walkover to Clare.'

Cork awaited Tipperary in the hurling semi-final, while Limerick had already reached the Munster final by beating Clare. Cork were then on the brink of the only four-in-a-row hurling All-Irelands in history. The first in that sequence was to be controversial. Scheduled for 17 August, the Cork-Tipp match was dramatically called off when the Department of Agriculture forbade Tipperary to travel. 'It wasn't just that match,' says King, 'but all the club activity within the county as well.'

The Central Council of the GAA now had a dilemma. Already Kilkenny – in many people's eyes favourites for that year's All-Ireland – had been hit by the epidemic. Despite being granted a bye to the provincial final by the Leinster Council,

The smash of the ash . . . hurleys broken during the delayed 2000 Offaly county hurling final between Birr and Seir Kieran at Birr. Photograph: Matt Kavanagh.

Kilkenny were prohibited from playing Dublin unless a clear three weeks had passed since the last outbreak. It was a condition the county couldn't meet.

Apprehensive that the All-Ireland would never get played, Central Council turned down a request from Tipperary for a postponement and ordered that Leinster and Munster nominate their representatives. In the event of either winning, they were to be recognised as All-Ireland champions. Dublin was the clear choice in Leinster, but Munster decided to offer its nomination to the winners of a specially convened match between Cork and

Limerick. On 14 September, Cork flattened the All-Ireland champions Limerick – minus it has to be said the Mackey brothers – 8–10 to 3–2.

There was no way back for Tipp and Kilkenny. The rest was perfunctory. Dublin edged out Galway in the All-Ireland semi-final before going down heavily to Cork in the final.

Yet the business of the season wasn't complete. In October the epidemic was deemed to have run its course. At the end of the month, Cork and Tipperary were scheduled to play their postponed Munster final. On 26 October in Limerick, the newly crowned All-Ireland champions were thrashed by Tipperary. According to King, there weren't really any hard feelings in Tipperary at the aborted season. 'They just got on with it,' he says.

Cork and Munster GAA historian Jim Cronin believes that the postponed provincial final gave Tipperary a certain amount of slagging rights. 'They wouldn't have let Cork forget it that easily,' he says, 'but it was mainly banter.' There remains to this day, however, scepticism about how seriously Cork took the rearranged Munster final. 'No one can prove it either way,' says Cronin, 'but Cork would say that they weren't as keen to win it as Tipperary. And a few weeks later in the Thomond Tournament (for Munster hurling counties) – which was a big thing in those days – Cork introduced some new players and won the

tournament well. It was really the first sign of a number of young players who were to feature in the All-Ireland wins which followed, people like Sean Condon and Con Murphy [future president of the GAA].'

Paddy Downey, this newspaper's former GAA correspondent, has heard direct evidence concerning the 1941 Munster final. 'I later interviewed a few people in Cork like Jack Barrett and Jack Lynch. They said that on the way to the match, Cork players stopped off in pubs to drink. They were all travelling in different cars. There was one particular place in Croom where they were supposed to have called. I'm not sure if that's the match in which Jack Lynch said they remembered seeing three balls, but a number of them had drink

Offaly time . . . Damien Murphy (Seir Kieran) tries to block a shot by Gary Hanniffy (Birr) during the 2000 Offaly Hurling Final which was eventually played on 25 March. Photograph: Matt Kavanagh.

taken. There was certainly an imbalance of motivation between Cork and Tipperary.'

If Cork were in the process of launching an era of unparalleled achievement – having whacked the reigning All-Ireland champions, taken their crown and about to win three more in succession – Kilkenny were coming to the end of their cycle. All-Ireland winners in 1939, finalists in 1940 and favourites in '41, they weren't to win another for a further six years by which time most of the team had changed. In November 1941, Kilkenny were beaten in the delayed Leinster final as Dublin saved the authorities further embarrassment.

Jimmy Phelan, whose goals had helped win the 1939 Thunder and Lightning final against Cork, feels to this day that the foot-and-mouth epidemic hastened Kilkenny's decline. 'There was no hurling in Kilkenny that year because of restrictions.'

For Phelan himself, the situation was particularly difficult, as he had been living in Carlow working with the Sugar Company since 1937. 'When the restrictions got worse,' he recalls, 'the only way of travelling was on a bicycle.'

The year of enforced idleness was the last straw for him. Although only in his mid-20s, he retired from hurling altogether. 'I gave it up in '41. I'd no facility of getting down to training and I couldn't keep up the cycling there and back and there was no hurling in Carlow.'

He has no regrets about the circumstances of his premature departure. 'Nothing was on our minds but the foot and mouth scare. Everything else was secondary. And it was different to today. There wasn't as much movement of people and no way of moving animals except driving them along the road.'

The 1941 epidemic came and went. In his definitive history of the GAA, Marcus de Burca passed this judgment: 'It was almost two years before the war made any major impact on the GAA. Even then a serious cattle disease had a temporarily more disruptive effect on the events run by the GAA than the war had.'

10 MARCH 2001

Windfall May Still Have Its Fall Guy

Emmet Malone

After the bitter divisions of the past two years, Eircom Park was formally consigned to history yesterday with barely a sentimental sigh from the FAI delegates who gathered at Dublin's Green Isle Hotel to decide between it and becoming tenants at the proposed Stadium Ireland.

The association's chief executive, Bernard O'Byrne, described the deal agreed with the Government in return for abandoning the project as 'stunning', and few can disagree. Certainly not the members of the FAI's 55-strong National Council, who unanimously voted in favour of its adoption.

O'Byrne estimated that the association will have between £80 million and £125 million to spend on football over the next 13 years. FAI treasurer Brendan Menton put the figure at 'at least £125 million'.

Subsequently it was agreed that the potential funds available to the organisation between now and 2014 could run to £165 million.

Of that, the association would, under normal circumstances, have expected the sport to have received around £78 million in Government grants, as the average subsidy at present is around £6 million per annum. Even that, however, values the move to Abbotstown at £87 million.

All sides agree that the five-page document – and its three pages of explanatory notes – is complicated. The main elements of the package, though, are: (1) an additional £9 million per annum in grants and loans for the next three years; (2) the right to keep the estimated £40 million they earn from advance box and ticket sales at Stadium Ireland (out of which they will be expected to repay £16 million); (3) savings of around £3 million per year once they switch their internationals to Stadium Ireland from Lansdowne Road.

In addition, there will be around £30 million in matching funding provided by the Government for various development projects, although some of this will be offset against the association's regular annual grants.

In the circumstances, it was no great surprise that the deal was accepted without the need for anything approaching serious debate. First, the officer board agreed unanimously to recommend it, then the board of management followed suit.

Finally, at the end of one of the shortest National Council meetings of recent times, they did no more than go through the motions of a vote.

Addressing the media afterwards, O'Byrne admitted to feeling some private disappointment that Eircom Park was now officially dead.

'But that has been more than balanced over the past couple of weeks when we saw the quality of support on offer from the Government,' he said. 'The figures promised in this deal are unheard of in terms of Irish football.'

Asked for his reaction to the agreement, Menton, who had long championed the idea of doing business with the Government, said: 'It provides something that soccer never had. We've never had the resources to support our game, and now we will, at every level.'

O'Byrne, pressed about his position and whether he would come under pressure as a result of the collapse of Eircom Park – a scheme on which the FAI has spent more than £3.5 million – said he didn't believe so.

'The reason I don't think so,' he remarked, 'is that there was a clear mandate to bring the stadium idea forward. I did come up with the idea, but after that I was doing my best to progress something that was the policy of the association.'

'The fact is,' said FAI president Pat Quigley, 'if we hadn't shown vision two or three years ago, we wouldn't have this offer now.'

While O'Byrne said that he enjoyed his job, did it to the best of his abilities and intended to stay in it, he added that if he were to depart, it would only be as a result of a move initiated by his employers.

However, there were signs at yesterday's meeting of the pressure he will now come under. The board of management broadened the brief of the subcommittee established on Wednesday to look into O'Byrne's use of an official credit card so that 'other issues' could be looked into as well.

Next Friday the board will meet again to consider some of the negative implications of yesterday's deal. In particular, they will have to decide how to handle outstanding commitments to companies such as IMG.

Last night, however, few wanted to think about next Friday. With the increased funding coming on stream late this summer, they were far too preoccupied looking further down the road than that.

12 MARCH 2001

Sonia's Confidence Takes a Hit as Ambitious Double Attempt Backfires

Ian O'Riordan

A World Indoor Championships which started out with Sonia O'Sullivan's exciting attempt on double gold ended in the worst case scenario yesterday when she trailed home a distant last in the 1,500 metres final.

It was hoped O'Sullivan would find some consolation for the seventh place finish in Saturday's 3,000 metres. Instead, she leaves Lisbon with two

Presidential boat . . . Emma McAleese, daughter of President Mary McAleese, feels the strain during the women's annual University Boat Race on the Liffey. Photograph: Bryan O'Brien.

THE IRISH TIMES SPORTING YEAR 2001

of her most disappointing performances in recent years and, perhaps more worryingly, a significant crack in her confidence ahead of the World Cross Country Championships in a fortnight.

It wasn't the first time that the Irishwoman came to a major event and threw the book of logic out the window. She thought about the double sometime last week and it looked possible. If she'd thought hard about it, then she may have decided otherwise.

There is little doubt Saturday's 3,000 metres final, which came just an hour and 45 minutes after she completed her 1,500 metre heat, could have provided her with at least some hardware. Yet by then, the demanding schedule of four championship races in a little over two days was already taking its toll and she never once threatened the leaders with her presence.

Yesterday, she at least put herself in front at the start in an effort to dominate the proceedings. After leading through 800 metres in a casual two minutes 22 seconds, however, it was clear the big kickers were just lining up behind her. When Portugal's Carla Sacramento then burst to the front with three laps to go, almost the entire field flew past in tight succession. Shortly afterwards, a gap of some five metres had opened and O'Sullivan's race was over.

Flat out ... Sonia O'Sullivan in action at the IAAF World Indoor Athletics Championships in Lisbon.

As Hasna Benhassi of Morocco took the surprise win in 4.10.83, O'Sullivan appeared distraught and exhausted when coming home ninth in a pedestrian 4.19.40.

'I have nothing at all to say about that,' was the only thing she could offer. Yet the fact does remain that the cross country championship in Ostend was always going to be her main target at this stage of the season. It was confirmed over the weekend that she is concentrating solely on the short course race, and having come to these championships in exciting form after her winter training in Australia, it is still possible that this weekend's failure may well be turned around.

Just how much the succession of disappointing races will affect her confidence remains to be seen. For a start, Saturday's 3,000 metres confrontation with Gabriela Sazbo was expected to provide the first chance for revenge since the Sydney Olympics, but instead offered the first suggestion that her ambitious attempt on a double was about to backfire.

Szabo immediately hit the front in an effort to draw the sting out of O'Sullivan, but she ended up taking the sting out of herself as well. Olga Yegorovia from Russia stole that show by winning gold in 8.37.48, over two seconds clear of the Romanian.

O'Sullivan had dropped to the rear after just two laps and only closed to seventh as the runners ahead of her dropped back, eventually clocking 8.44.37. That she improved her national indoor record offered no consolation.

Part of O'Sullivan's problem there undoubtedly came from the 1,500 metre heat so soon before, which she ended up running almost flat out in order to qualify for the final in third in 4.11.27. Yet she couldn't be sure just how much she had drained her tank.

'Obviously it's not something you normally do before a race,' she said. 'I did feel very ordinary, although I felt quite good in the 1,500. I don't

really know where the gap opened in the 3,000 metres but it did, and I never got back on. If I did then I might have had a chance but I never gave myself that chance.'

There was never any question that she would come back yesterday and give herself another chance in the 1,500 metres, but the quality of athletes in the field meant that a medal of any sort would be hard earned. Sacramento, even with the home support, ended up fourth.

Yet it reflected the sort of gamble that O'Sullivan was taking over the course of the last three days. If there is any consolation to be found, then at least she will go into the cross country championships with plenty of races in her legs.

Celtic's Golden Boy Secures the Silverware

Michael Walker

Celtic – 3, Kilmarnock – 0

Not a cloud in a blue Glasgow sky. Not a cloud on the green Celtic horizon. Yet, such is the empowering influence of Martin O'Neill, Celtic even have a silver lining on good days. Yesterday was emphatically one of those for Celtic and this morning the first silver pot of the O'Neill era sits gleaming in Parkhead.

More will surely follow, probably – rather than possibly – two more this season. A Scottish Cup semi-final awaits and 12 more points will ensure the league title. If Henrik Larsson keeps scoring at his astonishing rate, then a Celtic treble is a certainty.

Yesterday, with Celtic not wholly convincing against a durable Kilmarnock side, Larsson popped up to deliver his 45th, 46th and 47th goals of the season in the space of 32 second-half minutes. The Swede is now one goal behind Charlie Nicholas'

1982 total and is even closing in on Jimmy McGrory's record of 50. That's legendary company.

It is company his manager thinks Larsson deserves to keep. 'A fantastic player,' said O'Neill for the umpteenth time. 'He would score goals in any league. His third would have graced any cup final anywhere in the last century. Is he my type of player? You bet he's my type of player.'

Larsson's contribution was more welcome than usual as his partner Chris Sutton was sent off by referee Hugh Dallas on the hour for a reckless high challenge on Gary Holt. Sutton had not been booked previously and O'Neill thought the dismissal slightly unjust.

'Initially I thought it was a bit harsh, and having seen it on TV since I'm disinclined to change my mind.'

Celtic were one up at the time, courtesy of Larsson's 49th-minute opener, but they were not dominating. But as O'Neill said, after the red card, 'If anything we got stronger'.

They did. Larsson snaffled two more, Kilmarnock withered, O'Neill had his first trophy. How did it feel to be a successful Celtic manager, he was asked. 'I think that's premature, I've got a million miles to go.' As someone commented, about four weeks premature.

Just as they had done at Celtic Park in January, Kilmarnock clearly arrived with a tight game-plan, one based on energy and commitment. Then they were beaten 6-0, but here, for 48 minutes, it worked.

From the opening seconds when Gus MacPherson clattered into Bobby Petta, it was apparent Kilmarnock had a physical agenda. Three of their players were booked by the 41st minute and the antagonistic tactics had a verbal edge to them as well, Christophe Cocard, in particular, doing his best to wind up Neil Lennon.

But there was some calm intelligence from Ian Durrant until the former Rangers player limped off after 37 prosperous minutes. 'It could be the end of the big ball game for me,' Durrant said afterwards.

Then there was Kilmarnock's other notable attribute – ceaseless running. From Craig Dargo, a willing if lightweight centre-forward, through to the under-rated Garry Hay on the left and the resilient Kevin McGowne at the back, the men in blue ran and ran, hustled and harassed.

If they could not equal Celtic for skill and power, then Kilmarnock could try and match them for work-rate. They did, and until Larsson's first Kilmarnock looked very much like Leicester City. Celtic had been restricted to a couple of shots from Lubo Moravcik in the first half, though at the other end Jonathan Gould, playing with Robert Douglas cup-tied, was as under-employed as Gordon Marshall. It was the interval that changed things.

Prior to that, Sutton had been almost invisible. How his profile was to rise. Within three minutes of the re-start, Sutton supplied Colin Healy with an astute pass that left Healy free in the box. Only Marshall stood between Healy and glory, but the Irishman hit him with his shot. 'Healy was immense for us in the second half,' said O'Neill.

And the deflection off Marshall meant a corner. Once Moravcik had accepted the ball short, he swept in a cross that Sutton and Ramon Vega jumped for. The ball fell somewhat awkwardly for Larsson but this remarkable player turned it into a goal-scoring volley.

The next short spell was something like WWF as Paul Lambert, Cocard, Lennon and Chris Innes let the ball do its own thing. The rising tension exploded when Sutton launched himself at Holt and there were few complaints from his hooped colleagues when Dallas produced a red card.

Kilmarnock must have sensed a way back but were unable to enforce their numerical advantage, not least because Celtic played better football with 10 men than they had with 11.

They also had the luck. When Moravcik stabbed a short pass through to Larsson with 16 minutes remaining, the angle was not promising, Marshall was standing tall and Innes was closing in.

Wild Rovers . . . Patrick Deans celebrates with his team-mates after scoring for Shamrock Rovers against Shelbourne at Tolka Park. Photograph: Frank Miller.

Larsson, as he does, had a go anyway. The ball hit Innes and looped over Marshall. It was cruel on Kilmarnock and it effectively ended the game.

Seven minutes later Larsson made sure just in case. Collecting the ball on the halfway line, Larsson sprinted away from McGowne, who fell, approached Marshall, sold him a dummy of monumental proportions and slid the ball in with his left foot. 'The third oozed class,' said O'Neill.

It was a Larsson hat-trick. Now for the Celtic treble.

CELTIC: Gould, Lambert, Petta (Crainey 13 [Boyd 88]), Lennon, Valgaeren, Healy, Larsson, Moravcik (Smith 83), Sutton, Mjallby, Vega. Subs Not Used: Johnson, Kharine. Sent Off: Sutton (60). Booked: Lambert. Goals: Larsson 47, 74, 81.
KILMARNOCK: Marshall, MacPherson, McGowne, Cocard (McLaren 52), Holt, Durrant (Reilly 39),

Mahood, Dindeleux (Canero 73), Dargo, Innes, Hay. Subs not used: McCoist, Meldrum. Booked: Dindeleux, Dargo, McGowne, Hay.
REFEREE: H. Dallas (Scotland).

24 MARCH 2001

Up to its Neck in Bad Blood

Northern Ireland football, as well as Neil Lennon, is hurt by fans' bigotry, writes Michael Walker

> 'And the North, where I was a boy
> Is still the North, veneered with the grime of Glasgow.'
> Louis MacNeice

The venue now seems an unlikely one: Bootham Crescent, home of York City. The date, 22 October 1996. But the words said remain fresh. After a tricky

2–0 League Cup victory in which Leicester City had finally overcome their hosts with a Neil Lennon breakthrough goal on the hour, the Leicester manager Martin O'Neill said to reporters: 'I sigh when Neil Lennon gets the ball.' O'Neill meant with relief. Over the past two weeks, however, there has been sighing of a different sort altogether when the subject of Neil Lennon has arisen.

A lot of it has been sad, a mournful response to the sectarian abuse Lennon received during the recent Northern Ireland game with Norway at Windsor Park and what that said about Northern Irish life today.

A lot of it has also been weary, tinged with anger. In the 'whatever you say, say nothing' culture of the North this has come from people who don't want to know because they are tired of knowing.

And a lot of it has come from Lennon himself, a natural half-sad, half-angry reaction to his plight as an Ulster Catholic from Celtic playing in a Protestant, bluenose-Rangers arena. It can wear you down.

Tough as he is, Lennon's Lurgan-born world view must have altered. He is a gregarious character, always one of the lads. 'Lenny.' He used to share Old Firm laughs with Rangers fans such as Tommy Wright and Barry Hunter, but those jokes can't seem funny any more. Facts such as his Gaelic football youth, his love of Celtic, and that scores of family and friends make the trip to Scotland each weekend are now held against Lennon. Not just facts any more.

A good talker, Lennon has spoken since the Norway incident, tried to explain his and his family's position and dilemma. 'A very traumatic experience,' was his description of 7 March in its immediate aftermath. He had left the ground early with an uncle and brother, shaken. To those who said The Booing was not as bad as was being made out, or that the 'Neil Lennon RIP' hang-man graffiti was an isolated prank, Lennon replied: 'They're not in my shoes.'

Indeed. The morbid truth is that the minute Lennon decided to fulfil his 'boyhood dream' of joining Celtic, those shoes became less comfortable. If Lennon did not know that before, he has since acknowledged the effect upon Martin O'Neill of being in the 'Glasgow goldfish bowl', as Lennon put it. O'Neill is a much more guarded character than at Leicester. So, too, is Lennon. Prior to the last Old Firm game, his first, he said: 'I'll try not to get embroiled in all the hype, although in Glasgow it's all or nothing.'

Yesterday, though, Lennon spoke optimistically, if briefly. 'The reception I've had in Belfast this week has been really good. I think most people are behind me. If what happened last time has made people think about the situation a wee bit more, then maybe something positive has come out of a lot of negatives.

'I have thought about what will happen the first time I touch the ball and hopefully it will be positive. But I don't know if it will be. I feel more relaxed. There have been more positive vibes but if it happens again I'm not saying I won't walk away. I would have to think about it.'

Having witnessed the divided reality of Glasgow, and the quiet development in O'Neill, the allegation that Lennon used a loaded term such as '32-county team' when expressing his some-day wish to play for an all-Ireland football side is all the more difficult to believe. Lennon denies it; the journalist insists he said it.

What does not seem to be disputed is that Lennon said of his friends: 'Most of the people I know follow the Republic.' But, from a geographically and politically split town such as Lurgan, Lennon would know the danger of the alleged 32-county remark.

One Scottish journalist said last week that for them The Booing is 'a dead issue'. But not in Northern Ireland. Not in Lurgan. As a sporting example of just how far the alleged peace process has to travel, The Booing of Neil Lennon is fundamental to understanding where we are now. To downplay its significance is to bury the head.

Manager Sammy McIlroy has been accused of that. There are those who point to McIlroy's staunch east Belfast upbringing as evidence of his Protestant loyalties; it's the way others point to Lennon's childhood. Yesterday all McIlroy would say of The Booing was: 'That was unacceptable. We're looking forward to the game. Neil's looking forward to the game. Neil Lennon has nothing to prove.' McIlroy wants to get back to the football. Norway beat Northern Ireland 4–0.

Lennon does too. But getting back to football is hard given that if Lennon endures a similar experience this afternoon he will almost certainly retire from the international scene. He will be 30 this summer, not 20. He doesn't need all this. Celtic would probably not be too unhappy at that. They will want a player they paid £5.75 million for to be as ready as possible for a Champions League campaign.

But for the Irish Football Association, and Irish football, it would be a disaster if Lennon was forced out by bigotry. The signal it would send out would be more than symbolic. Already Northern Ireland footballers are suffering from their decline on the pitch and the continued sectarian menace off it.

In the last four years almost a dozen young players from the North have opted to play for the Republic. Religion is a say-nothing issue, but most are Catholics. 'I get calls on a weekly basis from people telling me this player wants to play for us and not the North,' the Republic's youth football director Brian Kerr said last month. 'It has almost become embarrassing the number of calls I get.' Lennon touched on the subject yesterday.

Disregarding the politics, in purely numerical terms this is a trend the North cannot allow to grow. The IFA has expressed its concern to the FAI. It may be too late. 'We've got a Provo on our team,' was one of the chants heard at Windsor Park against Norway. Soon the people singing this could get the all-Protestant team they want.

Yet, only on Wednesday, Rangers chairman David Murray announced that the Ibrox club, concerned at the off-putting nature of much of the atmosphere at Rangers games, will open a new family section where, Murray said: 'Sectarian, racial or foul language or actions will not be tolerated.'

It would be easy to deride the attempted cleaning of Glasgow's grime as a cosmetic gesture, just as it would be easy to dismiss the IFA anti-sectarianism campaign as irrelevant. But, even if reluctant, they are the beginning of a recognition that change must come. That players so identifiably 'Ulster Prod' as Iain Dowie have spoken out against Lennon's treatment is another indication that a moment has been reached.

Dowie, a former Northern Ireland captain, has an English accent, but as he said after the Norway match: 'My mother is from the Donegall Road and I was born at the bottom of Tate's Avenue, so Windsor Park was like a second home to me. But if this is what's going to happen to our own players, then perhaps the time has come for Northern Ireland to move from Windsor Park.

'It sticks in my throat to say that as a life-long Linfield fan. But we can't tolerate our own fans giving one of our own players the sort of abuse we heard. If a new international stadium is the answer to getting rid of that minority, then that's what the IFA must work towards.'

Symbolically, it would be the IFA's trump card. Windsor Park has too much history. From shots being fired regularly during games with Belfast Celtic in the opening decades of the last century; to the violent demise of Belfast Celtic there in 1948; to the abuse which Pat Jennings has spoken of; to the attack on Donegal Celtic; to the night in November against the Republic; and now to this. Windsor Park has been a theatre of hate.

So today should be pivotal, not just for Neil Lennon, but for Irish football. Ten thousand leaflets with 'Give Bigotry The Red Card' will be handed out before kick-off. A mascot called EDI –

Green blur . . . The Republic of Ireland squad on a training spin in Clonshaugh before travelling to Cyprus for the World Cup qualifier. Photograph: David Sleator.

meaning 'Equality, Diversity, Interdependency' – has been born. Stewards have been employed to weed out the shouters. The tension will be great.

But, whoever wins, you will hear the sighs all the way to Glasgow.

26 MARCH 2001

Flat Display Still Delivers the Goods

Emmet Malone

Cyprus – 0, Republic of Ireland – 4

It had been a week full of unpleasant complications for the Irish party in Cyprus, and, while the win that rounded it off was as good a result as anybody in the camp could have dared to hope for, it was scarcely a straightforward affair either.

By this morning, of course, that won't matter too much to the players or their manager. The three points earned moved the Republic up to second in the Group Two table, just a couple of points behind Portugal. The scoreline makes it Mick McCarthy's best away win since his first competitive game in charge of Ireland – the 5–0 defeat of Liechtenstein four-and-a-half years ago. And the relative strength of the opposition made this a much more impressive result than the one in Eschen.

The quality of the display, though, was another thing altogether. During the build-up to the game the thinking had been that an early Irish goal would kill off the hosts and, quite possibly, open the floodgates, just as a late one had for the Dutch here back in October.

Instead, Stavros Papadopoulos's side defied expectations by mounting an impressively spirited challenge to McCarthy's outfit, even after Roy Keane and Ian Harte had put the Irish in what should have been a commanding position. If the statistics don't lie, then 4–0 is at least economical with the truth. The shots-on-target tally, 6–3 in favour of the visitors, reflects more accurately the nature of this contest.

In fact, it was hard to believe the Cypriots did not convert even one of the chances they managed to create either just before the break, when Gary Kelly was forced to clear off the line twice in quick succession, or during a strong 20-minute spell immediately after it.

At the end of that period errors by Mark Kinsella and Kenny Cunningham allowed Michael Constantinou to get in one-on-one with Shay Given, but the goalkeeper stood his ground and the striker fired directly at him.

Ten minutes from time Marios Christoloulou should have scored from close range but blasted over. How the Irish would have coped with having had to defend a single-goal lead through the closing stages we were, happily, spared from discovering, and less than 60 seconds later a Gary Kelly shot from 25 yards out found the net with the help of a deflection.

Finally the Cypriots gave up the ghost, and after Robbie Keane was unlucky to have a tap-in disallowed for an alleged foul by David Connolly on the goalkeeper, his namesake scored the goal of the night, a wonderful individual effort in which he beat two defenders inside the box before sending a crashing shot in off the near post.

That strike rounded off a tremendous personal performance and ensured beyond doubt that, even if the milestone meant nothing to the Corkman himself, his 50th game for his country will be widely remembered as having been one of his best.

Others will prefer recalling the result to the performance. Of the back four, only Kelly did well. Harte, in particular, was beaten too often down the Cypriot's right flank and Cunningham, who picked up a booking, looked uncharacteristically clumsy in the centre.

Robbie Keane's display, which included a missed chip in the 64th minute that he would surely score nine out of any other 10 nights, was one of his most subdued for his country, while Kevin Kilbane struggled after a decent first half and was replaced late on by Damien Duff.

Jason McAteer's contribution, meanwhile, grew increasingly erratic with the result that it was no surprise, even to him one suspects, when he too departed 12 minutes before the end.

Aside from Keane Senior's outstanding showing in central midfield (as well as just about everywhere else), Connolly was probably the night's main Irish success story. The Feyenoord striker rummaged tirelessly in amongst the home side's three-man defence, and his close control and acceleration from a standing start proved far too much for his marker to handle.

Late on he forced a wonderful save from Nikos Panayitou with a close-range volley after a couple of interchanged passes with the Manchester United midfielder, and moments later he created what should have been that goal for his striking partner by getting quickly on to a parried shot on the edge of the six-yard box.

It was a particularly strong conclusion to an impressive 90-minute display. Twice early on his crosses from the right might have provided the basis for an opening goal, but in the end it took a ball from a similar position from Kelly to set up Roy Keane for a straightforward eight-yard finish.

After Robbie Keane had stepped over a low Kinsella pass into the box for Kilbane three minutes before the interval, the Sunderland winger had the legs taken from under him as he waited for the ball to pass him so that he could recover his stride.

From the penalty spot Harte calmly sent the goal-keeper the wrong way.

For all their dawdling, Ireland again showed themselves capable of keeping pace with their more illustrious group rivals all the way to October's final round of qualifying games.

CYPRUS: Panayiotou (Anothosis); Theodotou (AEK), Konnafis (Omonia), Melanarkitis (Anorthosis) (Filippou (Apollon), 55 mins), Charalampous (Olympiakos), Chrostodoulou (Aris, Greece); Pounnas (Anorthosis) (Malekkos (AEL), 44 mins), Spoljaric (Apollon), Ioakim (Omonia); Constantinou (Iraklis, Greece), Okkas (PAOK, Greece) (Agathokleous (Aris, Greece), 76 mins).
REPUBLIC OF IRELAND: Given (Newcastle United); Kelly (Leeds United), Breen (Coventry City), Cunningham (Wimbledon), Harte (Leeds United); McAteer (Blackburn Rovers) (Holland (Ipswich), 78 mins), Kinsella (Charlton Athletic), Roy Keane (Manchester United), Kilbane (Sunderland) (Duff (Blackburn Rovers), 83 mins); Robbie Keane (Leeds United) (Doherty (Tottenham Hotspur), 90 mins), Connolly (Feyenoord).
REFEREE: F. De Bleeckere (Belgium).

26 MARCH 2001

McAllister Earns Victory for Terenure

John O'Sullivan

Terenure College – 21, Blackrock College – 19

Four minutes from the final whistle, David McAllister surveyed a 45-metre penalty opportunity, the Terenure out-half aware that his side trailed by a single point, 19-18. A case of déjà vu: a little over 12 months ago he faced a difficult penalty opportunity. McAllister missed and Clongowes won the Leinster Schools' Senior Cup final.

Yesterday at Lansdowne Road, he found himself in a similar position, the destiny of the final entrusted to his right boot. He struck the ball magnificently, the touch judges raised their flags and to watch the player wheel away in delight was to witness a great sporting moment. It was the decisive score in a pulsating finale, though it was not the final act.

Blackrock demonstrated great character and resilience, traits that had brought them to within touching distance of the trophy. Referee Donal Courtney awarded them a penalty for Roy McDonnell's high tackle on John Ronan, 28 metres from the Terenure line. Into a strong breeze and denied the presence of first choice place-kicker Keelan McGowan who had been replaced, Blackrock had little option.

Scrum-half Daragh Geraghty kicked for the corner, the line-out was secured and the Blackrock pack rumbled to within five metres of their opponents' line. Three times ball carriers hit the deck in the tackle and from the fourth, second row Andrew O'Reilly was obliterated in a double-tackle, the ball squirting forward.

Blackrock were penalised from the ensuing scrum and when McAllister delightedly hoofed the ball into the upper echelons of the West Stand, he concluded a wonderful final. It was a classic confrontation. The pundits had suggested that there was nothing between two fine sides; the game reinforced that supposition.

At one stage it didn't look as if there would be any doubt about who was going to prevail. Eight minutes remained, Terenure led 18–9 and for all Blackrock's domination of possession and the powerful mauling and driving of their pack, they appeared to lack the inspiration and the patience to unravel the Terenure defence.

From the precipice of defeat, Blackrock dug deep and found a chink. Conor Sharpe, who had moved to out-half on McGowan's departure, was held up inches short of the line but Terenure had

High anxiety . . . A colourful Blackrock supporter looks worried during the Leinster Schools' Senior Cup final at Lansdowne Road. Photograph: Dara Mac Dónaill.

transgressed. From the ensuing tap penalty the colossal frame of O'Reilly cut a swathe through the defenders. The television cameras suggested that he may have lost the ball over the line but Courtney was closer, satisfied that he did not.

Left wing Alan Henry, who had a fine game, kicked the conversion and two minutes later, Sharpe added a neat drop goal to nudge Blackrock in front, 19–18. It was a remarkable comeback and spoke volumes about the character of the Blackrock team. But they may rue several handling errors behind the scrum, over-complication of attacking gambits and an inability to translate the progress of the forwards into points.

The Blackrock pack as a unit had a towering game, none more so than second row David Gannon, O'Reilly and outstanding number eight

Colm Treston. Yet a reliance to rumble their way from their own 22 at times suggested a tactical naivety. They did make headway but each yard was hard fought.

Terenure, though physically lighter, battled tenaciously up front and managed to completely disrupt the Blackrock line-out, particularly through Roy McDonnell, whose performance matched his stature. But Terenure's outstanding player up front was there – blindside flanker Jonathan Barretto, who quite apart from his try, had a huge presence both in attack and defence.

Behind the scrum McAllister produced another top-quality performance, his pin-point accuracy a festering sore on the Blackrock consciousness. He kicked two penalties, a conversion and a superb 35-metre drop goal. Outside him Killian Coleman

Terenure's man of the moment . . . David McAllister, who kicked the late penalty which gave Terenure victory in a thrilling Leinster Schools' Senior Cup final at Lansdowne Road, takes on Blackrock's John Ronan and David Gannon (right). Photograph: Dara Mac Dónaill.

conjured a magnificent individual try and was another to produce a towering display.

With Terenure leading 8–6, Coleman received a short pass, running an angled cutback. He barged his way past three tacklers, accelerated away from Ruairi Kerr and handed off Sharpe on a journey that spanned 45 metres. McAllister's conversion and drop goal took his side to an 18–9 lead; but when their world threatened to crumble in on top of them when Blackrock surged back to take the lead, Terenure responded like worthy champions.

SCORING SEQUENCE: 1 min: McAllister pen, 3–0; 4: McGowan pen, 3–3; 10: Barretto try, 8–3; 13: McGowan pen, 8–6; 22: K. Coleman try, McAllister con, 15–6; 37: McGowan pen, 15–9 (half-time); 59: McAllister drop goal, 18–9; 62:

O'Reilly try, Henry con, 18–16; 64: Sharpe drop goal, 18–19; 66: McAllister pen, 21–19.

TERENURE COLLEGE: D. Cazabon; O. Pugh, K. O'Toole, K. Coleman, J. Donnelly; D. McAllister, P. Coleman; J. Anthony Lee, G. Doyle, F. Cronin; E. Wallace, R. McDonnell; J. Barretto, D. Dunlop (capt), C. McGinn. Replacements: A. Dunlop for Wallace (63 mins); R. Hegarty for Doyle (65 mins).

BLACKROCK COLLEGE: C. Sharpe; R. Kerr, J. Quigley, J. Ronan (capt), A. Henry; K. McGowan, D. Geraghty; E. McBennett, J. Mannion, M. Whelan; D. Gannon, A. O'Reilly; G. Noonan, C. Treston, D. Price. Replacements: O. Busteed for Price (33 mins); J. Waldron for McGowan (52 mins).

REFEREE: D. Courtney (IRFU).

THE FINAL WHISTLE

Taking Things Seriously

Joyce Onwuka had a good giggle last weekend when a friend of hers, a middle-aged Nigerian man, vowed to top himself if Nigeria failed to beat Ghana in a World Cup qualifying match, just as we chuckled when Olivier Dacourt (Leeds) and Paolo Di Canio (West Ham) threatened to kill themselves in the not-so-distant future if their respective teams didn't win a trophy or two. Result? Nigeria 0, Ghana 0. 'Surprisingly, immediately after the match, he took out a small bottle from his pocket and drank the contents,' said a gobsmacked Joyce. 'It was when he started foaming in the mouth a few minutes after and subsequently died that we realised it was not a joke'. Well, you would, wouldn't you?

19 MARCH 2001

from Mary Hannigan's Planet Football

These Boots were Made for Walking

Jim Craig has illustrated how times have changed at Celtic since he was a player at Parkhead in the 1960s. The European and Scottish Cup winner describes on the 'free' Celtic FC website how he once arrived at the office of Bob Rooney, the club physiotherapist-cum-equipment man, a few weeks before the club's European Cup final against Benfica.

'Bob,' says I in bright fashion, 'I've burst my boots,' writes Craig.

'What foot?' asks Rooney.

'My left,' says Craig.

'Ah, that's all right, you don't use that one too often. We'll tape it,' replies Rooney.

That's not the sort of exchange you would hear between Henrik Larsson and Martin O'Neill.

24 MARCH 2001

Johnny Watterson

English Invasion

The Lansdowne clubhouse and particularly the bar staff would have been a little surprised at the demand for drink prior to Saturday's game against Galwegians. Augmenting those attending the pre-match dinner were about 400 Englishmen who had travelled to Dublin despite the fact that the Ireland-England Six Nations Championship game was postponed. Looking for a little action they were directed to Lansdowne Road but quite what they made of the AIL game – it finished 9–7 to Lansdowne – is another thing. Unmoved by the fare produced, a few offered a rendition of 'Swing Low Sweet Chariot' but even they lost heart and, like the majority of their counterparts, repaired to the bar long before the final whistle.

26 MARCH 2001

John O'Sullivan

Bayern Blunder

We liked this yarn, as reported by the *Sun* last week, even if we're not entirely convinced it's 110 per cent true. After the draw for the European Cup quarter-finals paired Bayern Munich with Manchester United, the Germans decided to send their scout, Wolfgang Dremmler, to Old Trafford for the game against Leicester. With two minutes to go, and the game still scoreless, Wolfgang left, having seen enough. What happened next? Do you really need to ask? United scored twice in two minutes. But then a Bayern representative should have predicted that, really, eh?

26 MARCH 2001

Mary Hannigan

Kilkenny kitten … While Kilkenny's top-cats hibernate for the winter, Dermot Grogan gets his chance to impress.
Photograph: Matt Kavanagh.

A P R I L

2 0 0 1

HIGHLIGHTS

1 April: David Coulthard ends Michael Schumacher's six-race winning streak with victory in the Sao Paulo Grand Prix.

3 April: Manchester United go down 1–0 to Bayern Munich at Old Trafford in the first leg of their Champions League quarter-final.

4 April: Leeds United claim a 3–0 win over Deportivo La Coruna in the first leg of their Champions League quarter-final at Elland Road.

5 April: Liverpool draw 0-0 with Barcelona at the Nou Camp in the UEFA Cup semi-final.

6 April: The GAA will receive £60 million in Croke Park development funding from the Government over the next three years.

7 April: The GAA votes against the opening of Croke Park to other sports at their annual congress in Dublin.

8 April: Tiger Woods takes his place in history by winning the US Masters in Augusta and becomes the first player ever to hold all four major titles at the same time.

9 April: Australia set a world record when they beat Tonga 22–0 in their Oceania World Cup soccer qualifying game.

13 April: Munster beat the Rest of Ireland 24–22 in a European Cup warm-up match.

15 April: Connacht grab a National Football League monopoly as Galway, Mayo, Sligo and Roscommon all qualify for the semi-finals.

16 April: The West rules Croke Park as Athenry and Crossmolina win the All-Ireland club hurling and football titles.

17 April: Arsenal fail to progress to the Champions League semi-final after falling to Valencia 1–0, but Leeds advance despite a 2–0 defeat by Deportivo.

18 April: No escape for Manchester United this time as Bayern Munich progress to Champions League semi-final with a 2–1 win in Munich.

19 April: Liverpool stay on treble trail after a 1–0 win over Barcelona in the UEFA Cup semi-final second leg.

21 April: Munster suffer a controversial loss to Stade Français in the European Cup semi-final in Lille.

22 April: Lennox Lewis loses his World Heavyweight title to Hasim Rahman of South Africa after a fifth-round knock-out in Johannesburg.

23 April: Bernard O'Byrne ends his term as chief executive of the FAI.

24 April: The Six Nations Committee reschedules Ireland's next game against Scotland for 22 September.

25 April: The Republic of Ireland beat Andorra 3–1 in a World Cup qualifying game best forgotten.

26 April: GAA President Sean McCague answers critics and defends the £60 million funding to the Association.

27 April: Istabraq falls at the final hurdle at Leopardstown for the second time this season.

29 April: Mayo upset Galway to win the National Football League title in Croke Park.

7 APRIL 2001

Clarke Sweeps into Contention

Philip Reid sees Darren Clarke proving the value of patience by keeping his cool to shoot one of the finest rounds of his life

Americans remember Darren Clarke. They remember him as the man who first proved Tiger Woods's fallibility. Americans think they know Darren Clarke. They know him as a car-loving, cigar-smoking Irishman whose girth shows a fondness for the good things in life.

Image is everything in the United States, and that's the way they see him. Darren Clarke is a player whom the great American public can relate to, and that, as much as the influence of sports psychologist Bob Rotella, probably explains his relaxed demeanour this week. It's also why they shout his name from outside the ropes. Few foreign players have bonded as well with them as Clarke has. The whooping and hollering normally reserved for their own crosses the boundaries when he hits form. And what they discovered at Augusta National yesterday is that the really big golf tournaments bring out the best in Clarke, who rebounded from a moderate opening round by shooting a 67 for a midway total of five-under-par 139 to jump right into the thick of things.

'I just want to play as well as I can, to do my own thing and keep on playing the way I am,' said Clarke. 'I'm happy with the way I am swinging the club and, if my putter works, then I will certainly give myself a chance.'

In fact, Clarke, who switched to a slightly heavier Scotty Cameron putter for yesterday's second round, reduced his putting figures to 28, down from 30 in the first round, but the real factor was a marginally more aggressive mindset, particularly with his approach shots.

The result was that he gave himself far more genuine birdie chances and, more times than not, he took them.

'The key is to be patient, as more learned players than me around here keep saying. But it's true. You try not to hit the ball into the wrong places, which I did on a couple of occasions today and paid the penalty, but you don't go looking for birdie all the time. You have to know the moment.'

Yesterday, that moment arrived on the first hole when he rolled in a 15 footer for birdie. However, he had to be patient by playing par golf until the 7th hole. There, he played a superb approach shot to 10 feet above the hole. As Clarke settled over his putt, the crowds broke into applause to welcome Jack Nicklaus, Gary Player and Arnold Palmer on to the third tee-box that adjoins the green. Instead of breaking his concentration, Clarke – watched by the three legends – rolled in the putt.

It kick-started the most productive stage in his round. At the 8th hole, Clarke's bold approach was reflected in his decision to go for the green in two. After nearly 10 minutes of a wait, he turned over the fairway wood and pulled the shot into the pines.

'I got lucky,' he confessed later. There were no trees in his way, but he still had to play a delicate flop shot over a mound on to the putting surface. He pitched to 10 feet, and sank the birdie putt.

At the 10th, he played his shot of the day. Left with 218 yards to the pin, with the ball on a downslope, Clarke played a 'career best' five-wood that actually hit the flagstick and left him with a three footer for birdie, which he sank.

The run was continued at the 11th where he hit a wedge approach to four feet and holed out for his fourth birdie in five holes, moving to five-under-par. His momentum, however, was halted at the 13th hole.

'What happened there stalled me a bit,' he admitted. Having pushed his drive behind trees,

Rushes Point . . . Michael McDermott (Stackstown) seems lost in the long grass during the West of Ireland Amateur Golf Championship at Rosses Point. Photograph: Brenda Fitzsimons.

with the ball nestling on pine needles, he again played a brilliant recovery to the left fringe.

However, the putter caught in the grass behind the ball as he played his eagle putt and it only got halfway to the hole, leaving a 20 footer for birdie which he put four feet past the hole. He held his nerve to hole out.

Another pushed drive at the 15th, again behind trees, meant he couldn't go for the green in two and he did well to claim a par, two-putting from 40 feet. His only dropped shot of the round came at the short 16th where his seven-iron tee-shot missed the green to the left and did well not to find a watery grave. Instead, it clung to the grass between green and water, but Clarke's recovery pitch finished four feet above the hole on a glass-like surface. He barely touched the ball, but it slid by for his only bogey.

Clarke, however, responded in style at the penultimate hole. He hit a massive drive and then hit a wedge approach to a sucker pin position and rolled in the four footer for his sixth birdie on the way to equalling his best round at Augusta, his third in 1998. He has everything to play for heading into the weekend!

9 APRIL 2001

GAA Embraces Ignominy Again

Seán Moran

It was a Yeatsian occasion. The GAA's annual Congress may rarely count as great drama but faced with the opportunity to act in a spirit of generosity, the association duly emulated

All the president's men . . . three former presidents of the GAA at the annual congress in the Burlington Hotel, Dublin, with Peter Quinn (centre) and Jack Boothman (right). The speaker is John Dowling. Photograph: Dara Mac Dónaill.

those old Abbey audiences and disgraced itself yet again. Twelve hours after being handed £60 million of public money, the GAA was happy to take the money and lock the gates of Croke Park.

If there was any consolation, it was in the extraordinary tightness of the margin. Director general Liam Mulvihill expressed surprise on Saturday evening at how far the pendulum had swung on the issue. From being a strictly minority view, the repeal of Rule 42 now looks inevitable but for another year at least, the association has to live with this regressive provision on its books.

On the eve of the debate, it was obvious what was at stake. One delegate spoke of the PR disaster that would break if the motion were defeated. There was a strong appreciation that the isolationist image of the GAA did the association few favours.

Talking to a journalistic colleague, *The Irish Times* suggested that the positive atmosphere generated by the Government bonanza might benefit the motion. 'You mean they'll be magnanimous about it?' Laughter all around.

On Saturday afternoon the arguments were made. The financial aspect never really arose, so the influence of the £60 million was hard to assess, but when you've won the lotto, you'll place less emphasis on renting out rooms.

The language used defined the parameters. Proponents spoke of 'generosity', 'openness', 'self-confidence' and 'putting the Fáilte Isteach sign over Croke Park'. Opposition arguments referred to 'the thin end of the wedge', the necessity for (in an uncomfortable echo of that old apologia for apartheid) 'parallel development' of sports and at one stage urged delegates 'to hold fast to the past'.

There were also disingenuous suggestions that other sports neither wanted nor needed Croke Park now that the national stadium was on stream. No reference to what soccer and rugby would do in the next five years or to why other sports would request the use of a ground barred to them by rule.

Then there was the vote. Three-hundred and nine delegates were registered but 44 didn't vote. Of those who did, 176 supported and 89 opposed the motion. One switched vote would have delivered the two-thirds majority. President Sean McCague was surprisingly adamant that he wouldn't countenance a recount. He probably had a point but conducting a vote of this nature on a show of hands is plainly daft.

One of those who had supported the motion said in the disappointed aftermath that you only had to look around to see what was wrong. He was referring to the average age of the congress delegates. Older and more conservative than the rank-and-file membership, annual Congress is still the GAA's supreme body.

How heavily this weighs on the average delegate is open to question. One opponent of the motion was accosted after the debate.

'What were you up to in there at all?'

'Sure soccer had their chance to build a stadium.'

'What's that got to do with it? This was about the GAA making decisions.'

'Ah look, I couldn't give a b★★★★cks.'

On such convictions swing great issues.

9 APRIL 2001

Destiny's Child has his Dream Fulfilled

Philip Reid

Destiny's child answered the call at Augusta National last evening, and took his place in history. Tiger Woods, as a ten-year old, used to stay out to practise in the dark and dream of winning the Grand Slam.

Technically this may not count as the real thing, but Woods's victory in the US Masters — for his second green jacket — ensured he became the first player ever to hold all four professional majors at the same time.

Call it what you will, a new configuration of the Grand Slam, or even the 'Tiger Slam', but his feat in winning his fourth straight major, and his sixth in all, has signalled Woods out as the greatest golfer in modern times.

A final round 68 for 16-under-par 272, having held off the concerted challenges of David Duval and Phil Mickelson in an absorbing battle, was sufficient to give Woods an emotional win, by two shots from Duval.

Before the final round, Mark Calcavecchia made the observation that 'Tiger is only a human being like the rest of us.' In golfing terms, he is a super being. Although he dropped a shot at the opening hole to show some degree of frailty, Woods – playing in the final pairing with Mickelson – refuted all-comers to ultimately stake his claim to be the greatest living sportsman.

'It's very difficult to win any of these major tournaments, and to have your game in the right place at the right time is an astonishing achievement. This is an accomplishment for Tiger that I'm not sure you can quite compare to anything else,' said Duval.

All through the championship, Woods had first crouched, then pounced on Saturday to take the 54-hole lead and, yesterday, in bright Georgian sunshine with no more than a gentle wind that swirled around the course, he devoured the field with a display that, not for the first time, belied his 25 years. In his five previous major wins, Woods had led going into the final round and, so, 231 days after his last major win, in the USPGA, he maintained that dominance. What made this win arguably more impressive than any other is that he fended off Mickelson, the world number two, and Duval, his predecessor as world number one, down the straight.

'To go toe-to-toe with David and Phil and win is great. I was grinding so hard out there, had to make some big putts to keep myself in the ball-game. As a kid I dreamt of competing against the best players in the world and winning majors, and I think this is the biggest accomplishment I have made,' said Woods.

It was an intriguing contest, fit for any amphitheatre. That it should be played out on a course steeped in history was fitting to match Woods's achievement, something that had evaded legendary figures like Jack Nicklaus and Arnold Palmer.

But he had to do it the hard way, as, after some early shaping from the likes of Angel Cabrera and Mark Calcavecchia, the tournament developed into a three-way fight between Woods, Duval and Mickelson.

The roars from the crowd that accompanied one putt after another from Duval, two groups ahead, kept Woods focused on the task ahead. Indeed, Duval, who had started the day three shots adrift, had an amazing front nine that featured just one par (at the 9th) as he jumped right into contention. Duval reached the turn in 32 strokes and, in some contrast, Woods was still level par for the day after six holes. However, back-to-back birdies at the 7th and 8th moved Woods into the lead on his own at 14-under, although a Duval birdie a matter of minutes later on the 10th meant they were again tied. All this time, Mickelson was searching for inspiration that just never came.

With one eye on Mickelson, and an ear on what was happening to Duval ahead, Woods made a clutch putt for par at the 10th, picked up a birdie at the 11th but then watched as his tee-shot at the 12th finished in the bunker. 'I played safe, because if I got it any way wrong it was in the water,' said Woods, who failed to get down for a par. It was to be his last bogey of the championship.

While Duval's approach to the 13th finished in the Creek, but not in the water, and he did well to make a par, Woods reckoned that his tee-shot on that hole some 20 minutes after Duval was 'probably the best I hit all day. It's one I've been practising on the range all week, just in case I needed it,' said Woods, who birdied.

It was gladitorial warfare from there on in. When Duval birdied the 15th to join Woods on 15-under, but then bogeyed the next, it seemed that Woods would close things out on the 15th.

He didn't. Although he had an eagle putt, he put it three-and-a-half feet past the hole and missed the birdie putt back.

Down the stretch, Duval gave himself birdie opportunities at the 17th and 18th holes ... but failed to make either. So, when Woods hit his approach to 15 feet on the last, he effectively had two putts to win. He needed only one, and that gave him his place in history.

9 APRIL 2001

Thrills and Spills as Marauder Triumphs

Brian O'Connor

After one of the most lunatic and compulsive races in history, what in the world can the Martell Grand National throw up in 2005?

It's a bit far away to be sure, but the world's most famous steeplechase has developed a habit of throwing up its specials every four years. There was that knicker-elastic incident in 1993, the phone a friend in '97 and now there has been just about the most eye-boggling, head-scratching race anyone could ever dare imagine.

Inevitably there will be those who say the thing shouldn't have been run at all. The HQs for those viewpoints vary from Camp Purist to Fort Hugger, but although Richard Guest and Red Marauder have now entered the history books, the Aintree Grand National itself is possibly the biggest winner of all.

The void race and the bomb evacuation kept the National at the forefront of the public's view of horse racing, but they were hardly for the most

Schools' hockey . . . Muckross number two, Rachel Keegan, and Linda Byrne, the Loreto, Bray captain, contest possession during the Leinster Schools' Senior Cup final at Three Rock Rovers' ground in Rathfarnham. Photograph: Brenda Fitzsimons.

positive of reasons. But on Saturday the National kicked against time and took us back to the reason why it is the world's most famous race.

This really was a stick-a-pin-in and hope-for-the-best Grand National. The sort of National that is the legend the once a year punters have been weaned on. The race where any of the runners can win if enough happens to the others. However, the trend had begun to grow of horses being backed to the hilt on the day and then winning as if the National had been reduced to just another follow-the-money tease. Try telling that to punters next year.

This was the most modern National but of an old black-and-white type. It's just that the old-timers would have dismissed the plot as science

GAA democracy in action . . . delegates at the annual congress vote by a show of hands not to allow soccer to be played at Croke Park. Photograph: Dara Mac Dónaill.

fiction. For one thing, no matter how much carnage there had been in the past, at least there was never a hint of nothing finishing the race. Not even with the 100 to 1 Foinavon in 1967. But as Red Marauder and Smarty approached Beechers second time around on Saturday, with the remnants of the seven that had survived the first circuit stretched behind them, who would have confidently laid odds of there being no finisher to the 2001 Grand National?

One reporter was heard to ask the question and was told to shut up by a normally obsequious bookmaker's representative. There was too much going on. To watch Red Marauder and Guest struggle over the last two fences and slog their way

to the line was to watch one of the most compelling of Aintree legends unfolding before your eyes. Rarely can there have been more unlikely Grand National heroes.

Guest's story of how he threw his jockey's licence into the stewards' room at Perth three years ago and told them how to fold it, has been flashed around the world to an estimated 650 million TV audience but the rider's verdict on his gallant mount is equally compelling.

'He is probably the worst jumper ever to win the National but he is a survivor. He must have made 10 mistakes out there, and it wasn't pretty, but you couldn't knock him down today,' said the 35-year old.

Red Marauder's owner-trainer Norman Mason was keen to hand every drop of credit over to Guest, who is also his assistant trainer, the rider passed it on to the horse and if Red Marauder could talk he would probably pass the congratulatory baton to luck.

Marauder was in the middle of the greatest pile-up since Foinavon's when the blinkered and loose Paddy's Return exited stage left at the Canal Turn and brought most of the field to a standstill. Eight horses exited, including the fancied Mely Moss. On such heavy ground, such a casualty rate so early on didn't bode well.

Red Marauder somehow survived the pile-up and continued to survive as the Chair claimed one of the co-favourites, Edmond. Then the 19th saw both Papillon and Blowing Wind come to a halt. Carl Llewellyn gave way to gravity and broken reins on Beau at the 20th.

Guest and Red Marauder survived best but the same credit if not the prize is due to Timmy Murphy, who somehow kept Smarty going when Mark Pitman's horse was clearly out on its feet. Blowing Wind and Papillon were remounted to be third and fourth.

The cup of the Aintree authorities overflowed with the report that all horses and riders returned safely despite the appalling conditions, and although Guest admitted he thought the decision to go ahead with the race was 'borderline', there were other riders such as Llewellyn who said conditions were perfectly raceable.

That seemed to be borne out yesterday when Papillon's trainer, Ted Walsh, reported the horse 'as fresh as paint' after his effort. He added: 'There's no plan for him at the moment except to come back here next year.'

The good news for Aintree is that he won't be alone. The Grand National 2001 may have been freakish as hell, but it's also a contender for the most compelling sports story of the year. Quite what the old race will do to top it next year is hard to imagine, but if it can't quite equal the weekend drama, just look forward to 2005.

14 APRIL 2001

This Self-inflicted Wound will Fester

Just when its interests met those of society, argues Tom Humphries, the GAA spurned both graciousness and pragmatism.

The most depressing aspect of the past seven days has been the reversion to peasant sleeveenism of those old accomplices, Fianna Fáil and the GAA. Like a pair of native rogues codding the Anglo folk in an episode from Somerville and Ross, they have made us endure the hammy lines of a pair of clumsy chancers.

When it was announced at GAA Congress in the Burlington last Friday night that the Government had given £60 million to the GAA in order to take a few games away from Croke Park, that was all the signalling that was needed. The following day, 43 delegates abstained on the biggest motion of the weekend. One leading exclusionist stood up and said quietly that not wanting to embarrass the Government was a good reason to vote No. Three past presidents of the association spoke against the Roscommon motion. Peter Quinn, the past president who had first floated the possibility of Croke Park's expanded usage, spoke not at all. A probable future president left the hall on personal business as the vote was about to be taken.

They added a touch of Florida politics and a dash of Tammany Hall. The decision was made by a show of hands, a recount was asked for, a recount was denied. The trustees who counted the votes are evidently unimpeachable. Yet when the presidential election comes around next year, independent auditors will be used to count the votes. So almost everyone went away whistling. The Government announced that it was 'disappointed' the GAA wasn't offering a home to the very sports the Government is so keen to offer a home to. The GAA announced that, well heck, it was close, and expressed bafflement at all the fuss. Both sides knew the vote had given Bertie Ahern a year with which to have his colossal vanity project set into contractual concrete. By midweek the heat hadn't quite gone away. Ahern, in best Flurry Knox mode, was telling people that, having failed to interest the GAA in the thin end of what they perceived to be a wedge, his main concern all along had been getting them to consume the whole wedge and share not just Croke Park but all their grounds. This is an insult to the intelligence of taxpayers.

Ahern knows that this will never happen (local GAA facilities have not just been built on sweat and blood and tears, but are overused as they stand), but it is a nice stick with which to muddy the waters.

In reality, Ahern, who made his grant to the FAI conditional on them abandoning Eircom Park and made his grant to the GAA conditional on them bringing fixtures to the BertieBowl, didn't attach any other conditions because he didn't want to. It would have been wrong to coerce the GAA into ground-sharing, but there were ways of leaving them to their own devices. He could have pushed the GAA a certain way by asking that, in all propriety, the announcement of the £60 million be delayed till after the vote. Instead, he gave a nod and a wink to the backwoodsmen.

We need only examine the case of the Dublin vote to be assured that the Taoiseach got his way. The Dublin County Board had a meeting on the Monday night before Congress. The use to which Croke Park was to be put didn't figure in the discussions, but a board member raised it briefly late in the night. Some of the problems inherent with the motion were immediately evident when Finbarr Donovan, a Corkman attached to the St

Brigid's club, raised the matter. Donovan was surprised to find that one of the main voices suggesting the thin end of the wedge scenario was coming from a club colleague of his. It wasn't exactly brother against brother, but still …

Most of the speakers had questions about the financial implications of renting out Croke Park. It became clear a large majority of Dublin clubs were in favour of transforming Croke Park from a drain on vital resources into an asset. It was agreed informally that the 11 Dublin delegates would support the Roscommon motion.

Most of the Dublin delegates met again on Tuesday, the following night, and in a run through the motions once again agreed to support the Roscommon motion. That was how matters rested until Friday night at the Burlington, when the GAA announced that it had struck a gusher.

The following morning the nature of the Dublin vote had changed radically. From being 11–0 in favour, the vote had become 7–4 in favour – a swing of eight votes. Con Roche, Sean O'Mahoney, Noel Murphy and an Under-21 delegate from the Erins Isle club all voted No.

There were cracks in the Limerick and Galway delegations also. The top table spent the longest time totting up the votes, and while the addition was being done the feeling went around the hall that this was going to be one of those absurd, Kafkaesque GAA moments. So it proved.

In the aftermath, the peculiarly cackhanded opportunism exhibited by the Progressive Democrats missed the point as it conveniently rode the wave of festering resentments which the GAA decision stirred up. The junior Government party continued to keep quiet about the proposed £1 billion being expended on the BertieBowl, despite complaints from the Department of Finance that the manner in which the Cabinet had approved the project had been a breach of procedures. As it stands, it is virtually impossible to get an accurate figure on the costing of one of the biggest capital projects ever undertaken by the State, let alone a decent rationale for proceeding with it.

A Government presided over by a man who once boasted happily of his abilities to consume a gallon of Bass without impairment now speaks out of the corner of its mouth about drink culture in this country and the possibility of removing drinks sponsorship from sporting events. A billion pounds would build a lot of leisure centres in a lot of towns as an alternative to drink culture. A billion pounds, if spent wisely, could actually inject some life into that jaded catchphrase 'sport for all'.

That's the Government's business, though, and even if the PDs did pile in for the kicking, what happened at GAA Congress last weekend was almost unique among the litany of self-inflicted wounds which the association has administered to itself in the last decade or so. For once the GAA had arrived at a junction when the interests of the association precisely met those of the society it exists in. It was a time for graciousness and pragmatism. Both were spurned.

Instead, the decision taken grows more absurd the more it is examined. If the Government is convinced (rightly) that it would be wrong to coerce an amateur body like the GAA into opening up its ground to rival professional sports, but is at the same time disappointed that it declines to do so, why dangle a £60 million solution on the eve of Congress? Why add to the costs of the great white elephant of Abbotstown by purchasing events with which to fill the thing? Those who study the economics of stadiums have long since noted that as businesses they are only productive when they make sports an export industry, i.e. if they attract outsiders, or if they prompt the sale of new rights in terms of broadcasting and merchandising. Stadium Ireland so precisely lacks what a major stadium needs for viability that it seems like a criminal misuse of funds.

Most of what will be spent in Stadium Ireland, on the rare occasions when it is full, is money which would have been spent anyway. Just less of it. The profit derived from GAA games played there will inevitably trickle down into the pockets of the Government's private sector partners in the business, rather than into the clubs and schools which built the GAA. Bertie Ahern should go and take a look at Toronto's ailing Skydome facility before he goes any further. In a city of 3.5 million people, with a professional baseball franchise which plays 81 Major League home games a year, and with a serious Olympic bid behind them, and a serious Olympic bid ahead of them, Toronto's 12-year old dome is a disaster.

The cost overruns which are inevitable with such a project led to the dome costing $600 million instead of the planned $150 million. After five years, private interests had to bail the government out.

So take a look at Toronto, or take a look even at the model for Abbotstown, Homebush Bay in Sydney, a suburban ghost town, struggling for viability. Virtually none of the reliable revenue generators which a major stadium should have are present in Stadium Ireland. There are insufficient events there to attract big deals from food, beverage and merchandising concessions or car-parking operations. The infrastructure for Abbotstown in terms of the road network is disastrous. Imagine regular Wednesday evening traffic on the M50 with another 14,000 cars (the Government estimates) added in heading to a soccer international. The facility merely replicates another one several miles away and brings nothing new in terms of franchise teams, historic resonance or a niche capacity.

Nor will the BertieBowl contribute an iota to urban development. Stadiums work best when set centrally in a pedestrian friendly environment near restaurants, bars, hotels, parks, shops, etc. Visitors and fans spend more money, bring more life, and have a better quality of experience. The only modern rationale for the remote location of stadiums is to maximise parking and concession revenues. The

BertieBowl doesn't have a fixture list strong enough for that. Ideally, Croke Park should be open for business now, and realistically such business would be minimal. Most international rugby games would fit into a 50,000-seat stadium if the Government had a mind to build one. Ditto almost all Irish soccer fixtures. At most, Croke Park would be asked – at its convenience and usually out of season – to hold three or four extra fixtures a year. It would still have its £60 million. It would have cauterised a cash haemorrhage and turned it into a money-maker.

For this it would reap goodwill and positive exposure. Last week's decision brought opprobrium, division, a loss of income and credibility and, one assumes, a slew of questions from box holders bemused to see the GAA agreeing to strip fixtures out of Croke Park. Last weekend was a chance lost amidst a welter of embarrassing cutery and poor leadership. All week it has been easier to get Beverly Cooper-Flynn to see the funny side of lawyer jokes than it has been to get a figure of any weight in the GAA to come to the telephone. The GAA should expect more of itself, even if nobody else does. As for the man they went so willingly into cahoots with? Well, the populace may hiss, but

Tipperary discovery . . . Lar Corbett, who came from nowhere to nail down the left corner forward position on the Tipperary team, in action in the league game against Waterford in Nenagh. Photograph: Alan Betson.

when Bertie contemplates his Bowl, well, Bertie applauds himself.

14 APRIL 2001

Tipping Game has Yet to be Mastered by the Tiger

Dermot Gilleece's Golfing Log

Events on the 11th hole at Augusta National last Sunday would have been watched with particular interest by two members of the club staff. And they could be forgiven for having decidedly mixed feelings when Tiger Woods, with a birdie to a bogey, achieved a potentially decisive two-shot swing over playing partner, Phil Mickelson, one of his closest challengers.

Long-time locker-room attendants, Richard Germany and Roland Gray, were clearly interested in all aspects of the climactic battle. But judging from their delight when last year's champion Vijay Singh peeled off several $50 bills by way of a parting gesture, it would have been entirely understandable had their thoughts strayed from the Grand Slam to monetary matters. In that context, they would have been aware of how Kultida Woods imbued in her son a keen sense of thrift. Granted, Woods has shown himself to be quite generous in certain situations, but he would not be rated in the same league as Mickelson, a locker-room legend.

While on the subject, Darren Clarke, with $200 tips, has a reputation for generosity in the US. So has Billy Andrade. And while USPGA Tour policy requires each player to leave a minimum tip of $20 per tournament, two-time US Open champion Lee Janzen is among those who are happy to give considerably more.

'They're very helpful,' he said of locker-room attendants. 'They shine your shoes, replace your spikes, take care of your dry-cleaning, make rest-aurant reservations and give you directions. A lot of little things go into the job.'

In return for such services, some players are notoriously tight-fisted. But Mickelson, who has been known to tip $50 for an on-course drink, is the leading benefactor, closely followed by John Daly. In the locker-room, the game's top left-hander gives a standard tip of $500 if he misses the cut; $1,000 for a top-10 finish and $2,000 to $3,000 for a win. And he has been known to tip a further $500 to security guards.

'I know it sounds like a lot, but you've got to remember that we're taking over their entire facility for a week,' said Mickelson, who has also been known to enjoy a flutter. 'That's a week's worth of members' tips they don't get. We have an obligation to make up for it.' Meanwhile, Janzen still blushes at the difficulty he found himself in after winning his first US Open at Baltusrol in 1993. 'I was in a total daze, didn't have any cash, so I ended up writing the locker-room guy a cheque for $250,' he recalled. 'When I got home a few days later, I couldn't remember who I'd written the cheque to, so I stopped payment on it.'

The upshot was that the newly-crowned champion got a letter from a crushed Baltusrol attendant complaining: 'Hey, I thought you were legit.' Janzen made good on the original amount, with a few extra dollars thrown in by way of compensation, but the embarrassment remains.

So, what did Tiger leave the locker-room at Augusta National last Sunday night? Nobody's saying, but whatever the amount, the suspicion will remain than Mickelson would have left more.

'Green is kind of a tough colour. Tiger doesn't look as good in green as he does in some colours.'

(David Hagler, director of apparel for Nike Golf and co-ordinator of Woods's outfits, when asked why the Masters champion rarely wears green.)

17 APRIL 2001

Rabbitte Pulls Win Out of Hat

Seán Moran

Athenry 3-24, Graigue-Ballycallan 2-19 (after extra time)

Athenry won a second successive AIB club hurling championship at Croke Park yesterday. That bald statistic hides the fact that the Connacht side virtually lost the title before regaining it in extra time against an unlucky Graigue-Ballycallan.

The hurling mightn't have always been off the top shelf but the match was exciting, unpredictable and gave a crowd of 20,025 the first genuinely competitive All-Ireland final in six years.

Many things went right and wrong for each team but Athenry always looked the superior unit despite a failure to translate that fact on to the scoreboard. In the end, it was their greater reserve option that stood as the most obvious difference between the teams, as Pat Nally and his selectors shuffled their players around to achieve maximum effect.

Yet that superiority very nearly came to nothing as the Kilkenny champions turned the tables once, and nearly twice, by making the best of what came their way. Only a goal in the last moment of normal time – Eugene Cloonan lunging at the ball to finish a final, frantic attack – saved Athenry from a surprising defeat. But Graigue-Ballycallan would have deserved the title for their second half efforts and the manner in which the champions squandered a winning platform.

Extra time told against Graigue-Ballycallan. Without the replacement strength to remount their challenge and surely dispirited by the manner in which the trophy was knocked off their mantelpiece, they found the champions reinvigorated. Despite a lively opening half, which nearly delivered a number of goals for them, the Galway team led by only two points. As ever most of the damage was done by Eugene Cloonan, from placed balls, but, in general play, Cathal and Donal Moran were lively, the veteran Pat Higgins energetic and cunning. At the back, goalkeeper Michael Crimmins was utterly dependable, the defence efficient, and in the case of Brian Higgins at right wing back, outstanding.

Higgins won an awful lot of the aerial battles for someone of 5 feet 7 inches. His forward movement was also impressive and he landed a magnificent point in extra time to underline that fact.

In the opening stages Graigue were a disappointment. The attack, which had sparkled so much against Sixmilebridge, seemed in difficulty. Neither Adrian Ronan nor Denis Byrne was commanding, Tomas Dermody was anonymous and only John Hoyne – with two well-struck points – maintained his performance level.

Defensively, however, they were in better form. Although Athenry cut through on a number of occasions, Graigue held their composure – scrambling a flick from Eugene Cloonan off the line in the 15th minute. Goalkeeper Johnny Ronan was in superb form and two point-blank saves from Cathal Moran in the third minute and Pat Higgins 20 minutes later prevented certain goals.

The start of the second half suggested Athenry were going to win by a mile. In the 42nd minute, Joe Rabbitte stuck up his paw and scored a point for a 0–12 to 0–7 lead for the champions. Instead of that being the springboard for a comfortable win, it was the signal for an unanswered 1–5 from the Kilkenny team in eight minutes.

Adrian Ronan was the inspiration, from the point he nonchalantly swung over from tight in the right corner, to the goal he craftily poached. It came after Tomas Comerford's long ball created a dangerous attack which was broken up, by an apparent foul, but completed when the ball bobbled loose.

With the match now on its head, Athenry struggled and their opponents grew in confidence. Instead of preserving the width in their attack, the Connacht team bunched horribly and were generally surrounded by hard-working opponents. In defence full-back Pat O'Dwyer was excellent, whipping the ball away from Shane Donohue during one frantic attack. It really looked as if the champions had blown their title by failing to take their chances.

A goal difference between the teams was maintained for the closing 10 minutes until Cloonan's decisive touch. Although he ended with 1-11, Athenry's scorer-in-chief did great work out the field, after the management decided to switch him to the wing, and send the hitherto ineffective Rabbitte in on the square as a target man.

This gambit effectively decided the match at the end of the first half of extra time. Athenry had incrementally added to their score with some good points, when Cloonan dropped a ball into Rabbitte. He caught and kicked to the net for a 2–20 to 1–17 lead.

Late goals from James Young – briefly threatening another comeback – and David Donohue cancelled each other out and Athenry had become only the second club to retain the All-Ireland hurling championship.

ATHENRY: M Crimmins; E. Keogh, G. Keane,

Barrell of Murphy's . . . Dublin forward Vinnie Murphy tries to muscle his way past Galway's Michael Comer in the National Football League game at Parnell Park. Photograph: Dara Mac Dónaill.

J. Feeney; B. Higgins (0–1), B. Feeney, P. Hardiman; B. Keogh, B. Hanley; J. Rabbitte (capt; 1–1), P. Higgins (0–1), D. Moran (0–4); C. Moran, E. Cloonan (1–11, two 65s, eight frees), D. Donohue (1–3). Subs: S. Donohue for C. Moran (48 mins); D. Burns (0–2) for Hanley (48 mins); D. Cloonan for D. Donohue (61 mins); D. Donohue for Feeney (67 mins); D. Higgins (0–1, a free) for P. Higgins (89 mins).

GRAIGUE-BALLYCALLAN: J. Ronan; J. Butler, P. O'Dwyer, J. Ryall; P. McCluskey, T. Comerford, A. Hoyne; J. Young (1–0), E. O'Dwyer (0–1); D. Byrne, J. Hoyne (0–2), M. Hoyne (0–2); A. Ronan (1–9, six frees), T. Dermody, E. Brennan (0–4). Subs: D. Hoyne (0–1) for McCluskey (42 mins); J. Young for Dermody (73 mins); J. Lynch for A. Hoyne (88 mins).

REFEREE: J. McDonnell (Tipperary).

19 APRIL 2001

No Escape to Victory this Time for United

Michael Walker

Bayern Munich – 2, Manchester United – 1
Bayern Munich win 3-1 on aggregate

Alex Ferguson has one chance left if the Manchester United he has built up over 14 years is to justify its greatness by winning the second European Cup. Ferguson believes this necessary to warrant comparison with the great teams of the past. On the evidence of a fairly convincing 3–1 aggregate defeat, against a Bayern Munich side which may be some way short of special itself, Ferguson has a lot of work to do.

Goals from Giovane Elber and Mehmet Scholl in the fifth and 39th minutes last night, added to the strike from Paulo Sergio at Old Trafford a fortnight ago, finished United's interest, and their season. Ryan Giggs managed a 49th minute reply that briefly restored a measure of faith, but it had been decisively undermined by United's chaotic defending.

It was such that Gary Neville and Wes Brown swapped positions after the interval to alleviate Brown's discomfort. But the damage had been done by then. United made two changes from the first leg at Old Trafford. David Beckham's suspension meant a wider than usual role for Paul Scholes on the right, and Ole Gunnar Solskjaer was downgraded to the bench having been on the wing in Manchester.

There had been only the mildest of sparring when Scholl sprayed a pass from Bayern's midfield to Michael Tarnat, who had advanced from left back.

Tarnat found space behind Gary Neville and sent in a daisy-cutter of a cross that was horrible to United's back-pedalling defenders but which was perfect for Elber at the far post. From four yards the Brazilian made no mistake.

In a way, United's situation had not altered: they had needed two goals to win at kick-off and they still needed two. At least as long as Bayern did not get another. Some hope.

Bayern, attacking with confidence as United defended with nervousness, almost scored with their next move. Scholl and Elber were central directors as United were carved apart with two simple passes.

The second of those left Carsten Jancker free in the area with just Fabien Barthez to beat. But Jancker saw his volley rebound off the woodwork. Eight minutes had gone.

The distress, even at that stage, of the Manchester back line was obvious. It was made all the more conspicuous by the contrasting composure of, for example, Bixente Lizarazu's stand-in Willy Sagnol.

Neville and Mikael Silvestre were both suffering from poor distribution and in the 18th minute it was Brown's turn to be at fault. Another Bayern probe down the United right created room for Elber this time to deliver a centre. It was comfortable for

Brown, but his attempted header back to Barthez was soft and short. Jancker stepped in but could only poke the ball weakly at Barthez. Realistically, United could have been three down. On aggregate they would be soon.

That said, United could also have scored an equaliser in the 26th minute. Their previous attacking had been somewhat haphazard, over reliant on physical pressure and, supposedly, crosses from Giggs. Too often Giggs failed in that department, although it was from his corner that Keane managed a tiny flick with his head. The ball fell at speed to Andy Cole, he stabbed it goalward, but there was the pivotal figure of Scholl to boot the ball off the line.

Scholl's next work was at the other end, this time kicking the ball over Barthez's line. Bayern moved forward via the injured Jancker's replacement Alexander Zickler and Elber. As the ball skidded across the United area having been sent in by Sagnol, it came to Scholl at the far post. From 10 yards Scholl found the back of the net. United's players stared at each other motionless.

Now they required three to reach the semifinal. A first nearly arrived before half-time, though, Keane surging into the box and teeing up Dwight Yorke. Yorke's side-footer was straight at Oliver Kahn but somehow went through him and ended up on top of the net.

The second half began with the Germans continuing to open United at will, and yet, it was the English champions who scored. A good goal it was too, Giggs charging onto Scholes's alert lob to put another one over Kahn. The aggregate score was 3–1 now. Some hope.

The 4,000 Manchester United fans present had it raised on the hour when Giggs met a loose, bouncing ball with an improvised volley that Kahn stretched every sinew to palm away.

Munich might have wobbled then, but instead steadied themselves and started worrying Barthez again, the rangy Zickler, in particular. Ferguson

threw on Teddy Sheringham and Solskjaer, but the game ended with a blast of whistles as Zickler fell under a challenge from Silvestre in the United area. No penalty, but the next whistle was the final one.

BAYERN MUNICH: Kahn, Kuffour, Andersson, Linke, Sagnol, Tarnat, Jeremies, Effenberg, Scholl (Sergio 88), Jancker (Zickler 35), Elber (Santa Cruz 64). Subs not used: Dreher, Weisinger, Hargreaves, Kling. Goals: Elber 5, Scholl 40.
MANCHESTER UNITED: Barthez, Gary Neville, Brown (Chadwick 85), Stam, Silvestre, Scholes, Keane, Butt (Solskjaer 78), Giggs, Yorke (Sheringham 66), Cole. Subs Not Used: Van Der Gouw, Johnsen, Phil Neville, Wallwork. Goal: Giggs 49.
REFEREE: V.M. Pereira (Portugal).

23 APRIL 2001

Munster Run Out of Miracles

Gerry Thornley

Stade Français – 16, Munster – 15

For a team that has given so much to so many, cruelly, they are going to be left with more than their fair share of ghosts. Certainly, if losing one final by a point could be considered harsh, to lose a semi-final as well by the narrowest of margins could almost give you a persecution complex. Once again, Ronan O'Gara will be left to rue three penalty misses, but to saddle him with the blame would be grossly unfair. One was into the wind, one was from almost half-way and the other looked, quite conceivably, to have curled inside the far upright before being hesitantly decreed wide. And ultimately, he once again showed his bottle to then step up and nail the last two.

At least this was only a semi-final, but even so if anything there will be more to gnaw over. For

Strong Constitution . . . Bryan Sherbourne of Galwegians finds himself surrounded by Cork Constitution players when he tries to make a break during the All-Ireland League game at Crowley Park. Photograph: Frank Miller.

starters there was the outrageous denial of a per-fectly legitimate and well-executed try. And, it should be noted, it began with John O'Neill's well-timed run from an onside position.

Most of all, though, Munster didn't play to anything like their capabilities. Even ignoring last season's memorable semi-final, they've since per-formed better and duly beaten better sides than this Stade outfit. Another match or two, and this Stade would have been taken.

Reluctant as he was to make excuses, Declan Kidney applied an apt golfing analogy in likening the difficulties Munster had in getting to the pace of a representative game and re-applying their normally innate team-work. 'It's like trying to get your swing back and play a championship course at the one time.'

As with the one-point defeat to Northampton in last year's final, the minor miracle was that Munster managed to engineer themselves to within a point of their opponents. What got them there was their sheer desire. The second-half recovery was made all the more remarkable by the low base which their first-half performance provided, primarily in their use of the ball. Certainly, six points were rather needlessly coughed up by unco-ordinated attempts to run ball out of defence, leaving Jason Holland and John Hayes isolated and then penalised for not releasing.

Against that, though, the maximum for touch finds into the wind was about 35 metres, and Stade's second-half difficulties hammered home the point.

However, Munster's crunch problem, as in mud-bath defeats to Northampton and Bath in the past 12 months, was an inability to adequately control their own set-piece ball. Between the jigs and the reels Munster must have coughed up a dozen of their own line-outs and scrums, and only they could defy that handicap, albeit with the help of a heavy penalty count in their favour.

Munster's line-out has rarely experienced so many difficulties. At their morning work-out, Frankie Sheahan was throwing only bull's-eyes. In the heat of battle Frankie initially missed a few, but Stade also compete better than most (effectively marking John Langford) and also defend better than most, cleverly preventing the catchers from landing and so starting the drive. To utilise their old spring chicken Mick Galwey, and actually revive the line-out as a weapon in the second half, was a helluva turnaround.

Donnacha O'Callaghan has come in for a bit of flak, primarily because his handling errors were so exposed – from the kick-off, a couple of line-outs (though one was so off-beam that it hit his thigh), and a wayward pass to no one in particular, suggesting it was more a communication problem elsewhere. In fact he put in some good hits, ran the ball back gamely and worked honestly, a prime example being when he ripped the ball out from a ruck just as Chris White had put his whistle to his mouth to give Stade a turnover scrum in the build-up to O'Gara's third three-pointer.

For sure, David Wallace didn't have his customary dynamic impact as one of Munster's prime strike runners, but given where he'd come from it was a herculean effort. For sure, too, the Munster back-row were beaten continuously to the breakdown, primarily by the excellent Richard Pool-Jones. Witness his continuity play for Cliff Mytton's match-winning try (along with the ubiquitous Morgan Williams) but as that move showed the Stade loosies also had more targets beyond the gain line.

From the base of a retreating or skewing scrum, Anthony Foley's pick-ups were water out of wine vintage. He carried the ball and laid it back

every time as usual, and a couple of second-half big hits on Christophe Juillet and David Auradou helped keep Stade pinned into their own half.

Munster lacked penetration, save for Foley and O'Neill. Defensively sound, no one had a better go in running straight at the near impenetrable blue and red line (at one ruck there were 11 of them fanning out across the pitch) than the ever-improving and gamey Shannon wing. In what was largely a war of attrition across the gain line, those attributes mattered more than any other.

To have had his legitimate try disallowed, to have suffered from the disruptions of the past two months, to have been forced to play several key players recently sidelined by injury, all after being drawn away to the competition favourites at the semi-final stage for the second year running, then you have to wonder if the gods were against them.

Then to have played rustily and well below par on the day, to have suffered especially in the set-pieces and then to somehow get within a point of superior opponents on the day, well, you can only wonder at this lot really.

SCORING SEQUENCE: 3 mins: Dominguez pen 3–0; 5 mins: O'Gara pen 3–3; 21 mins: Dominguez pen 6–3; 29 mins: O'Gara pen 6–6; 33 mins: Dominguez pen 9–6; 35 mins: Mytton try, Dominguez con 16–6; (half-time 16–6); 49 mins: O'Gara pen 16–9; 71 mins: O'Gara pen 16–12; 79 mins: O'Gara pen 16–15.

STADE FRANÇAIS: C. Dominici; T. Lombard, C. Mytton, F. Comba, R. Poulain; D. Dominguez, M. Williams; S. Marconnet, F. Landreau, P. de Villiers, D. Auradou, M. James, C. Moni, C. Juillet, R. Pool-Jones. Replacements – D. George for Gomes (81 mins), A. Gomes for Juillet (73–81 mins).

MUNSTER: D. Crotty; J. O'Neill, M. Mullins, J. Holland, A. Horgan; R. O'Gara, P. Stringer; P. Clohessy, F. Sheahan, J. Hayes, M. Galwey (capt), J. Langford, D. O'Callaghan, A. Foley, D. Wallace.

REPLACEMENTS – M. Horan for Clohessy (81 mins), D. O'Cuinneagain for O'Callaghan (70 mins). REFEREE: C. White (Eng)

24 APRIL 2001

O'Byrne and FAI Part Company

Emmet Malone

Scarcely six weeks after the project he staked his reputation on collapsed, and those who had battled with him over its completion insisted he must go, Bernard O'Byrne conceded defeat again yesterday when he agreed to start negotiating the conditions on which he would end his term as chief executive of the FAI.

After another day of prolonged meetings, involving football's leading officials and administrators from around the country, the FAI issued a statement last night confirming the Dubliner's fate had been sealed, and he would depart by the first day of next month.

O'Byrne had, it stated, on the basis of 'the immense pressure on himself and his family … asked the association to discuss a confidential voluntary retirement package. 'These talks,' it added, 'would take place over the coming days.'

The feeling seems to be that with talks due to start tomorrow morning, a deal could be reached by the end of the week although it is not clear whether the international game against Andorra will necessitate the postponement of a final agreement.

Opponents of O'Byrne had expressed confidence prior to yesterday's meeting of the association's board of management – effectively its board of directors – that a report of a four-man subcommittee into alleged irregularities involving the official's handling of his company credit card and questions over the way he handled some of his expenses claims would make his departure inevitable.

As it turned out, the suggestion that O'Byrne should step down was first put to him by the association's president, his long-time ally Pat Quigley and National League chairman Michael Hyland, who met with O'Byrne in the city centre after a meeting of the officer board at a hotel near Dublin Airport.

At that stage he refused and it was late in the afternoon before the directors got around to considering his position. Before any substantial discussion about the issue took place, however, the meeting was adjourned at O'Byrne's request. A further session of talks took place, with Quigley and Hyland apparently talking directly to the chief executive, while Brendan Menton and Des Casey received updates in another room on how things were proceeding.

By then both sides had taken legal advice, and while the two opinions differed dramatically, O'Byrne is reported to have made the request to enter talks over a severance package.

When the meeting of the board resumed at just after six o'clock, news of what had transpired was relayed to the directors. It was agreed that the content of the report into O'Byrne's behaviour would remain confidential until after any talks had been concluded and the officers sought permission to negotiate the package. A motion granting them the power to do so was proposed and seconded by John Byrne and John Delaney.

Menton, Casey, Hyland and Quigley then held a press conference to announce those talks will start tomorrow and, all made it clear that they do not expect the process to be long or drawn out.

'The work of the association will continue,' said Quigley, 'and Bernard will continue to work on its behalf for the next few days but there will only be a few days involved. Everything will be concluded by 1 May.'

'It has been a very difficult time for the association,' said Menton, 'but the events of the day overtook the content of the report, which will remain private. The officers will discuss the terms of a settlement over the next few days and we are

Corinthian spirit . . . Olly Close (Corinthians) takes a tumble over Pembroke Wanderers' captain Paudie Carley and Duncan McKeen during the Leinster Senior Hockey Cup final at Serpentine Avenue. Photograph: David Sleator.

looking to conclude a legally binding agreement. That will be an end to the matter.'

The main issue at stake in the discussions will be the value of the package O'Byrne takes away with him. In recent days supporters had floated the figure of £200,000.

Quigley, subsequently, paid tribute to the contribution made by his friend during his time at Merrion Square, remarking O'Byrne had 'done a lot of development work and taken the association a long way.'

Less upset, though clearly anxious not to appear triumphant, Delaney said he felt 'vindicated by all that happened. I felt that Bernard wasn't the person to unite the association in the aftermath of the Eircom Park affair and I was consistent in

saying that he should go.'

O'Byrne was not available for comment last night.

26 APRIL 2001

Points in the Bag but a Match to Forget

Emmet Malone

Republic of Ireland – 3, Andorra – 1

Three goals, three points and Mick McCarthy's still perched impressively at the top of Group Two. Irish teams have had far worse nights at Lansdowne Road. While the result might look adequate in the record books, most of those involved in last night's defeat of the weakest international side ever to play at the stadium will be glad to forget a game that should have yielded so much more.

They certainly won't want to be reminded of the manner in which they fell behind, to a team that has never avoided defeat in a competitive international, nor of the way in which they almost monopolised possession of the ball in the second half, and yet only managed to add once to their 2–1 half-time lead.

That goal, a close range strike by the team's stand-in skipper Gary Breen after 77 minutes, doesn't even start to reflect the home side's domination of the game's later stages.

The reality, however, was the Irish strikers never managed to score and David Connolly, after some promising away displays last month, failed miserably to produce the sort of performance that might have impressed McCarthy.

With a little luck, of course, the scoreline might have had a far healthier look about it. Ian Harte struck the angle of the woodwork late on with a free that, nine times out of 10, might have flown into the top corner, while Alfonso Sanchez, the goalkeeper who did so much to impress in Barcelona, again made an enormous contribution.

If this World Cup campaign comes down to goal difference, the Irish players may well look back on this game in the knowledge that they should have done much better, particularly in the final third of the pitch where the massed defence was no excuse for the lack of imagination or the repeatedly poor quality of the finishing.

McCarthy had said beforehand that patience would be required against a team that, while packed with amateurs, had become adept at making things difficult for much better international teams.

But even the Irish manager must have been sorely tested as the home side, well on top but still looking for their initial breakthrough 32 minutes in, managed to allow the Andorrans to score their first

away goal in four World Cup qualifying games.

In the absence of any serious attempt to mark the big defender, there was little that Shay Given could have done to prevent Ildefons Lima's perfectly judged header from a Justo Ruiz free finding the back of the net. Breen was the guilty party, allowing the big defender to get first run.

But, prior to that, there were plenty of candidates for blame, with the original failure to clear an Andorran corner adequately, eventually leading to the rash challenge by Ian Harte on Juli Sanchez which led to the well-executed set-piece.

The Lansdowne Road crowd's reaction to the goal was a mixture of irritation and bewilderment. But they were cheering two minutes later. Matt Holland's high ball into the area was neatly helped into Kevin Kilbane's path by Gary Doherty, and the winger slipped the ball between the approaching Alfonso Sanchez and his post.

Having kept their heads fairly well early on, the Andorrans suddenly looked rattled. All the more so three minutes later when the Irish added a second goal. This time Mark Kennedy was the creative force, beating his man down the right-hand side, then floating in a wonderful right-footed cross that was almost turned home by the head of Doherty.

The striker's attempt came crashing back down, off the underside of the crossbar though, and as Sanchez and a couple of his defenders tried to recover, Mark Kinsella arrived, just wide of the right-hand post, to drive the loose ball back into the roof of the net.

At that point, another couple before the break really didn't look to be out of the question. There would, presumably, have been one at least, had David Connolly's penalty appeals not been turned down, following what looked to have been a challenge from behind, inside the area. Doherty also forced another decent save from Sanchez when he made a good headed contact with Harte's cross.

Like a boxer, after taking a heavy blow and is looking to make the bell the Andorrans clung on and managed to survive the last minutes of the first half.

When they came back for the second half they somehow managed to steady the rocking ship, although their pride had to be repeatedly saved by the continued heroics of Sanchez, despite his mistake for Breen's 77th minute goal.

McCarthy's decision to bring on three full-backs, in the closing 25 minutes, suggested the margin of victory was good enough for him. In a group where goal difference may well yet prove to be of crucial importance, we can only hope that, come October, we're not all talking ruefully about the lost opportunity.

REP OF IRELAND: Given, Gary Kelly, Breen (Staunton 85), Dunne, Harte, Kennedy (Carr 66), Kinsella (Finnan 79), Holland, Kilbane, Connolly, Doherty. Subs not used: Foley, Robbie Keane, Farrelly, Alan Kelly. Booked: Kinsella. Goals: Kilbane 34, Kinsella 36, Breen 76.

ANDORRA: Alfonso Sanchez, Escura, Antoni Lima, Delfons Lima, Roberto Jonas, Txema, Emiliano (Francesc Soria 87), Jimenez (Pujol 81), Oscar, Ruiz, Juli Sanchez (Fernandez 90). Subs not used: Gil, Ferron, Buxo, Poli. Booked: Txema, Jimenez. Goals: Delfons Lima 32.

REFEREE: K. Jakobsson (Iceland).

Down and out . . . Garth McGimpsey of Bangor Golf Club misses a putt on the sixth green during the West of Ireland Amateur Open Golf Championships at Rosses Point. Photograph: Brenda Fitzsimons.

30 APRIL 2001

Mayo's Trials All in the Past

From Seán Moran, at Croke Park

Maybe it's all this Arms Trial stuff. Thirty-one years ago when the crisis was breaking, Mayo won the National League. As the Government archives have yet to prove a link, it's obviously a coincidence, but yesterday at Croke Park, with the recriminations of 31 years ago again in circulation, Mayo have regained the NFL title for the first time since beating Galway 0–13 to 0–12. They were admittedly helped by Galway's failure to import sufficient weaponry to score even a point in the closing 28 minutes of the match but no one was too interested in launching an investigation amidst all the celebration. Since those heady days of 1970, Mayo have lost about 10 national senior (men's) finals between League, club and All-Ireland. But the times are changing. Yesterday, before a modest crowd of 22,623, Marty McNicholas's winner added the NFL title to Crossmolina's club All-Ireland of only two weeks to make April 2001 a month of months for the county.

Few titles have been as hard earned but it was all the sweeter for that. Captain Noel Connelly told a happy crowd from the presentation dais that he hoped the trophy would make up in some small way for the disappointments of 1996 and '97 when All-Ireland finals were lost.

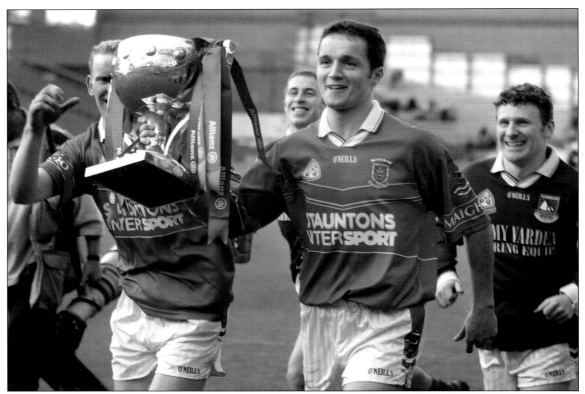

Western values . . . captain Noel Connelly leads his Mayo team-mates on a lap of honour after their win over Galway in the National Football League final at Croke Park after four Connacht teams had reached the semi-finals. Photograph: Cyril Byrne.

Opponents Galway suffered the galling experience of losing a second national final at Croke Park in the space of little over six months. Manager John O'Mahony had no complaints about the victory of his home county. 'We didn't play well enough to win,' he said. 'We died. There were a few chances at the end and a couple of decisions that went against us but this was a special day for Mayo and I sincerely and heartily congratulate them. When they left the pitch in Sligo [after defeat in the championship] last year, people thought they'd be gone for a few years, so I'm delighted for them.' O'Mahony's counterpart Pat Holmes was happy and relieved after the nervy, one-point victory.

'I'm very happy with the manner in which we won. My heart was in my mouth thinking "will he ever blow it up?"'

'We've been unlucky in the past but that's football and we weren't thinking about the past today.'

One of the players sharing the county's bleak history was David Brady who put in a Trojan display at centre-field. By his own reckoning he had been involved in seven losing All-Ireland finals from under-age to club and senior. 'I'm dying to wake up tomorrow,' he said, 'and realise that I've won something. This means more than anything else to me because we've been losers up to this.'

THE FINAL WHISTLE

Sore Subject

A big thank you to Niall Conway, webmaster of www.derrycityfc.com (in Planet Football's humble opinion the smartest National League website in cyberspace) for his e-mail last week. Niall alerted us to the fate of Finn Harps goalkeeper Damien Bradley, who was ruled out for the rest of the season after picking up an injury — while watching telly. Damien tore his Achilles tendon while celebrating Gary Doherty's goal for Spurs against Arsenal in the FA Cup semi-final.

All of which reminded us of our top five favourite injuries of all time: (5) Southampton goalkeeper Michael Stensgaard spent three months in plaster after dropping an ironing board on his foot; (4) Portsmouth's John Durnin broke his arm when he overturned a golf buggy; (3) Hadjuk Split's Milan Rapaic missed the start of a season after poking himself in the eye with a boarding pass at an airport; (2) Southampton's Claus Lundekvam damaged his back picking up a frying pan; and (1) Dave Beasant missed the start of a season, when he was at Chelsea, after dropping a jar of salad cream on his foot. Damien Bradley? You're in fine company — get well soon.

16 APRIL 2001

Mary Hannigan

DLSP deliver . . . Eddie Devitt, the DLSP full-back, dives over the line to score the first try in the All-Ireland League game against Lansdowne at Lansdowne Road. Photograph: Eric Luke.

MAY

2001

HIGHLIGHTS

1 May: Liverpool move into third in the Premiership with a 2–0 win over Bradford City.

2 May: Ken Doherty's fighting spirit is not enough to see him past John Higgins in the quarter-final of the World Snooker championships at the Crucible.

6 May: Bohemians clinch the National League title in the last stride as they beat Kilkenny 5–0 and Shelbourne fall to Cork City 1-0. Tipperary win the National Hurling League final and championship warm-up over Clare.

7 May: Ronnie O'Sullivan finally realises his dream and wins the World Snooker Championship final over John Higgins.

8 May: Valencia end the hopes of Leeds United with a 3–0 win in the Champions League semi-final second leg.

9 May: Bayern Munich continue their run through Europe with a 2–1 win over Real Madrid in Munich.

10 May: Paul McGinley takes a first round lead in the International Open at the Belfry.

12 May: Michael Owen helps end Liverpool's nine-year wait with two goals in the FA Cup win over Arsenal.

13 May: Bohemians win the double by claiming the FAI Cup over Longford Town. Sweden's Henrik Stenson wins the International Open trophy at the Belfry. Fermanagh draw with Donegal in the first high-steam clash of the football championship.

14 May: Arsenal manager Arsene Wenger indicates that he is to extend his contract to stay at Highbury.

15 May: Niall Buckley returns from America to assist Kildare in the All-Ireland.

16 May: Liverpool's treble has a golden hue as they defeat Alaves 5–4 with a golden goal in the UEFA Cup final in Dortmund. Controversy hits Galway football as the Donellan brothers John and Michael don't turn up for training.

17 May: Former Meath captain John McDermott announces his retirement.

18 May: Brendan Menton takes over as new FAI Chief Executive.

20 May: Eagle-eyed Tiger Woods wins again at the TPC of Europe in Heidelberg. Tyrone's hunger consigns Armagh to second sitting in the Ulster football championship.

21 May: Manchester City sack manager Joe Royle as the club stumbles to another crisis.

22 May: The Donnellan brothers return to the Galway football panel and make peace with manager John O'Mahony.

23 May: Goalkeeper Oliver Kahn is the Bayern Munich hero by saving the decisive penalty in the Champions League final shoot-out with Valencia. The feud between the Olympic Council of Ireland and the Athletics Association of Ireland continues as athletes are withdrawn from the European Youth Olympics over the gear issue.

24 May: Kevin Keegan returns to football management by taking the vacant job at Manchester City.

26 May: Dungannon prove class act by becoming the first Ulster side to win the All-Ireland League Rugby title.

27 May: Cork fall on home turf to Eamonn Cregan's Limerick in the Munster hurling championship. Eddie Irvine finally makes some noise on the Grand Prix circuit by taking third in Monte Carlo.

28 May: Venus Williams crashes out of the first round of the French Open at Roland Garros. Bolton Wanderers gain promotion to the Premiership with a 3–0 win over Preston North End.

7 MAY 2001

Bohemians Work the Miracle

Philip Reid

He doesn't look like a messiah, but they reckon that Roddy Collins is something of a modern-day miracle worker. Yesterday, just two-and-a-half years after assuming managerial control of a club in turmoil, he led them to the Promised Land as this one-time giant of Irish football captured the Eircom Premier League trophy after a 23-year gap.

'This is where this club belongs,' said Collins, shortly after his side's 5–0 away win over Kilkenny City, coupled with Cork City's win over long-time leaders Shelbourne, gave Bohemians a championship win that had seemed improbable just four months ago. At that stage, Shelbourne were 12 points ahead in the title race and apparently out of

Bohemian rhapsody . . . Tony O'Connor (left) is congratulated by Stephen Caffrey after he had scored the goal which won the FAI Cup final against Longford Town and clinched a league-cup double for Bohemians. Photograph: Eric Luke.

reach. However, Bohemians won seven of their last eight games and defied logic. Collins, for one, wasn't the least surprised.

'A few months ago, a little woman from the Liberties, Jimmy Fullam's granny, gave me rosary beads and a card. I hadn't seen rosary beads since my First Communion, but I was stood in the hotel before our first cup game and I had a strong premonition that I'd be sitting on the sofa in that same hotel having a pint after we had won the league,' he remarked.

Such clairvoyance skills aren't normally a requisite for a football manager and, even so, Collins was forced to leave his favoured touchline position three minutes before the end of yesterday's match. 'My stomach was churning so much I just couldn't take it,' he said, by way of explaining his retreat to the dressing room.

Indeed, as soon as their match finished, all of the Bohemians players were shepherded into that same dressing room as the match in Tolka Park hadn't yet concluded. One player used his mobile phone to ring a friend who was at the Shelbourne-Cork City match and relayed the final moments to the rest of the squad. No champagne was uncorked until the final whistle sounded, and then sheer euphoria took over.

'This day two years ago we were in UCD fighting for our survival as a club,' said Collins in emphasising how far they have come in the interim. Now, as league champions and with the FAI Cup final just a week away, Bohemians appear to have regained their place in the pecking order.

Collins, who doesn't have a contract, isn't ruling out a possible move to a managerial position in English football. 'I want to go to the top. I have my ambitions,' he said, adding that the club need to move on and 'look at the overall situation, the youths. We've got to work to get this, get that. If we could have a Rosenborg here, why would you want to leave? But things can't continue the way they were.'

Such a statement of intent has obviously struck a cord with the players. One of them, Glenn Crowe, already named PFAI Player of the Year, capped off a memorable season by scoring two goals yesterday to break two records: Kevin O'Flanagan's all-time club record and Jonathan Speake's all-time league record.

Crowe's two goals yesterday brought his league total to 25 and his season's tally to 35.

'It's brilliant to get this reward, winning the league, and hopefully I'll be back next season and score more goals ... and we also have the Champions League to look forward to. I have my own ambitions. I've played in England [with Wolves] and enjoyed it.'

7 MAY 2001

Tipperary Win First Battle But Not War

Tom Humphries

What do we talk about when we talk about Tipperary and Clare in a league final? Shadow boxing or a rumble in the jungle? More the former than the latter if yesterday's game at Limerick was anything to go by.

It was lively stuff, but the boys tended to float like butterflies. We came away yearning for 3 June when the stinging like bees bit begins.

Nothing but the same old story then in many respects – a league final which left us talking once more about the supremacy of the championship over all other forms. Even the teams don't pretend any more.

Tipperary won, of course, taking their 18th title in a match which offered nuggets of hope to both teams. Clare will be sustained by the fact that Tipp goalkeeper Brendan Cummins was man of the match, a fitting award in the light of the five clear goal chances the losers carved out.

League finale . . . Clare full-forward Niall Gilligan gains a yard on Tipperary full-back Philip Maher and keeps his eye on the sliotar at the Gaelic Grounds in Limerick, but Tipperary take the first serious title of the year. - Photograph: Dara Mac Dónaill.

Tipp will know that they competed where they had to, hauled back a deficit and strung together a necklace of shining scores to secure the game. Not a lot more could be asked. Sufficient unto the day etc. …

Funny how times have changed. Only 25,142 were interested enough to make the jaunt to watch the two teams who provided the most compelling rivalry of the nineties. The league has fallen a long way.

Back in the sideburned seventies, Clare's league titles were great emotional wrenchings which were supposed to joyously presage the good times to come.

Yesterday, neither team viewed the attainment of the secondary national title as a ticket to anything other than more hard work.

Nor was there any of the sizzling spite which has attended games between Clare and Tipp in recent years, just two teams with furrowed brows playing a little poker. In these changed times neither side has an ascendancy worth resenting.

None of which should detract from Tipp's achievement in skipping through this league season unbeaten.

The learning curve for Nicky English's young team has been as steep as this disjointed spring could have allowed and, if there was a distinct absence of champagne and high fives yesterday, it was just because league titles are no longer appropriate occasions for such things.

Tipp need only look back two years to appreciate how long league wins live in the memory.

All that matters for both sides is what happens when they meet in Cork on 3 June. 'That was a nice win for us today,' said full-back Phillip Maher, encapsulating the mood, 'and we'll have a nice night, but it's back to training on Tuesday night'.

The bright points have been plentiful for Tipp, though, and even yesterday hampered by a string of injuries there were reasons to be cheerful. The form of young Lar Corbett gave the most cause for rejoicing.

It would be easy and fashionable to dismiss the entire thing as a phoney war, but some of the themes which have run through the epic relationship between these counties in the past decade recurred yesterday.

John Leahy was big and irreducible for Tipp. Brian Lohan was thunderous for Clare.

Rather than rubbing each others' noses in it, they made to plamás each other with respectful words afterwards.

The Tipperary dressing room noted that Clare would find plenty of cause for good hope; Clare conceded the point, but felt Tipp had lots to be happy about, too.

'Clare are going to be a better team the next day,' said Tipp forward Eddie Enright. 'It's always nice to win, but there were only a few points in it today and that will mean nothing on 3 June.'

'It's kind of worrying if you look back,' said Clare manager Cyril Lyons. 'We created good chances in last year's Munster championship and didn't take them. We created good chances today and didn't take them.'

They went their separate ways, the team buses turning at the signs that said. 'To the drawing board'. Nobody sang and nobody cried.

National League titles are like one-night stands – fun while they last but not something that grown-ups boast about.

As for respect the next morning? Respect is earned elsewhere.

9 MAY 2001

European Dream Ends in Nightmare for Leeds

Michael Walker

Valencia – 3 Leeds United – 0
Valencia win 3-0 on aggregate

Leeds United's engrossing Champions' League campaign finished last night in much the way it had started last September – with a heavy defeat on Spanish soil yards away from the Mediterranean. Nine months ago David O'Leary's young team had been well and truly beaten 4-0 in the Nou Camp in Barcelona and been mocked in Spain for the poverty of their performance.

Last night, down the coast in Valencia, it was a similar scoreline as this individually and collectively excellent Valencia side progressed to a second consecutive European Cup final. However, while the score was nearly the same, the Leeds performance was considerably better.

That the night ended in shame with Alan Smith being sent off for a two-footed lunge at the substitute Vicente in injury time was a shame in itself because Leeds had been undone by quality, not by themselves. The Yorkshire club could point to the legitimacy of Valencia's opener, scored by Jaun Sanchez, the man Lee Bowyer trod upon, with Sanchez's left bicep, but ultimately it was Valencia's superior defending and attacking movement that won the game in such a decisive fashion.

It was sealed in the space of four electric minutes, soon after half-time, when Sanchez got his and Valencia's second, and Gaizka Mendieta added a fine third. There was still 40 minutes to play after that and though Leeds, principally through Harry Kewell, tried to rally, it was Nigel Martyn who was making saves at the other end.

It means the Valencia manager Hector Cuper will have guided a club to a third European final in a row, a unique achievement. In tactical terms, O'Leary forsook the opportunity of bringing Gary Kelly in for Bowyer on the right and went with his instinct which, when it comes to sending out teams, is always progressive. Eirik Bakke lined up in front of Danny Mills.

Otherwise the Leeds team was as expected, although Hector Cuper surprisingly chose his brilliant young Argentinian creator, Pablo Aimar, when the view in Spain had been that Cuper would plump for a more defensive beginning.

In a stadium where literally hearing yourself think was difficult, it was easy to understand why Cuper thought he would have the tide of noise behind his side, a volume that would increase every time Aimar threatened something special. The slightest hint of this, and that did happen, Mendieta raising expectations with an early volley that Martyn saved smartly.

Mendieta clearly had the taste and it was from his curling invitation of a cross that Valencia went ahead. Swung in from the right touch-line, Mendieta's centre cut out both Rio Ferdinand and Dominic Matteo and Sanchez met it on the dive. Whether Sanchez' connection was with his hand, shoulder or head was hard to tell from a seat high in the stands, but the ball went in and Leeds circled the referee, Urs Meier, immediately. Meier did not bother to consult his linesman. The goal stood.

Nevertheless, Leeds still needed just an equaliser to go through. They set about getting it admirably, inspired by Kewell on the left and Olivier Dacourt in the middle. In the 27th minute, after Kewell had rounded Jocelyn Angloma, the resulting corner caused a goal-mouth scramble; Kewell then sent a fierce drive fizzing over Santiago Canizares' bar and Dacourt followed that with a superb run past three opponents and a shot from 20 yards.

Mark Viduka kept the momentum going with some great footwork to set up David Batty. Batty's shot was weak but Leeds had reasserted their right to be here, though there was a dubious moment shortly before the interval when Kily Gonzalez went to ground in the Leeds area under a challenge from Bakke.

However, Leeds' first-half recovery and any heroic interval speeches were not merely rendered redundant by Valencia's second-half surge, they were obliterated. Two shots of breath-taking precision

National hero . . . David's Lad, ridden by Timmy Murphy, clears the last behind Rathbawn Prince, but goes on to win the Irish Grand National at Fairyhouse. Photograph: Joe St Leger.

nestled in Martyn's bottom left-hand corner.

The first came from Sanchez. As he raced across the front of the Leeds box it seemed Sanchez had reached a dead end; moreover Bakke was closing in, yet Sanchez whipped the ball with his left foot back across himself and beyond Martyn.

Leeds' response was an amazing dribble from Kewell but the possibility of a romantic comeback was nullified by Mendieta's goal just four minutes later.

Leeds had gone for it, pushing numbers forward, when suddenly Valencia broke away at speed. When Mendieta was played in by Kily Gonzalez's perfect pass, the Valencia captain found himself alone in a green acre. He could have run on but instead chose to shoot. It was a good choice, the ball zooming low past Martyn.

Even Leeds fans should have saluted Valencia at that moment.

VALENCIA: Canizares; Angloma, Ayala, Pellegrino, Aurelio, Albelda, Mendieta (Angulo 73), Aimar (Deschamps 70), Kily Gonzalez (Vicente 65), Carew, Sanchez. Subs Not Used: Palop, Djukic, Zahovic, Alonso. Booked: Sanchez, Aimar. Goals: Sanchez 15, 46, Mendieta 52.

LEEDS: Martyn; Mills, Ferdinand, Matteo, Harte, Bakke, Dacourt, Batty, Kewell, Viduka, Smith. Subs not used: Robinson, Kelly, Woodgate, McPhail, Wilcox, Burns, Maybury. Sent Off: Smith (90).
REFEREE: Urs Meier (Switzerland).

14 MAY 2001

Pegasus Show their Mettle

Mary Hannigan

It is probably as foolish as it is perilous to ever attempt to write off Pegasus but after two lacklustre performances at the All-Ireland Club Championships in Belfield there was a suspicion that maybe the Ulster side had lost their edge and that the win they needed against Hermes in yesterday's tournament decider would be beyond them. So much for that.

Once again the Ulster champions showed their mettle. They beat Hermes 1-0 to secure their fourth successive national title — and their passage into European competition next season.

'Magnificent,' is how Pegasus coach Graham Quincey described his team's first-half display. Seven short corners in the first 16 minutes underlined their dominance and if it wasn't for heroic defending from Daphne Sixsmith and Sinead McDonnell they would have gone in at the break with a comfortable lead.

However, they had to wait until the 46th minute to get the goal that ultimately clinched victory, with Irish sweeper Arlene Boyles firing home through a crowd of players from her team's ninth

Champagne reception . . . Pegasus celebrate in grand style after beating Hermes 1–0 to win the All-Ireland Club Hockey Championship at Belfield. Photograph: Brenda Fitzsimons.

short corner of the contest. By then, McDonnell had cleared a Pamela Magill corner strike off the line, with Susie Martin, Kim Mills, Claire McGookin and Claire McMahon all going close to opening the scoring for the Belfast side.

The closest Hermes came to snatching the point they needed for their first All-Ireland title was when a Sixsmith shot, from a corner, flew inches wide in the 50th minute.

The measure of the competitiveness of the tournament is that Alexandra finished without a point – yet were the only team to score against Pegasus – through a sublime Trish Conway lob from a short corner in Saturday's 4–1 defeat.

Loreto, who beat Alexandra 4–1 yesterday to take third place, had their title hopes ended by Hermes, on Saturday, when they lost 1–0 – Aisling Keane got the Hermes winner after 21 minutes.

17 MAY 2001

Liverpool's Treble has a Golden Hue

Michael Walker

Liverpool – 5, Alaves – 4 (after extra time)

Epic. No other word for it. Epic. European football was given one of its great finals here last night, and anyone who thinks that overblown should consider that Liverpool consummated their beloved cup treble and yet no one cared one jot. Last night was all about last night.

At various stages 2–0 up, then 3–1 and finally 4–3, Liverpool were three times reeled in by the magnificent players of Alaves. With just over one minute of normal time remaining Jordi Cruyff equalised to take the game to its golden goal scenario, and there, after Alaves had been reduced to nine men, a man called Delfi Geli headed an own goal to give Liverpool their first European trophy

since 1984. It was the 117th minute of a brilliant compelling evening.

Despite the huge squad he has assembled over the past two seasons, Houllier had pointed out on Tuesday that over the past six or seven games – crucial games all – he had kept his team changes to a minimum. He maintained that attitude last night, bringing in only Gary McAllister to the side that had started against Arsenal in Cardiff last Saturday. Vladimir Smicer gave way, as he had when McAllister had come on in Wales.

That was a like for like switch, but the Basques were more cautious. Instead of their usual 4–4–2 formation, the Alaves manager, Jose Manuel 'Mane' Esnal, went for a 3–5–2 line-up.

The idea was to add some height to the back line, and much of the Alaves warm-up was taken up by big men heading away long punts. When it mattered, though, just over three minutes into the match, the warm-up looked like a cold memory for the Alaves defence.

McAllister's free-kick from the right flank was, as usual, fast, accurate and dangerous. That, however, should not have precluded any of Alaves' three centre-halves from getting to it first. Instead, they allowed it to skim over the lot of them to Babbel. Babbel scored his fourth goal of the season with a downward header from barely six yards. 1–0. The voyage had begun.

As dream starts go this must have been Houllier's Tuesday night's slumber. Yet it got even better, and quickly. Thirteen minutes and what seemed like several attacks later Dietmar Hamann, already having a night to remember, worked the ball to Owen. Owen is not often credited for the insightfulness of his vision or the precision of his passing. But, at that moment, he picked out Gerrard haring through the Alaves defence. Gerrard took the ball on a couple of strides before powering it underneath the left arm of the unprotected goalkeeper, Martin Herrera; 2–0 and it felt like the end of the match.

But it was only the beginning of a Basque fight-back that was uplifting for the neutral to behold. Oscar Tellez, the fat-as-a-landlord central defender, made Sander Westerveld move swiftly to save a free-kick, but Alaves' turning point came with the introduction of Ivan Alonso for Dan Eggen in the 23rd minute. If that was an admission by Mane that he had got it wrong at the start, then he is a brave man.

He must have been punching the air when, four minutes after he came on, Alonso rose above Babbel at the far post to direct a careful header past Westerveld. The cross had come in from the right, where Contra now began to live up to his billing as the best right back in Spain. 2–1.

Alaves were back in it. Five minutes later only a last-ditch challenge on Javi Moreno by Babbel prevented an equaliser, and Westerveld then denied the same man, with a point-blank block after Moreno had left Stephane Henchoz writhing in embarrassment on the turf. Westerveld was also hit fortuitously by a shot from Ivan Tomic. And then Alaves threw all that away. Hamann threaded another pass through Alaves, Owen seized it, rounded Herrera and was brought down before he could shoot. Herrera should have been sent off but was shown only yellow. Nevertheless, he paid as McAllister stroked in the penalty. 3–1. Forty minutes, 36 seconds had gone.

Half-time brought a welcome breather. But then it all started again. Contra, really doing himself justice now, twisted and turned Jamie Carragher and floated in a ball to the far post. There Moreno out-jumped Gerrard to place another header past Westerveld. 3–2. Our bemusement was matched only by our amusement.

Three more minutes, a free-kick on the edge of the Liverpool area. Worryingly for Liverpool, Moreno stood over it. Then he ran up and kicked it – under the leaping wall. Westerveld stood motionless as the ball raced past him. It was 3–3 and it was magnificent.

But not over. In the 63rd minute on came Fowler for Emile Heskey. Ten minutes later Fowler collected a short pass from McAllister and sort of stumbled into the Alaves box. The ball was on Fowler's right and as he went past one, then two opponents, he looked half-balanced. Then, around the penalty-spot, came his chance. He had wasted them in Cardiff, but not now. With his right Fowler passed the ball into the bottom corner. 4–3.

And yet still not over. Alaves, superb Alaves, rallied themselves again. Two minutes left and a corner from Pablo. Westerveld came to punch. Cruyff got there first, his blond locks setting up a golden finale. It was 4–4 and it was still game on.

21 MAY 2001

Jam Rolls for Some and Jars for Others

Tom Humphries

At the risk of sounding unpatriotic, isn't it like a little death when the English soccer season ends? I reckon that 60 per cent of my small talk, 80 per cent of my teletext usage and 78 per cent of my trivia store relates to The Premiership. From now till August, I will be a social vegetable. (As if you readers need telling.)

I have already been trying out my close season conversational gambits and am honing them for the dark days when the teletext has nothing more substantial to offer me than Leeds being 'linked' with somebody's 'wantaway' star followed by Chelsea making a 'surprise swoop' for said star.

Best small-talk results, so far, have been achieved by my strident assertion that Liverpool are jammy. They are so jammy that they actually redefine our understanding of jam and all its derivative substances. New university departments

Champions collapse . . . Tyrone back, Ryan McMenamin, seems under pressure, but not as much pressure as Ulster champions Armagh who bite the dust in Clones. Photograph: Frank Miller.

must be opened to study this extraordinary strain of jamminess.

I mean ... c'mon, having played a light programme of what looked like pre-season friendlies to win the League Cup the jam should have ended then. Instead, it continued spreading endlessly until we were all nauseous yet curious about what sort of receptacle was being used.

Some cases in point. Liverpool are playing Everton, about to drop two league points when Gary McAllister gets a last-minute free-kick at a point so distant from the Everton goal that one wouldn't mount an attack without using sherpas.

He footles a low little free and finds, to his delight, that the Everton goalie has not just built an inadequate wall but is standing on the wrong side of the goal filling out his betting slips.

McAllister's celebrations are almost marred when he comes close to dying from laughter. Houllier is on the pitch with his big jammy grin too. We are jammy. Nous sommes les jamants! they are saying to each other! Bah.

I need not remind you that, while the gods were giving to Liverpool, they had just done with taking away from Leeds. The Wes Brown business cost Leeds two points at the time. Ended up costing £20 million sterling despite Leeds having embarrassed Liverpool at Anfield on Good Friday. The city of Leeds has been a jam-free zone since the mid-sixties.

In passing, I like to cite Liverpool's other two cup campaigns when, having been outplayed by an ailing Arsenal side, they won the FA Cup and then the whole ugly UEFA business when, having mounted a conspiracy of boredom with Barcelona, they sleep-walked into a final which unfolded like a Sunday morning seven-a-side.

They then won it with a jam-topped own goal. So they end up with three cups and a Champions League place with all those former Liverpool defenders who now work as analysts wetting themselves with pleasure.

This usually kindles the conversation, especially with women who like nothing better than arguing the toss over lucky free-kicks from a few months back. 'Wow,' they gush, 'talk about needing to get a life.'

And, by way of demonstrating that they haven't seen anything yet, I segue straight into my 'Leeds are the unluckiest team in history' riff, into which I have worked a nice hook, to wit that Leeds fans know the good times have returned because the team are banjaxed by misfortune once more.

For appreciative audiences I recall the seminal injustice of the 1970 Cup final against Chelsea, forever known as the Eddie Gray final. I throw in the five runners-up spots the great team got and finish the medley with a little number which takes in the Jeff Astle goal, several cruel end-of-season scheduling tortures and the 1975 European Cup final when Leeds had a cracker of a goal disallowed and Bayern scored twice, once on each visit to the Leeds half.

I then cut to modern times. I keen a lament about the mighty Manchester United corporation getting all the decisions lest their shares slump or Roy Keane says something mean to somebody.

I describe in detail, which will be invaluable to social historians centuries hence, how a brave group of young babies became so susceptible to injuries that Rio Ferdinand actually strained his leg muscle while watching television with his foot up on the coffee table. Was the table yellow carded? You know it wasn't.

Bravely, the team fought on. In all the great cities of Europe the babies travelled (half-fare) and

dazzled with their play only to have Lee Bowyer taken from them on the eve of the European Cup semi-final.

Which brings us on to Manchester United. Avoid at all costs by way of small talk. I have found it to be a fairly incontrovertible article of conversation that United aren't the same team without Roy Keane. Indeed, everyone in the world has virtually the same opinion as regards just about anything to do with Manchester United.

Beckham and the Nevilles are gloriously over-rated. They badly need a striker, a creative midfielder and another winger. Even Manchester United fans who have been following their team for as long as two years have nothing to offer here. They are bored, sated, flatulent almost with the good times, sick of following a club which does everything right.

My hope for this fallow summer is straight forward therefore. That Manchester United be restored to us as an object of derision as they were in the years when Leeds and Blackburn last won league titles.

Let the Ferguson era end in blood and spite and a row with Posh Spice, let their new kit be comically effete, let tonsorial fashions make a cruel joke out of Barthez and Stam, let the drinking club be reinstigated, and finally, let Alfe Inge Haaland be made player manager.

21 MAY 2001

Red Robbie Will Never Walk Alone

Keith Duggan

It was interesting to observe the differing interpretations of Liverpool FC in a week when the club experienced a rebirth. The decline of the Merseyside giants must have been of deep concern to those in the FA engine room, particularly, given the predictions that the

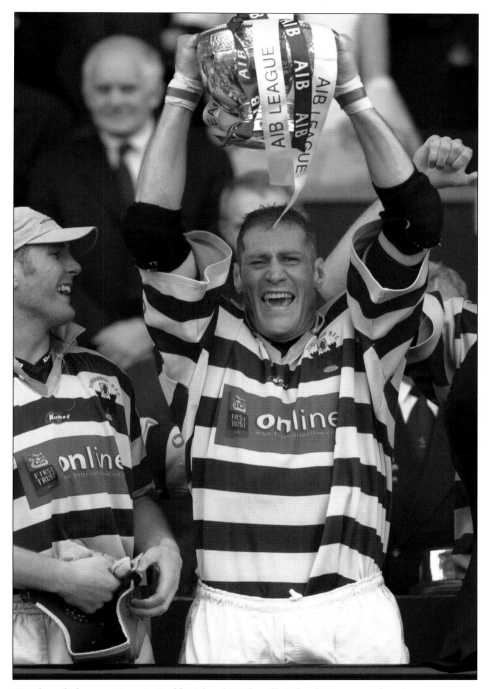

*Northern lights . . . Captain Paddy Johns lifts the All-Ireland League trophy after
Dungannon had set Lansdowne Road alight — and outclassed holders Cork Constitution —
with scintillating rugby. Photograph: Alan Betson.*

First classic . . . Imagine, ridden by Seamus Heffernan, wins the Irish 1,000 Guineas at the Curragh to complete a Guineas double for trainer Aidan O'Brien. Photograph: Brenda Fitzsimons.

arrest would prove terminal. The club, went the argument, was married to arcane traditions and the city was simply not hip or cosmopolitan enough to attract the exotic stars from abroad. This is Anfield: so what?

After Wednesday night's childishly fantastic UEFA Cup win, it was clear that the commentators were correct about one thing: Liverpool is definitely not cool. Its players will never have Chelsea chic, or the ineffable glamour that wearing a Man United shirt affords or even the big city slickness that mid-table Spurs can always rely on. The year was 1996.

Come to play for Liverpool and you are a Scouser, a Scally, a Corkhill.

Once, on FA Cup final day of 1995, the Liverpool team actually believed that it had achieved genuine coolness and the manifestation of that – those off-white, Del Boy suits – remains the most embarrassing episode in the club's history.

Liverpool's apparent reclamation of old glories has been greeted with polemical viewpoints from the TV pundits. While Kop legends Alan Hansen and Mark Lawrenson were giddy with glee on BBC 1, the domestic pairing of Giles and Dunphy were not best pleased on Network 2.

Eamo', in fact, could hardly contain his outrage and in recent times seems to acknowledge every Liverpool victory as a personal insult. Still smarting from Arsenal's failure to beat the Scousers by the 4–1 margin they probably should have in the previous Saturday's FA Cup final, he raged, like Lear on the heath, against the Merseyside's first European triumph since 1984.

'I can deny them. It should be about the skill to win. Look at this Liverpool side – it's a mess. He's a bad coach. I say he is a bad coach. He took Owen off, he put Gerrard at right back when he should have been running the game at midfield and he left Danny Murphy on for 110 minutes …'

More restrained, but equally nonplussed by the hooking of three Cups in one season was John Giles, who warned that Houllier had not built a team for the future. Dunphy contended that the run of 60-odd cup games was down to some sort of luck. For many weeks, he had predicted an abrupt end to the streak.

After Liverpool made it to the UEFA Cup semi-final, he happily assured us that Barcelona would eat them alive. It wasn't born out of any bias from Dunphy's part, simply that he believes that the current Liverpool style – boring pragmatism – is a betrayal of the Shankly/Paisley/Dalglish tradition and that they are imposters, not worthy of the praise.

There is little doubt that anyone with the interests of English football at heart – including the cross-channel soccer media – will welcome the return of a resurgent Liverpool without dissecting the blueprint for success too deeply. But it is worth looking at what a strong Liverpool side represents in the neon world of Premiership soccer.

BBC's documentary, 'When Liverpool Ruled the World', broadcast as an appetiser to the final against Alaves was a fairly straightforward review of the club's continental adventures of the 1970s and '80s. What one was left with was not so much an admiration for the great victories so much as for

the warmth of the city: the unforgettable quote about Dalglish's dialect – 'He's never injured and even when he tells you he is, you can't understand him'; the 1977 crowd banner: 'We've eaten the Swiss rolls, had the Frogs legs and now we're Munching Gladback'.

Best of all was the 'perm' craze which spread from Phil Thompson and Phil Neal on to Lawrenson and into the terraces until practically every Scouser in the city had a big frizzy perm. That in turn led to the scene in *Boys from the Blackstuff* where Yosser Hughes, with regulation 'tache and perm meets a sulking Graham Souness and says, solemnly, 'you look like me – and Magnum'.

Liverpool's first European Cup final, in Rome, was remembered for the startling number of fridges and other household appliances sold by fans determined to make the trip. Twenty-five thousand turned up. Always swimming against the economic tide, Scousers had football and wit to sustain them.

That is why of all the current generation, Robbie Fowler will always be god on the Kop. After his goal on Wednesday night, George Hamilton observed that for Liverpool fans, it was the one they'd cherish most.

Fowler is one of them – far from hip, full of flaws but burning with talent and a sense of identity, of what it is to be a Liverpudlian. That infamous mimic of his alleged cocaine habit, when he bent over to snort the end line after scoring – that was part of it.

Mischievous, yes, but witty too. Even his inflammatory gesture to the preppy Graham Le Saux, insulting and wrong though it was, still earned many a private chuckle. Fowler isn't PC, he's a Scouser, an Anfield hero with butty legs and a stupid breathing apparatus on his schnozz. He will never make the front cover of *Esquire* but he will always sell extra copies of the *Echo*.

Maybe the sceptics are right. Maybe this season was just a cosmic interruption of Liverpool's slide to irrelevance. What seems clear, though, is that the football club can never become unimportant to the city. It is the city and vice versa.

People who spend time in Liverpool testify that it is a brilliantly warm place, maybe the way Dublin used to be before all the Tiger crap was peddled. But it is also, in places, astonishingly destitute.

So it is pointless talking of the future. The future is the 90 minutes, the 'You'll never walk alone' anthem, the sense that even for an evening, the rest of the flashy soccer world is looking at their little red-bricked enclave with awe. In that sense even if Eamon Dunphy is right in the long term, he is still wrong.

22 MAY 2001

Random Pals Grin and Bear It

Colin Byrne
Caddie to Paul Lawrie

It was 7.30 a.m. on Wednesday at the St Leon-Rot Golf Club and the chauffeur driven cars (all German made) were queuing up to leave their passengers off at the main entrance to the clubhouse. Pro-Am day at the Deutsche Bank TPC Open and the sponsor's guests were arriving for a bite of wurst and a cup of

Senior citizen . . . Seiji Ebihara lines up the vital putt on the 18th which he birdied to win the Irish Seniors Open at Powerscourt. Photograph: David Sleator.

coffee before their assault on the course. This was most definitely an executive affair – there were no punters involved in this pro-am.

For professionals the pro-am is a necessary evil; if you are not in the pro-am it means you are not playing well, as it is normally the higher-ranked players who compete. If you are in, then you have the pleasure of spending up to six hours on the course, most of it in fear of your life, or of getting maimed by the frequently misdirected shots, or having to search knee-deep in hay looking for an errant approach.

Many of the amateur contestants agree that they would not like to be in a similar situation, of near chaos on the eve of their company's a.g.m., or a presentation of an important deal to the board. Professional golfers are expected to put themselves through such rigours every Wednesday as 'preparation' for the start of the tournament next day. They do, however, enjoy playing for the larger purses that ensue from inviting high rollers to join them for a pre-tournament round.

The shotgun broke the early morning tranquality on the course at 8.30 a.m. and Paul Lawrie hit his tee-shot off the 8th. His playing partners had introduced themselves. Mike, a plucky American in his forties with a handicap of nine bid us both a hearty good morning. His business partner Robert was less enthusiastic but none the less polite, off an 18 handicap.

Then Rolf Hess, the third member of the amateur team, presented himself. A well-built German in his late fifties, Rolf made his opening gambit with a beaming smile which exposed the glittering crowns on his back teeth. He told Paul that he had read an article written by an amateur, who had played with Lawrie in a pro-am in America last year, that was very interesting. Had he read it, Rolf enquired. Paul feigned enthusiasm at the German with the fixed grin, as he responded, that he hadn't seen the piece.

Rolf was the last to hit. As he shuffled about in his pre-shot preparation, a white band slid down his wrist, coming to rest just above his glove. Paul wondered what the band signified. Professionals tend to be reserved when it comes to the over-enthusiastic amateur getting just a little too close at such an early stage in the day. Rolf developed an early habit of grinning uncontrollably in your face after he made a comment that was not remotely grinnable at apart from the deliverer's expression as he did so. Paul perceived this as somewhat manic.

Professionals obviously have no concept of how batty they appear to the outside world as they carry on in reaction to a bad shot. The white band of course was the hospitality tag that got the guests into the lunch banquet. The round rolled on laboriously. An hour after we started we were still on our third hole: at this rate we were in danger of breaking the six-hour record. Rolf got on the card with, in his own words, a 'nice and easy par'. He chipped in from a thick lie in the rough. If it hadn't clattered the pin, head on, his ball would not have stayed on the green.

Paul asked Rolf if he was nervous, as he had complained of stomach trouble earlier. Paul's enquiry was more in connection with his eccentric behaviour, rather than the quality of his golf. After all, he was used to bad golfers. Rolf drew a serious expression for his reply. 'Nervous, me?' He turned out to be a chess grandmaster. 'A game of golf is not going to make me nervous'. This reply did have the effect of putting the critical golfer back in his place.

Michael, the financier from North Carolina, was teeing up on a different side of the tee to the grandmaster. He had just spent four days at Number 2 (Pinehurst, I assumed) playing with Nick Faldo. In his first sentence Michael had rattled off more famous golf courses than I could remember.

Shinnecock, Baltusrol, Winged Foot flowed from Michael's tongue like they were in his back yard. Golf nut and professional pro-ammer immediately sprang to mind. His brother usually played with him in pro-ams but he couldn't make this one. He was too busy buying a bank, back in the States.

Michael looked back at the third amateur, Robert, as he was tacking his way down a particularly long par four. 'That guy's got too much loft in his swing,' he exclaimed. Looking back down the fairway at the struggling golfer, I was trying to see if his back swing was very steep and somehow associate it with the loft that Michael was referring to. With a grin on his face he asked Paul and me if we could spot it. Then he proceeded to explain. 'You know, loft: Lack of F★★★ing Talent.'

The grandmaster proceeded to question every

yardage I provided him with throughout the day. Off a handicap of 14, the doubting boardman didn't know how far his shots were likely to go, whether the numbers he was basing his club selection on were accurate or not.

As a sort of compensation for his cross-examination of my figures I got to find out about his jousts with his old sparring partner on the board, Boris Spassky. Rolf is level with his Russian friend and rival in their chess games over the years. The pair, it seems, also held a Swiss doubles tennis title until last year.

As the shotgun signified the start of the afternoon torture session for the late starting pros, our

Les Sky Bleus . . . Wayne McCarthy weaves through the Longford defence to score Dublin's first goal in this year's championship at Croke Park. Photograph: Alan Betson.

group still had one hole to complete. We had reached a golfing form of stalemate. The authorities tried to relieve us from our state of fairway suspension by starting the afternoon contestants before we had finished. A *zugzwang* or forced move was going to be the only way to shift this lot.

28 MAY 2001

Limerick Invade and Dethrone

Seán Moran

Limerick 1–16, Cork 1–15

Cork, masters of the big surprise, are no longer Guinness Munster hurling champions. The title evaporated even more sensationally than their All-Ireland had last August against Offaly.

A resurgent Limerick, all youthful buzz and earnest endeavour, raided the once impregnable Páirc Uí Chaoimh for a second time in five years and won an exhilarating first-round contest by the slimmest of margins.

The young team had to win the match a couple of times. Nervy finishing meant a failure to give full expression to their first-half supremacy.

The second half would be different. Derek Barrett, switched to wing-back in place of the missing Seán Ó hAilpín, returned to centre-field and with the hard-working Mark Landers, got some sort of momentum going.

So, when Cork hunted Limerick down in the second half – Alan Browne's 39th minute solo-and-strike goal the key moment – and hit the front for the first time with 10 minutes remaining, there was hardly a soul in the unexpectedly big crowd of 37,792 who couldn't read the script.

Yet, Limerick battled back and, in an almost unbearably tense closing phase, they outscored the champions by three points to one. Cork were unable

to find the extra gear necessary to pull away and in the 67th minute Limerick captain Barry Foley drifted over a sideline cut, to put his team in front.

Shortly afterwards the crowd buzzed at the disclosure that there would be no injury time (assumed to be worth a couple of extra minutes to Cork) and the countdown began for real. Where do you start to convey the essentials of such an afternoon?

Was it Cork being complacent again? They certainly played poorly enough for long stretches, but there was more to it than merely the torpor of the champions.

Crazy as it must seem to anyone who saw their abject humiliation by Clare in the league last month, Limerick believed in themselves. They didn't fold under pressure and settle for the substantial moral victory on offer.

And there was more. They had the stomach to accept setbacks and come again.

Tactically, they were astute. Manager Eamonn Cregan remembered how Cork had comfortably absorbed Limerick's best efforts a year ago before pulling away to win well. They had posed too predictable a challenge.

Yesterday was different. Cregan shuffled his attacking deck continuously. No Cork defender had the opportunity to get comfortable on his man. The forwards moved around disrupting their markers and bombarding Cork with a constantly released energy.

The champions had their alibis. Brian Corcoran, fulcrum of the team that won the All-Ireland two years ago, was only recovered from injury and, although he shored things up when coming on for the second half, his absence from the starting line-up was a blow.

Ó hAilpín's car accident, coming only days before the match, was further, grave disruption. But the point was that no one foresaw these problems as in any way terminal to Cork's chances.

The overall effort was praised but Limerick's full-forwards were central to the drama. Full-forward Brian Begley gave a gigantic display on Diarmuid O'Sullivan. The achievement was enhanced by O'Sullivan's performance. This was no off-day.

During the intense tussles between the two, Cork's full-back won his share, including a super catch and clearance from a ball dropped in perilously by Mike O'Brien in the 16th minute.

And, in one of the moments of the season, two minutes into the second half, O'Sullivan raged out of his square after the ball and lofted a stunning point from nearly 100 metres.

Ollie Moran at centre-forward made light of his conversion from defensive pivot and, like Begley, hit three points. All around the attack, Limerick crackled with aggressive intent.

The half-time lead of 1–10 to 0–7 was backed up with 10 wides. The goal came when James Butler switched corners in the 12th minute, burned off John Browne before unleashing a fierce shot, which rebounded back out from the highly-strung netting.

Cork's attack was terribly disappointing. Sean McGrath, for a while, and the ever-dependable Alan Browne (another championship goal under his belt) showed in patches but Limerick's defence played their hearts out – from Timmy Houlihan, so calm in goal, to the tireless Mark Foley.

Foley was returning to the ground where he made such an auspicious debut five years ago, and he played it again – earning the TV Man of the Match award as he had back then.

LIMERICK: T. Houlihan, S. McDonagh, T.J. Ryan, B. Geary, C. Smith, C. Carey, M. Foley, J. Moran, M. O'Brien, P. O'Grady (0–5), O. Moran (0–3), M. Keane, J. Butler (1–1), B. Begley (0–3), B. Foley (0–4). Subs: J. Foley for Keane, D. Reale for Smith, O. O'Neill for J. Moran, C. Smith for O'Brien.
CORK: D. Óg Cusack, F. Ryan, D. O'Sullivan (0–1), J. Browne, W. Sherlock, P. Mulcahy,

D. Barrett, M. Landers (0–2), P. Ryan (0–1), T. McCarthy, A. Browne (1–2), J. O'Connor (0–1), S. McGrath (0–2), J. Deane (0–4), B. O'Connor (0–2). Subs: K. Murray for Mc Carthy, B. Corcoran for P. Ryan, N. Ronan for J. O'Connor.
REFEREE: P. Horan (Offaly).

29 MAY 2001

Venus Brought Down to Earth in Major Crash

Johnny Watterson

It is the day all top seeds fear – the first day, the day not to show feet of clay. Venus Williams, in theory protected by her number two seeding, will wonder how, after four matches going back to 1998 in which Barbara Schett never went further than two sets with her, she finds herself packing her bags.

Williams should wonder whether the French Open is going to be as cruel to her as it has been to her compatriots Pete Sampras and John McEnroe, who have never won here.

Well, no, Venus nor indeed her sister, sixth seed Serena, with whom family fortunes now rest, would ever entertain such a negative thought. The Williams' have always been quite heroically stoic in the face of tennis catastrophes.

'It was not the happiest day of my life. I'll move on,' she said afterwards. 'Nothing is a setback. It's just a loss. I just had a very rough day. It's too late now to turn the tables.'

Quite a contrast to the refreshingly jovial Schett, who sat back in her seat and laughed her way through the post-match inquisition. 'She went out and hit errors so…' chuckled Schett, 'who cares?… I don't'.

That's a fair summation of Williams' 43 unforced errors. A game that was never close to steady repeatedly failed her. Her serving was mediocre and she couldn't keep her normally blazing ground strokes on court.

Part of the problem was that her footwork was sluggish and tactically she refused to change by coming into the net. Another harsh 6–4, 6–4 lesson for the Californian, but not the only one yesterday.

Locally, Amelie Mauresmo's sharp exit to the German number 56 Jana Kandarr was more seismic than Williams'. The two would make uncomfortable bedfellows.

Mauresmo, ending her tournament being insightfully articulate and unafraid to speak of her own frailties, was a counterpoint to Williams' terror of even mentioning failure.

The fifth seed and player of form coming into the competition and the one who adorned every billboard and grinned from every magazine cover shouldered enormous French expectations. That appeared to beat her.

'I thought that my match was bad. Not a question of tactics, fitness or … whatever. It was just a state of mind I was in and I couldn't overcome it,' said Mauresmo.

'It is hard to put it into words but there is a feeling of powerlessness in addition to the stress. In fact, you feel as though you are being overwhelmed. I was trying to think of how to loosen up but I couldn't collect my thoughts.'

Like Williams, who had two service breaks in the second set to survive, before losing on the fourth match point, Mauresmo also had a chance to cling on going 5–2 ahead and earning the first set point before burning.

Jelena Dokic had the honour of launching the women's tournament on the Centre Court. The Yugoslavian number 15 seed, whose record on clay remains on two victories, one from last year and yesterday, indicated that she might just improve on her statistics.

Her father and coach Damir, thankfully taking a back seat these days, was nowhere to be seen as Dokic set about her Czech-born opponent Adriana Gersi waspishly.

She soon made it a French Open debut to remember for the 24-year old. The 40-minute 6–0, 6–0 match was a first for Gersi since she began on the circuit in 1996. Never before had she perished on court to what they call a double bagel.

Dokic has already won the Italian Open this year and on 21 May reached a career-high singles ranking of 18. In Rome she also treated Amelie Mauresmo, before Roland Garros, to only her third defeat of the year in 34 matches.

THE FINAL WHISTLE

A Farewell to 2000-2001

The things footballers say

'Yes, I was surprised about George's sacking – but as I always say, nothing surprises me in football.'

(Les Ferdinand)

'Yeah, I was a bit anxious when I got to the stadium, but in all fairness if I hadn't been anxious I'd have been worried.'

(Leeds goalkeeper Paul Robinson)

'Achilles tendon injuries are the worst you can probably have – they are a pain in the butt.'

(David O'Leary)

'My parents have been there for me, ever since I was about seven.'

(David Beckham)

Poem of the season

'Roses are red, violets are blue, I wish Henrik Larsson would go to Man U.'

(A St Valentine's Day message from a Rangers fan to his Celtic beloved (as published in the *Daily Record*))

Chant of the season

'Are you Tim Henman in disguise?'

(Shamrock Rovers led 4–1 ... but lost 6–4 to Bohemians)

'Phew' of the season

(1) 'I wouldn't pose nude for £3 million'. (Peter Beardsley),

(2) Terry Venables' wife's success in persuading him not to pose naked with a pair of Dobermans for *Cosmopolitan* magazine.

More things footballers say

'I've had an interest in racing all my life – or longer really.'

(Kevin Keegan)

'This is cup football now, it's all one-off games – and we have two of them against Valencia.'

(Rio Ferdinand)

'Paulo Wanchope is totally unpredictable – but you know what you're going to get when you buy him.'

(Alan Shearer)

'It got to the point where I owed one bookie £65,000, another £40,000 and a third £25,000 ... but thankfully my debts never got to what I would call crazy money.'

(John Hartson)

Bizarre No 1

Fulham captain Chris Coleman was ruled out for the second half of the season after breaking his leg in a car crash. A friend revealed that 'he swerved to avoid what he thinks was a deer. It all happened so fast'. He also said the animal could have been something smaller, like a rabbit.'

Bizarre No 2

Ceahlaul Piatra Neamt president Gheorghe Stefan's attempt to overturn the five-year ban from European competition imposed on the Romanian club by UEFA for 'offering the services' of prostitutes to match officials before their Intertoto game against Austria Vienna: 'They weren't prostitutes, they were members of a folk ensemble.'

Bizarre No 3

Sky Sport's Andy Gray's attempt at dispelling the theory that football folk have dodgy taste in music: 'I dispute that – in the car at the moment I've got The Corrs, Cher, Phil Collins, Shania Twain and Rod Stewart.'

Favourite pundits

(1) Barry Venison – 'Tempo – now there's a big word.'

(2) Ron Atkinson – 'Sometimes you just can't do nothing about anything.'

(3) Anonymous BBC Radio Five Live commentator – 'To be honest, I can't remember him scoring a goal that wasn't memorable.'

(4) Another anonymous BBC Radio Five Live commentator – 'Manchester City's Shaun Wright-Phillips, who is of course Ian Wright's son ... he doesn't look anything like him, though.' Note: Shaun is Ian's adopted son.

'We're saying nothing' 2000–2001

As part of a campaign by local libraries to encourage children to read more, the players of Leeds United were asked to name their favourite book of all time. Olivier Dacourt chose the autobiography of Francois Mitterrand, Nigel Martyn opted for *The Hobbit* and Mark Viduka? He nominated the picture book, *Where's Wally?*. 'It's the kind of book you can share with your mates,' he said, to which Dominic Matteo replied: 'absolutely'.

Charming

'In 11th place on the "most beautiful women in sport" list was our Minister for Sport Kate Hoey – I would hate to meet the girl who came 12th on a dark night.'

(Chelsea chairman Ken Bates)

'It was just his presence – he didn't have any.'

(Gerry Taggart on Lawrie McMenemy's days as Northern Ireland manager)

Question: Bohemians, UCD and Finn Harps are football teams in which country?

Answer: Finland.

(As heard on Channel 4's quiz show 15–1)

'We've sold our birthright down the fjord to a nation of seven million skiers and hammer throwers who spend half their lives in darkness.'

(The *Daily Mail's* Jeff Powell welcomes Sven-Goran Eriksson to the England job)

'He may be a good manager, but it's not as if he sells any strips.'

(The response of a Manchester United director on hearing of Alex Ferguson's wage demands for becoming the club's ambassador after he retires)

Saddest parents of the season

True, we were about 18 years late but still, the revelation that Emlyn Hughes named his daughter Emma Lynn was worth the wait. Close runner-up is Liverpool supporter Ronnie Chambers who only recently christened his daughter 'Anfield Shankly Paisley Houllier' – a little sister for 'Kopite Megan' and 'Ruth

Jamie Redknapp'. In time all three might forgive Ronnie, but we very much doubt it.

We get the drift

'It should be good, it will be good. We have got many good players and they will become a good team. He is a great manager. I think it will be a good thing.'

(David Beckham on Sven Goran Eriksson's appointment as England manager)

'It's another challenge. It's not a challenge that I would have liked – I'd rather have had the challenge of getting into Europe – but it's another challenge and it's a challenge that I relish. It's a challenge and I'm up for that challenge.'

(Paul Ince on Middlesbrough's relegation battle)

21 MAY 2001

Mary Hannigan

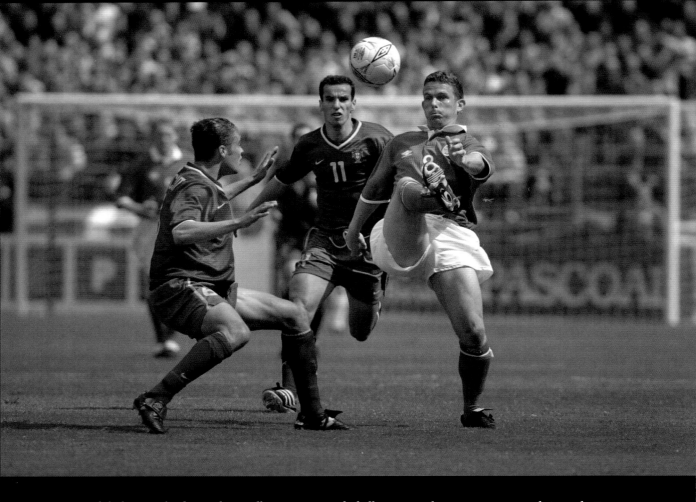

High kick . . . Ireland's Mark Kinsella gets a foot to the ball as Portugal's Nuno Bennetto and Arnando Teixeira move in to challenge at Lansdowne Road. Photograph: Dara Mac Dónaill.

JUNE

2 0 0 1

HIGHLIGHTS

2 June: Republic of Ireland draw 1–1 with Portugal in Group Two of the World Cup qualifier.

3 June: Tipperary survive battle of attrition by beating Clare 0–15, 0–14 in the Munster Senior Hurling Championship semi-final at Páirc Uí Chaoimh.

7 June: Giro d'Italia comes to a halt as riders go on strike following a police raid for drugs.

8 June: Lions maul the amateurs in a record-breaking victory as they beat Western Australia 116–10.

9 June: Jennifer Capriati captures the French Open title. Galileo wins the Vodafone Derby at Epsom.

10 June: Gustavo Kuerten claims his third French Open title. Ralf Schumacher takes the Canadian Grand Prix and leaves brother Michael in second place.

11 June: Limerick stage one of the great comebacks to beat Waterford 4–11, 2–14 in the Munster Senior Hurling Championship semi-final at Páirc Uí Chaoimh. Kilkenny cruise to victory with an awesome performance, beating Offaly 3–21, 0–18, in the Leinster hurling championship semi-final at Croke Park. Mayo stay on track as Sligo stutter and run out of steam in the Connacht Senior Football Championship semi-final at Castlebar (Mayo 1–12 – Sligo 1–11).

16 June: The Lions easily beat Queensland 42–8 at Ballymore in Brisbane. Sam Lynch wins gold for Ireland in the lightweight single sculls at the World Cup regatta in Seville.

17 June: No stopping revitalised Tyrone as they take the Ulster Senior Football Championship semi-final 3–7 to Derry's 0–14 in Clones. Dublin emerge from a morass to beat Offaly 1–12, 0–13 in the Leinster Senior Football semi-final at Croke Park.

18 June: South African Retief Goosen grasps second chance to win the US Open in a play-off with American Mark Brooks.

19 June: Lions alarmed by wake-up call as they go down 25–28 to Australia 'A'.

23 June: The Lions beat NSW Waratahs 41–24 during which Ronan O'Gara is repeatedly punched and left needing eight stitches to two lacerations below his left eye.

24 June: Normal service resumed as Meath rise to the occasion and beat Kildare 1–16, 1–11 in the Leinster Senior Football Championship semi-final at Croke Park. Cavan beat Monaghan 0–13, 0–11 in Ulster.

25 June: Martina Hingis falls at the first as she loses to unknown Spanish player Virginia Ruano Pascual 6–4, 6–2 in her first-round match at Wimbledon.

30 June: Roaring Lions tear apart the Wallabies 29–13 in the First Test at the Gabba Stadium, Brisbane.

Wholesome Homeboy Who Has The Gift

Tom Humphries finds Damien Duff's attitude to life and football as refreshing as it is rare in the modern footballer

So. What ails modern sport? Well, have a listen to Damien Duff, a walking, talking embarrassment to his spangled profession. In the course of the following interview, he states unapologetically that he loves his Ma and Da to bits, that's he's not really very interested in money, that he lives a really quiet life out in the sticks, that he had a tear in his eye when they played the anthem on his senior international debut.

Don't feel obliged to read on unless you sense that you must because here's where it all gets sick and twisted: Duff even claims that it's great being a well-paid young footballer.

Finally, with an insouciance that will shock you rigid, he gets up and shakes your hand and thanks you by name. And he departs for the Point to watch Ronan Keating. Disgusting.

What is wrong here? Can Damien Duff find nothing about which to be bad mannered, pouty and aggrieved. Does he lack the basic professionalism to be rude? Has he nothing to moan about? Why is he talking to a journalist anyway?

Where did it all go so wrong? It's his parents, Gerry and Mary, who must shoulder much of the blame – and yet it will be hard not to feel sorry for them if they have to watch their tearaway son zigging and zagging around Lansdowne Road this afternoon, with over 30,000 strangers tribally chanting Duffer! Duffer! That's the sort of thing that happens when you rear one of the best wingers in football and bestow on him the sort of shy groundedness and self-deprecating humour that soccer players usually can't access.

Whatever part Duff plays in this afternoon's proceedings, his presence will send a little electric shock of excitement around the ground every time he touches the ball. He's a throwback to another age, when dribbling was performed by slope-shouldered waifs in baggy shorts. It was an art form, the retailing of dummies, the throwing of feints and skips, the quicksilver feet. Duff has adhered to first principles all along. He was introduced to the soccer racket by his father, Gerry Duff, who at the time was a notorious Manchester United fanatic. Damien, the middle one of five kids, knew no better and was soon worshipping in the mainstream religion also.

Yet, when the time came, Blackburn was one of a few clubs he went to try out for. He made it one night at a trial game in Ewood Park. Alan Maybury was playing, Nicky Byrne from Westlife was there, too, as was Stephen Roche of Millwall. Duff was magical, though. Blackburn and himself chose each other and there was something right and fitting about that marriage. The blue and white quadrants and the grimy old town bear the same old-fashioned quality, as does Duff himself.

Brian Kerr had heard about him before he went away. One evening, with a couple of hours to put down, Kerr wandered up to Dalymount to see an Irish youths team play Poland. He wasn't employed by the FAI at the time and the names were largely unfamiliar. The PA man read through the teamsheet quickly, crackling out the squad numbers and names like an Eastern European railway announcer. Kerr didn't catch many of them, but as the game unfolded one kid stood out. That must be the famous Damien Duff.

There would be a twist, of course. Ireland scored an equaliser in the fourth minute of injury-time, leaving Ireland, Denmark and Portugal deadlocked in the qualifying group. It was decided to settle things by coin toss, there and then. Kerr hung around out of curiosity. Ireland won and went through to meet Norway in a two-legged play-off the following spring. By the time the play-off came about, Kerr was in charge of the team.

'I remember we went to Norway for the away leg. To Bergen. It was beautiful there. I remember it clearly – John Carew was playing for Norway, the groundsman in the place was Irish, and Duffer had turned out to be this quiet shy lad who didn't say much. You'd kinda worry about him, but he went out on to the pitch that day, though, and he was so good that the crowd were laughing at their own left back. He went past him and around him so many times that the back was dizzy. Duffer did extraordinary things that night.'

Ireland won 2–1 and took the return leg 3–0. The good times were about to roll. Duff was taking it all with a shrug. His progress in football has been

like a scorching run down the wing. Astonishing to watch, bread and butter for him.

'I started down the road with Leicester Celtic, went on down to Lourdes and finished at St Kevin's before I moved to Blackburn. Don't know why I moved around really. I'm usually just a homeboy. I found myself going from team to team.'

Kerr understands how Duff kept moving, though. His feet were scorching too many side-lines. When he and Noel O'Reilly decided to look at all the prospects for the Malaysia Youth World Cup, they set up a week of football in Limerick and, as well as a slew of players from the right age group, they brought four from the group two years younger – Duff, Maybury, Richard Dunne and Dave Whittle. After the first training session, Duff

Duffer . . . Damien Duff goes down after a challenge in the Ireland–Portugal match.

was going to Malaysia. Everyone else was playing for the chance to go with him. How good was he?

'I remember,' says Kerr, 'spending a lot of time telling the team about conserving energy in matches, not to be gung-ho, not to spend all their energy. We'd talk about tactics and patience. One day I called Damien aside and said to him: "None of this applies to you, you can do what you want, go with your hunches." And he looked at me, very suspiciously. "Why?" asked Duff.

"You're nearly always right," said Kerr, "go with your instincts."'

As Duff was leaving the room, his blond brow furrowed and still intensely suspicious, Kerr called after him: 'Hey Duffer.'

'Yes.'

'We all love you here! Relax!'

And Duffer burst out laughing. Kerr knew the kid was onside, he'd cracked the seal of his inhibitions.

By then Duff was on the way. The fact that he was Ireland's player of the tournament was no more of an indicator of his potential than his progress at Blackburn.

He'd realised quite young that he wanted a career in soccer. He remembers announcing it in school and, even though he was handy, people laughed. He attended school in De La Salle, Churchtown, a rugby college, and even abandoned soccer for two years to try rugby.

How did that go?

'Well I'm a soccer player!'

Pat Devlin had scouted him for Blackburn. What clinched it for Devlin was a match in Sallynoggin one day when Duff, just a little blond splinter of a kid, rounded two players and then chipped the goal-keeper while playing for Lourdes against St Joseph's Boys. Devlin's jaw dropped. He brought Duff across when he was 15. It was the season Blackburn won the Premiership and they met and chatted with Kenny Dalglish, whose accent Duff found virtually impenetrable but whose wit he came to enjoy.

'I thought Kenny was funny and I thought overall it was the place to be. I was just dying to go. There was the odd tearful night. When I got there I was a bit homesick and at one time they had to bring my parents across because I wanted to go home, but it was years ago now.'

Alan Irvine was the youth team manager, shepherding quite a group of Irish kids through it all. Chris Malone, Gary Tallon, Tommy Morgan, Graham Cassin, Kieran Ryan, Dave Worrell were also there at the time. The English lads would all skip home for the weekends. The Irish kids would look after each other, arrange cinema trips. On the pitch, Duff made an immediate impression. He made his debut on the last day of the 1997-1998 season and won the man of the match award.

Since then he has become a local legend. He was player of the year last year with Rovers and was narrowly pipped for the award this season by Matt Jansen. When people speak of him they don't stint on using words like loyalty and decency. In Dublin this week he took an evening off to go and watch old schoolfriends play in the Leinster League. Pat Devlin still looks after all his interests. He never considered jumping off the ship at Blackburn when they sank to planet Nationwide.

'It was devastating, but all I wanted to do was help us get back up. Then last season we under-performed big time. We came in 10th or something. Luckily we made it this year.'

And if they hadn't?

'Well, maybe the club would have wanted to cash in on a few of us. It was kind of make or break. I'm not interested in money, though. I just like playing football. I don't worry about what anyone else gets.'

Still, the impression is unavoidable that Blackburn know what they have on their hands. When player of the year Jansen renegotiated his contract this week, the club noted that they had brought it 'into line with players like Damien Duff and David Dunn'.

He has never grasped the superstar life which his skills entitle him to. He lives well outside Blackburn — 'up in the sticks near a load of old people' — and doesn't socialise much beyond the odd bit of golf or snooker. 'Some of the other lads live around, but they're all loved up with girlfriends and wives and kids and stuff. Mostly I just sleep.'

He has seen off a half-dozen managers during his time at Ewood Park. This year it's been Graeme Souness glowering across the training grounds.

'He's tough and he still likes to join in during training. He's still got the touches and he likes taking the mickey out of the lads. I stay well away from him over the other side of the pitch.'

Yet, tackling isn't as alien to him as most wingers. Kerr remembers him as being devoted to winning the ball back whenever it was lost and, this week in training, it was Duff's hunger which brought about the collision between himself and Steve Carr.

He'll be nervous this afternoon. Playing for Ireland gets the butterflies flying. He made his debut in Olomouc, in the Czech Republic, a few years back, an occasion marked by his apparent willingness to take on the entire Czech team.

'I played about 70 minutes that day and hoped to build on that. It was great. I remember having an old tear in the eye when the anthem was played and then the game was great. My job is going past people and I suppose back then I thought I'd have to beat people all day. I was trying to be Billy the Hero, but I was just a young lad and it was a great honour.'

He'd deny it, of course, but he has that old-fashioned Billy the Hero quality to him. The Premiership will enjoy him next year, Devlin feels. 'People forget he made his debut when he was 17 and he's had a few hard years. Different managers, a few injuries, but he's a determined fella. Next year people will be surprised by him all over again. The best is still to come and Damien deserves every good thing he gets. He's special.'

The bus is filling up for the Ronan Keating trip. 'Ah sure, it's better than just sitting around,' says Duff as he heads off for the night, a young man already freckled by greatness, with the best of the beautiful game stretching ahead of him waiting to be his, and without an enemy in the world to begrudge it to him.

Something must be done.

4 JUNE 2001

McCarthy Embraces the Game's Finer Points

Tom Humphries

Mick McCarthy comes into the band room looking dapper and determined. We media chickens are all over the coop, our feathers ruffled by the Portuguese who have circulated clichés among themselves without translating them for our benefit. Our phrase book tells us that right now we are as infirm as gaily coloured talking birds.

McCarthy is asked about the incident at the end, where he was dragged away from Antonio Oliveira by Eusebio. 'You know what there was before that?' says Mick, surprised, it seems, to be asked. 'There was a fantastic pulsating game of football which ebbed and flowed. We had some good spells, they had some bad spells. I think it was a terrific game. We could have won, we could have lost … that doesn't interest me, the other thing.'

Unfortunately for Mick we have just been through a press conference where people talked about that which was only of interest to themselves in a language comprehensible only to themselves. The spirit of journalistic enquiry must be restored. McCarthy acquiesces to the fourth estate. 'The story is I went to shake his hand. He wouldn't shake my hand. For what reason I don't know. I've always been led to believe … even as a player, I could go out and have a ding-dong battle no matter who it's with, and, end of game, I shake

Extra leg . . . Roy Keane is challenged by Roberto Severo, Portugal, at Lansdowne Road. Photograph: Dara Mac Dónaill.

hands. If he doesn't want to shake hands that's fine. I shouldn't have reacted the way I did and I apologise for that – it made me angry.' That wasn't so hard. We ask him if Luis Figo was a good hugger. If the game was all about hugging would he be the most expensive hugger in the world? 'I'd sooner have a hug off Figo than off their coach anyway,' says Mick with admirable certainty.

There follows an interlude of momentary sourness where McCarthy attacks us 'wallys' for making 'some filth' out of the hug thing, a thought which hadn't occurred to most of us. Behind me a voice says quietly, 'So Johnny Foreigner really doesn't like it up him.' Luckily it doesn't reach the ears of the Irish manager who has read that Figo is a gay icon in Spain and just can't afford to have the same status in Barnsley.

Much more important than all of this is the nitty-gritty of the football. Their goal, which looked like an inexpensive header granted to the rampantly heterosexual Luis Figo, arrived at a time when the Irish were in a state of some flux.

'Yeah, the goal came as we were trying to get Gary Doherty on. I went to 4–3–3 after we scored … I sent on information not to go 4–5–1, I didn't want to sit back. "Whatever you do don't sit back," were the words, but it happens. They were having a good bit of pressure but if we'd escaped that, got away with it, we'd have been okay. I'd changed it earlier (Niall Quinn coming off minutes beforehand) because I thought we were just sitting back. Maybe that sent a negative response to players which wasn't intended … Did they score because I went 4–3–3 or because the best player in the world snuck in?'

With a toothsome wind favouring the visitors in the first half, he had gone into the break knowing that his team would be a different proposition in the second half. He'd also gone in knowing that Roy Keane won't be getting on the plane to Estonia this morning (which rather makes the king-size seats a futile gesture).

'Having Roy in September (for the game against the Netherlands) might be the lesser of two evils. He was unbelievable this afternoon. Magnificent. We'll just have to play without him. There's that and Gary Breen gone. Apart from that life's just a bed of roses.'

The questions keep coming. Would he have done this if he'd known that? What about if this had happened and that hadn't? McCarthy is becoming exasperated.

'Look,' he says, 'these are things I can't do anything about.' He pauses. 'Where is it?' he says, and pats his breast pocket. 'Ah.'

He begins reading from the piece of card he has just fished out. 'God grant me the serenity to accept the things I cannot change, the courage to change the things I can, and the wisdom to know the difference.'

He rises and heads for the door, the sun is setting in a blaze of almost celestial light and a bluebird lights gently on his shoulder. As we are hushed, in wonder, the birdsong is strengthened by a choir of angels and cherry blossoms begin falling like snow.

'That's not true, is it, that thing about Figo?' says somebody. 'About him being gay?'

4 JUNE 2001

Unknown Visitors Given a Guarded G'day

Gerry Thornley

'Excuse me, who are these people?' It was a common enough refrain from some of the many bemused onlookers amongst the 50 or so people in the arrivals area of Perth International Airport on Saturday afternoon. The people in question were of course the neatly attired – if a little weary – Lions after their 20-hour journey from London via Singapore.

As entrances go this was more tradesman's than red carpet but all the better for that, most probably.

Perth is an ideal starting point really, more accessible than the more populated eastern half of the continent and with a relatively passing interest in rugby union. This is Aussie Rules territory. You had to plough through 13 pages of AFL coverage in the tabloid *Sunday Times* and then a couple of pages of tennis before finding the page devoted to the arrival of Martin Johnson and company.

Johnson cut his usually imposing presence, even dwarfing Donal Lenihan as they fielded questions jointly. The first official words emanating from the mouths of Lions were familiar stuff, Graham Henry reiterating his mantra of his recent weeks. 'We're hoping to play to our strengths and find one or two Australian weaknesses,' he smiled, knowing full well he was saying something close to nothing. Of necessity, of course, he cannot give the slightest clue as to the Lions' style of play and so they all trotted out the customary respectful comments about their hosts.

Henry reckoned they'd actually 'achieved more' than they'd hoped in that first preparatory week in Aldershot. 'It's hard to visualise what you're going to do in that first week and where you're going to get to, but I think we got about 40 per cent down the track when we thought we'd be about 25 per cent, so it was a positive start.'

The two primary purposes of the first week's exercise were to bond the squad and their four disparate national groupings, and also begin to evolve a style of play. 'We did a lot of team-building stuff. The Impact people who did the team-building exercises for the last (Lions) tour to South Africa worked with the group again,' said Henry. Aside from forming a band, more an orchestra really in which everyone had to take part, Henry revealed with a still incredulous smile: 'We did all sorts of things like climbing up great big things up in the air and then shouting like hell. And we did some dragon boat racing.'

By Perth airport standards the Lions' arrival prompted a kerfuffle of Heathrowesque proportions.

Its nearest major city is Singapore, over four-and-a-half hours away by plane. In covering almost a third of the Australian continent, Western Australia is roughly the size of India but with less than one per cent of that country's population. Of the state's 1.7 million inhabitants over two-thirds live in Perth.

The Lions have based themselves south of Perth, though effectively a southern extension of the city's flat sprawling suburbia, in Freemantle by the Indian ocean. Almost hitting the ground running, the squad checked into their hotel and within four hours of touching down had a light run-out at nearby Freemantle Oval. All bar Jonny Wilkinson (groin strain) and Dai Young (calf) of the 37-man squad took part over the opening couple of days.

On Sunday morning the Lions management decided the first training session would be at 7.30 a.m. local time, on the premise that the jet-lagged players would probably be up and about by then anyhow, even though their body clocks were telling them it was 1.30 a.m.

Even at that ungodly Sunday hour, there was a fair sprinkling of sprucely kitted out cyclists dotting the running/cycling track which lines the Swan River that runs into the heart of Perth – akin, you'd half felt, to a secret society and one taking its health a little too seriously.

Even at a delayed 8.15 a.m. only the birds were at the nearby Tompkins Park to greet the Lions for their first full-scale session. Adjacent to the Swan River, in the distance to a tree-lined, flat, scenic backdrop, were the cluster of skyscrapers in downtown Perth, which were initially shrouded in a sunny mist.

Before the end of the two-and-a-half-hour session the skyscrapers had vanished and the players had been submerged in rain. 'They brought the weather with them,' reckoned one of the dozen or so expats (an Irishman) who trickled into the ground. Several hundred or so attended the 3.30 p.m. session which followed a similar format.

Twenty minutes or so of warm-ups conducted by the booming baritone of Wales's Newcastle-born fitness adviser Steve Black were followed by a variety of continuity drills which were overseen by Graham Henry and Andy Robinson, interspersed with some defensive drills under the coaching of Phil Larder before the nucleus of Friday's opening selection against Western Australia broke away. This again enabled the offensive and defensive coaching units to work in tandem.

The spirit of camaraderie is clearly well established already but it was all highly serious, if highly skilled, stuff, before the squad attempts to conduct training behind closed doors on day two away from prying Wallaby eyes. And they, reputedly, pry better than any of them.

This being winter, with the temperatures reaching around 18–19 degrees Celsius, night comes early and the lights came on before the end of the second session. It had been the first of many long days and perhaps by the time they leave for Sydney six weeks hence, even the onlookers in the airport departure area will have some idea as to who they are.

4 JUNE 2001

Tuam Raiders Bury Tribesmen

Ian O'Riordan

Roscommon 2–12, Galway 0–14

Say hello to a little masterpiece, a perfect blend of vigour, colour and movement. Roscommon came to the heartland of Galway football yesterday and set it alight, producing enough fire and brimstone to ensure 1998 doesn't become a folk song just yet.

This may not be the greatest victory in Roscommon's history but none of their supporters coming out of Tuam Stadium could remember better. Littered match programmes were picked up as souvenirs. The flags were a sell-out. And no better excuse for loitering in the streets.

Of course, the championship will always move in mysterious ways but no one had the courage to say they saw this coming. Roscommon were down with injuries and down on their luck, especially if the 1998 Connacht final affair was the measuring point. Galway were on the rebound and out to prove a point, none more than the returning Michael Donnellan.

Yet one could only wonder how any team in the country would have beaten Roscommon here yesterday. They gave as good as they got from the start and before long it was clear nothing was going to stop them. Not Donnellan, not Padraig Joyce, not Ja Fallon. Nobody.

So where do you begin? With the sparkling Francie Grehan, Seamus O'Neill and Conor Connelly, with Fergal O'Donnell and Frankie Dolan flat to the boards, and with Nigel Dineen shooting sharp and fiery. With every man on the team busy being reborn or killing off all avenues of hope for Galway, and every man contributing to the overall effort.

Defensively, they soaked up as much pressure as anyone could have thrown at them but to a man, they held up with the minimum of fault. Denis Gavin and Martin Raftery in the two corners were gradually building a fort, and John Whyte didn't leave room for a view. Grehan was the inspiration of the half-backs, but the efforts of Clifford McDonald and Paul Noone were likewise majestic.

'There were so many moments that defined this win that I don't know where to begin,' said manager John Tobin. 'But there was no magic formula or Holy Grail involved in this. We did quite well in the league and we were really aiming for this game today.

'In fact, the defeat against Mayo in the league semi-final made us, because we did learn a lot from that. So we worked on a few extra things and then

Word of advice . . . Scoil Lorcan Naofa, Kilmacud, get some last-minute tips before defeating Scoil Mhuire, Marino, in Division 1 Junior Corn Oideachais Hurling final of the Church and General Cumann na mBunscoil at Parnell Park. Photograph: Bryan O'Brien.

we just played with great heart and great determination. The tackling back was very decisive, and we do have a big full-forward line and they are effective.'

By the end, Galway had blown out like an old tyre and now take on the unenviable tag of back-door men. It wasn't the first time in recent seasons they've tried to chase down a second-half deficit, yet rarely has their fate seemed sealed so early.

With the exception of the first 10 minutes, when Seán Ó Dómhnaill and then Tommy Joyce had Galway's only two genuine goal chances that could have put a whole different spin on the game, the reigning Connacht champions struggled to establish any sort of superiority. Roscommon

were a little tentative to start, but that didn't last long.

Through Alan Kerins and a Padraig Joyce free, Galway pushed their noses in front for as long as 11 minutes, when Dineen first split the posts. Two minutes later the thoughts of an upset were first sown when Dineen, freed up in front of goal by Gerry Lohan, cracked the Galway net with as much enthusiasm as he could produce.

By then, it was clear the long ball from Roscommon's midfield and half-backs was proving a source of major turbulence within the Galway defence. Panic may be too strong a word, but the confidence of John Divilly and Gary Fahey was shaken on more than a few occasions.

Michael Donnellan played with his typical range and with typical hunger and his first score on 23 minutes restored the balance at 0–5 to 1–2. After a couple more exchanges of scores, however, Galway started to bounce more freely, pushing two points clear thanks to the Joyce brothers, Padraig and Tommy.

That would be Rosommon's worst phase of the game but they would never again fall behind. Just before the call for the turnaround, they were back in front thanks to another long ball from the burning boot and phenomenal vision of Conor Connelly. This time Frankie Dolan got on the end and after skipping around Tomas Mannion, shot Roscommon 2–4 to 0–8 in front.

There would be one more definitive moment for Galway, spurred on by the introduction of John Donnellan. Bergin, Kieran Comer and then Padraig Joyce brought them back within range, although Comer's score was helped on by Frankie Dolan's injury that robbed Roscommon of possession (Stephen Lohan was the immediate replacement). With Donnellan's first free, coming on 50 minutes, Galway would once again see level scores on the board. So who wanted the next one more? The 18-year-old O'Neill was now winning every ball at midfield and he fired over two points within two minutes. Gavin pressed forward and got another. Gerry Lohan finally found the range from a free and then Stephen Lohan shot two more. Galway's sole response was two more frees from Donnellan – and even those had to be hard earned.

A magical win and totally deserved. 'Well we've had great days over the last three or four years in the Connacht championship,' said Galway manager John O'Mahony, 'but today wasn't one of them. It was just a bad day at the office.'

ROSCOMMON: D. Thompson, D. Gavin (0–1), J. Whyte, M. Raftery, P. Noone (0–1), F. Grehan, C. McDonald, S. O'Neill (0–2), F. O'Donnell, C. Connelly, J. Hanley, A. Nolan, N. Dineen (1–3) G. Lohan (0–1), F. Dolan (1–2). Subs: G. Cox for Nolan, S. Lohan (0–2) for Dolan, R. Owens for Raftery. GALWAY: P. Lally, R. Fahey, G. Fahey, T. Mannion, D. Meehan, J. Divilly, S. de Paor, S. Ó Domhnaill, J. Bergin (0–1), T. Joyce (0–1) J. Fallon, M. Donnellan (0–1), A. Kerins (0–1), P. Joyce (0–6), K. Comer (0–1). Subs: J. Donnellan (0–3) for T. Joyce, K. Walsh for Comer, R. Silke for Divilly, L. Colleran for Ó Domhnaill. REFEREE: B. Gorman (Armagh).

11 JUNE 2001

Galileo Shows He's a Star

Brian O'Connor

Michael Kinane glanced to his colleague Johnny Murtagh when weighing in after Saturday's Vodafone Epsom Derby and summed up the horse he had just ridden: 'Class, just class.'

Murtagh understood better than most. Sinndar, after all, was a fine Derby winner last year and matured into a genuine champion. But in Galileo, racing has a new star that could end up breaking every kind of mould imaginable.

Rarely in its 212 year history can the Derby have thrown up a victor who was so easily identifiable as the winner from so far out. From the moment the gates opened and Michael Kinane put the Sadler's Wells colt into the perfect position, just off the pace, there never seemed a doubt.

One kick at the two-furlong pole meant there wasn't even a 'seems' as the Aidan O'Brien-trained winner showed an astonishing turn of foot that allowed Kinane the luxury of looking around well before the line.

What he saw was Golan, a 2,000 Guineas winner whose stud rights John Magnier felt were worth paying $15 million to buy into only days before, struggling in second, and a double Group

Raining men . . . Fans watch Colin Montgomerie chip the ball on to the green in the Murphy's Irish Open at Fota Island in Cork. Photograph: David Sleator.

One winner in Tobougg back in third. It was a ruthlessly authoritative success that even had the virtue of being expected.

'I have never known Aidan so confident about a horse,' declared Magnier, who also had the satisfaction of seeing his champion stallion, Sadler's Wells, finally nail that elusive first Derby success.

'When we stepped him up in his home work he started beating the horses whom he had been working with by 15 to 18 lengths more than he had been before. At the time we thought the other horses must have been wrong. He really is an extraordinary horse,' said O'Brien.

The remarkable 31-year-old trainer from Co. Wexford is enjoying the sort of season that even his predecessor at Ballydoyle, Vincent O'Brien, would have been proud of.

Galileo is his fifth classic winner of the year, and O'Brien's confirmation yesterday that the colt will probably go next for the Irish Derby, while the filly Imagine will be aimed at the Irish Oaks, means the classic story is far from finished.

But Galileo is set to be the story within the story because this is a unique talent that could take a unique route to greatness.

Not for this latest Ballydoyle champion the traditional route to Paris in the fall and the Arc de Triomphe, which Sinndar followed so gloriously last year. There won't be the usual concentration on mile and a half races, and Galileo's real test won't even come on grass.

Instead, the focus seems to be heading towards a mile warm-up at Ascot in September, followed by a crack at America's best on dirt in the Breeders' Cup at Belmont Park on 27 October. It's a global trend that could hold huge significance for the career pattern of Europe's future champions.

A lot will depend on Galileo can buck the trend, but the suspicion at Epsom on Saturday was that if any horse can do it, this one can.

Kieren Fallon, who had to give up the ride on Golan through suspension, was yesterday still feeling aggrieved at having missed out on the big day, but admitted the runner-up would have 'needed an outboard motor' to have beaten Galileo.

His replacement Pat Eddery said: 'Galileo looks a champion. I followed him all the way round but when he kicked I couldn't go with him.' Frankie Dettori arrived late on Tobougg to take third, but even he will be relieved to see Galileo missing from Sandown's Eclipse.

It was that kind of Derby. The 11th Irish-trained winner since the war turned the classic into a procession, set the second fastest time in the race's history and still gave the impression the best is yet to come. Galileo really could turn out to be one of the greats.

11 JUNE 2001

Hoey's Thoughts Turn Toward Augusta

Dermot Gilleece

In a delightfully peaceful setting, far removed from the scene of battle, Michael Hoey tenderly fingered his glittering prize. Less than 24 hours previously, he had become only the fifth Irishman to capture the British Amateur Championship – and here was the medal to prove it.

The trophy was delivered to his club, Shandon Park, on Saturday night when the captain, Billy Bell, accepted it on behalf of the members. 'It's nice to be able to give something back, after all the help I've received at Shandon over the years,' he said.

We were in the garden of the Hoey residence in east Belfast, with sunshine filtering through the trees of the Stormont Estate. Michael's brother Edward, a 24-year-old doctor, was there. So were his proud parents, Brian and Pearl.

They had travelled to Prestwick GC on Saturday morning with Billy Black, president of the GUI, who had been invited to join in the 150th birthday celebrations of a club which had given birth to the British Open. And they were rewarded with the sight of Michael completing a remarkable week's play by gaining a one-hole victory over Ian Campbell of Wales in the 36-hole final.

Not wishing to deflect from the achievement of his son, Brian had to be reminded that it was only a short distance down the Ayrshire coast at Royal Troon that he, as a 50-year-old, had won three matches out of three at number one for Ireland, including a 4 and 3 victory over England's David Gilford, in the Home Internationals of 1984.

And Prestwick will be remembered for the triumph of Christy O'Connor Snr in the Dunlop Masters of 1956, when he carded a final round of 67 to beat Eric Brown by a stroke. And how the defending champion, Harry Bradshaw, had extended a congratulatory hand, before his compatriot had reached the recorder's hut.

Prestwick was also the scene of Irish celebration in 1992, when the Men's Home Internationals were won for an unprecedented third successive year.

Now, its ancient turf had delivered the highest individual prize in the amateur game. It is a prize which was captured by Jimmy Bruen at Royal Birkdale in 1946, by Ulster's Max McCreadie at Portmarnock in 1949, by Joe Carr at Hoylake (1953), St Andrews (1958) and Royal Portrush (1960), and by another Ulsterman, Garth McGimpsey, at Royal Dornoch in 1985.

'I felt greatly honoured when I looked at the names on the trophy,' said the latest recipient. 'And there are so many bonuses. I thought about going to the Tour School this autumn but that's all changed, given that I'm in the Open at Royal Lytham next month and in the US Masters at Augusta National next year.

'I played Augusta in May 1999 when I was a

student at Clemson. And though we were off the back tees and I shot something in the mid-'70s, it was only a bit of fun. This will be different. I wonder if I'll get to play with Tiger Woods. Miko Ilonen (last year's Amateur champion) did this year. They'd never put Tiger with the Amateur champion two years in a row, would they?'

During the week at Prestwick, Hoey's thoughts were dominated by what he felt he needed to do so as to maintain his prospects of making this year's Walker Cup team. 'That's been my main focus and I felt I had to reach the quarter-finals,' he said. By the time this was accomplished, he and his father both suspected it might be Michael's week.

'When you're as long around golf as I am, you tend to look out for certain signs,' said Hoey senior. 'And I felt we had one on the 19th hole of Michael's first round match with Nicklas Bruzelius.' His son agreed. 'I holed a 35-foot putt to stay in the match,' he said. 'That was a key moment.'

As it happened, he went on to win that match on the 24th. Then, in last Friday's semi-finals, when he was two down against Simon Mackenzie with four to play, he holed a 25-footer for a half on the 15th. Another key moment. Incidentally, that match went to the 25th, by way of strengthening the suspicion that Shandon Park players relish golfing marathons. It will be recalled that Hoey's club-mate, David Long, was taken to the 26th before beating Arthur Pierse in the final of the 1979 West of Ireland.

'When I played Prestwick in practice, I knew I would need to be patient and determined,' he went on. 'And I really drew on lessons learned from Dr Bob Rotella's (a leading American sports psychologist) books.

'There was also a big pay-off from Bobby Browne's (professional at Laytown and Bettystown) coaching. My competitive breakthrough came when I won the Irish Strokeplay at Royal Dublin in 1998, but my game seemed to stagnate the following year.

'That was when I went to Bobby. He has been a terrific help, especially where alignment, posture and course management were concerned.'

In Saturday's final, Campbell had a five-foot, left-to-right downhill putt on the 36th green to keep the match alive, but it slipped past the target on the right. It was all over. Hoey brought home a rather special gift from the host club — a limited edition print of a painting by Elizabeth McCrindle of Prestwick's two finishing holes, which he handled rather well.

11 JUNE 2001

Capriati on Top in Power Play

Johnny Watterson

Jennifer Capriati's victory in the French Open in Paris on Saturday has proved that the future of the women's game is moving further from the technical excellence of Martina Hingis and more towards the explosive striking of power players.

It barely needed to be stated but after a record-equalling 22-game third set at Roland Garros during which both Capriati and Kim Clijsters hit more winners and more errors than anyone could remember in a final, the level of power play has again taken a quantum leap.

The cornering of the market clearly no longer belongs to the Williams sisters.

Capriati, at the apex of the game once more and touted as a possible Grand Slam achiever (all four majors in the same calendar year), endured the relentless pummelling of 18-year-old Clijsters, for two hours 21 minutes, and finally nailed down the match in the 77-minute third set after service games were exchanged seven times.

Clijsters hit 76 unforced errors and Capriati 79, an unusually high amount with the Belgian actually winning more points in total than the American, 131 to 126, before losing the match 1–6, 6–4, 12–10.

'You see all the new upcoming players are all players who hit the ball very hard,' said Clijsters. 'Jelena Dokic, Justine Henin, Elena Dementieva, they hit the ball hard, like to go for points. I think this is probably the future of tennis.

'I wasn't feeling tired. I was pleased with the way I played and that I gave 200 per cent. I kept fighting for every point. I was happy to see that we still had very good rallies at 10–10 in the third.'

It was not the shape the match was expected to take with the inexperience of Clijsters in her first Grand Slam final being overshadowed by the reinvigorated Capriati.

Inevitably, the American's rise to her second Slam of the season was again being packaged as a tale of redemption and a triumph of the work ethic. Given her troubled past, when she dropped out of tennis for almost three years and her ever improving physical condition, few could argue.

The match itself was wholly defined by the third set, Capriati inexplicably dropping the first 6–1 before a significant 6–4 revival in the second threw it into a deciding third set.

Clijsters, playing with commendable poise, showed few signs of nerves and was the player who drew most of the gasps with her elastic retrieving of raking Capriati forehands.

But Clijsters' athleticism and power were not quite grooved enough for the 25-year-old and as the match approached its climax over the final four games, when nerves crept in and service games began to waver, it was the Australian Open champion who came up with the big points.

Clijsters had four breakpoints on Capriati's serve in the 14th game and another two in the 20th game but each time Capriati refused to concede. But neither could Capriati subjugate the first-time finalist, twice having opportunities to break.

Finally the 21st game offered the chance. Capriati took it and served out the match, a fore-hand to the corner fittingly ending the contest.

'Gee 155 errors. I think that's just the way the women's game is now,' said Capriati. 'If you are going to go for your shots, you're not always going to make it. You're going to make errors. I think it's better to take the chance. That's the way young players are playing. They're being brought up to play like that. I think you have to play like that.

'I just stayed in there and knew that I would pick up the level of my game. I knew there was going to be a time where she would just let up a little bit.'

Dedicating her win to cancer-stricken Corina Morariu, the doubles partner of Lindsay Davenport, Capriati refused to look towards Wimbledon but threateningly noted that she feels comfortable on grass.

'I'm not even thinking about it (Wimbledon) yet. I mean I like grass. I can't wait to get on it and play on it.'

WOMEN'S SINGLES FINAL: (4) J. Capriati (USA) bt (12) K. Clijsters (Bel) 1–6 6–4 12–10.
MEN'S DOUBLES FINAL: M. Bhupathi (Ind) and L. Paes (Ind) bt (13) P. Pala (Cze) and P. Vizner (Cze) 7–6 7–5 6–3.
MIXED DOUBLES FINAL: V. Ruano-Pascual (Spa) and T. Carbonell (Spa) bt P. Suarez (Arg) and J. Oncins (Bra) 7–5 6–3.

11 JUNE 2001

Limerick Stage One of the Great Comebacks

Seán Moran

Limerick 4–11, Waterford 2–14

It's hard to beat the sense of caught breath at a championship match when a team is unexpectedly cresting the wave. It's harder still to beat the buzz that tingles around the ground when a match belatedly erupts into a contest. But it's hardest of all to beat three goals in six minutes.

That triple hit – courtesy of James Butler and Brian Begley (twice) – was the centrepiece of Limerick's remarkable win in yesterday's Guinness Munster Hurling semi-final at Páirc Uí Chaoimh. Waterford gave it their best shot early on and looked to have destroyed this eagerly awaited fixture within a quarter of an hour, by which stage they led by a staggering 11 points, 2–6 to 0–1.

Afterwards Limerick's manager Eamonn Cregan said that the match had had many turning points. Throughout, those turning points were made possible by supreme composure under what must have been unbearable pressure. Scores patiently taken, tactical switches incisively made and performance levels undaunted by early catastrophes all played a role.

Twice Waterford looked likely winners. In the irrepressible opening movement, their forwards tore Limerick apart and the shocked attendance of 40,673 wondered what the precise dimensions of the rout would be. Then at the end of the second quarter when Limerick had failed to make significant inroads on the seven-point interval lead, it looked as if Gerald McCarthy's team would be able to stay at arm's length until the end.

But the second and fourth quarters told the more influential story. At the end of each half Limerick made a decisive impact on the scoreboard, cumulatively outscoring their opponents by 4–6 to 0–4.

Back to the start. Within seconds of the throw-in Paul O'Grady (whose nearly flawless – seven out of eight – free-taking sustained his team throughout) had given Limerick the lead but it was to be 18 minutes before they troubled the scoreboard operator again.

In that time Waterford ran amok. The strange thing about this passage was that the impetus didn't wholly come from the blessed trinity of Tony Browne, Ken McGrath and Paul Flynn. The debutants in the full-forward line, John Mullane and Seamus Prendergast, got off to rocking good starts. Mullane persecuted Brian Geary until the less tolerant Clem Smith dropped back. Eventually the corner forward had to be replaced because of an injury, which looked like a pulled muscle or hamstring. Prendergast gave T.J. Ryan the physical challenge Cork couldn't present and in the second minute he had plucked down a high ball, moved left inside his marker and pulled the ball back across Timmy Houlihan's goal and into the net.

Waterford then opened up and began to take their points. By the 16th minute every single forward had scored from play. Thrown in among the scores was Flynn's goal. Having been sent in by Mullane, the Ballygunner marksman swerved around Stephen McDonagh, picked his spot and Houlihan hardly moved. The scale of this domination was added to by Limerick's apparent ineptitude, fluffing the odd chance, racking up wides.

Drastic action was needed and taken. The switch that took Smith to the corner also brought Geary out to centre back and moved Ciaran Carey to the wing – ironically given that Waterford were thought likely to move McGrath on to Carey rather than vice versa. Things tightened up. At the far end, Ollie Moran worked tirelessly and effectively against the physical strength of Peter Queally to create a couple of chances but the scores weren't coming.

Until the 19th minute. Appropriately it was Ollie Moran who drove through on a single-minded run to within firing range and took the vital goal. It mightn't have seemed vital at the time, with Waterford still eight points ahead, but it set in motion the first phase of the comeback. By half-time the margin was down to seven points – 1–3 to 2–7.

Jack Foley replaced the injured James Moran at centre-field and got a point on the restart, but for a long time Limerick couldn't make the gap close significantly. Yet the scoreline obscured the extent

Solo run . . . Limerick's Jack Foley finds his own space in the Munster Senior Hurling Championship semi-final at Páirc Uí Chaoimh. Photograph: Eric Luke.

to which they were getting on top all around the field.

Mark Foley reproduced the form of the Cork match and won, scavenged and cleared a heap of ball. In the full-back line McDonagh was masterful, knowing when to commit and when to hold back. Impassively casting off the embarrassment of Flynn's goal, he dug in and seemed to be everywhere trouble threatened.

Carey's later move to centre-field was another success. Freed from the pressure of defending against McGrath, he used his experience and instincts to acquire ball and run at Waterford, creating time and space for his forwards. During the second half, it was McGrath who kept Waterford in it. His presence and accuracy earned three points for his team and kept them tantalisingly beyond Limerick's reach.

It was becoming clear that Limerick needed at least one goal to shave the margin, create a bit of momentum for themselves and pressurise their opponents. After a phase of loose shooting and prematurely desperate attempts at goal, Waterford cracked.

The second goal was as random as pinball, the sliotar ricocheting around the goal-mouth after Carey had soloed through to create an attack. Finally, it was James Butler who pulled on the ball for a cracking goal. Still three points in it but Waterford's blood was clouding the water.

A minute later, O'Grady nearly ended another episode of goal-mouth anarchy by squeezing in a goal but Brian Flannery preserved his line at the cost of a 65. O'Grady got his way however by dropping the ball into the square for a hitherto quiet Begley (in fairness, he was injured in a pre-match puck about) to catch, turn and goal.

Three minutes later the big full forward had done it again, this time from a Mark Foley ball. Although the time was still there, Waterford's cause looked out on a marble slab. In injury time Flynn hit the bar with a free which flew over for a point.

The last action saw Carey in his own goal-mouth fetching Browne's free and racing clear with an animated Cregan almost matching him step-for-step along the endline.

Suitably impressed, referee Pat Horan dispensed with 30 seconds of the recommended three minutes' injury-time (as he had at the end of the first half) and whistled Limerick into the Munster final against Tipperary and an eternity of fond reminiscence.

LIMERICK: T. Houlihan, S. McDonagh, T.J. Ryan, B. Geary, C. Smith, C. Carey, M. Foley, J. Moran (0–1), M. O'Brien, P. O'Grady (0–7), O. Moran (1–1), M. Keane, J. Butler (1–0), B. Begley (2–0), B. Foley. Subs: J. Foley (0–2) for Butler, O. O'Neill for Kane, D. Reale for Geary.
WATERFORD: B. Landers, T. Feeney, S. Cullinane, B. Flannery, J. Murray, P. Queally, J. O'Connor, J. Brenner, T. Browne (0–2), D. Shanahan (0–1), F. Hartley (0–1), K. McGrath (0–4), J. Mullane (0–1), S. Prendergast (1–0), P. Flynn (1–4). Subs: M. White (0–1) for Mullane, E. Murphy for Shanahan, A. Kirwan for Brenner.
REFEREE: P. Horan (Offaly).

On a clear day . . . Limerick fans celebrate their team's victory at Páirc Uí Chaoimh. Photograph: Eric Luke.

Harrington's Sunday School

Tom Humphries

The road less travelled. Many years ago Padraig Harrington was a Gaelic footballer. The last serious game he played was in Croke Park. He was centre back and marking a fair-headed young fella and he sprained his wrist chasing after him in the first minute. He got the run around all day and went off to play golf that weekend keeping his mouth shut about the wrist because he knew this was his sport from there on.

Yesterday Padraig was in Southern Hills playing the last round of the US Open with Tiger Woods. And the fair-haired young lad? Dessie Farrell was in Croke Park. You do what you do best.

So how did it feel to be Padraig Harrington yesterday at this particular stage of the journey? Sunday at the US Open. Walking from the practice green to the first tee parting an ocean of humanity.

Everyone is whooping. Three yards behind Padraig Harrington is Tiger Woods, wearing the claret red shirt he wears for final day play. All this goes into Padraig Harrington's data bank of experiences.

'I was delighted to be playing with him. It's a good situation to familiarise yourself with. It's like playing the last day when you are in contention. There is so much attention.'

Cutting through the crowd, Harrington has a kilowatt grin on his face. All that hollering.

'Just for me?' he says to Dave McNeilly his caddie.

On the first tee it's handshakes and best wishes. Woods and Harrington played against each other in company at the Ryder Cup in Brookline but this time there is a sense of tension which wasn't pres-

ent even then. Southern Hills Country Club and most of the people therein genuinely expect that Tiger Woods could pull back a nine-shot deficit.

Padraig Harrington is an extra in this production, but a key extra.

'Ladies and gentlemen this is the 12.45 tee-time. From Dublin, Ireland, Paw-Drag Hairington!'

He steps up in a talc-coloured shirt and slacks and whacks an iron shot into the blue yonder, looking as relaxed as he might for a Sunday morning foursome in Stackstown. He scarcely looks at Tiger Woods's drive.

'Lucky enough, with Tiger you aren't in a competition,' he says later. 'It's not like you are trying to out-drive him. He's playing his game. You play yours. Most of the time he's using different clubs. There's no sense of competition. He started on the first with a wood, which is tough, and by the back nine I was sort of wandering off on my own anyway.'

Still, down the first fairway they walk shoulder to shoulder, slipping into chat to soothe the nerves. Harrington asks Woods if he's coming to Ireland for fishing. Woods says he's going to Alaska.

They part. Harrington's ball has found the first light cut of rough. Woods is better placed. Time to step back and let the Tiger Woods show begin.

At this exalted level you need a fine instrument to calibrate the difference between success and relative failure, between genius and hard luck. It's a couple of lipped birdie putts, it's a bad bounce or a tough lie.

'Not again,' Harrington mutters on the second, as he finds light rough again. He and Woods have parred the first and are hitting their drives about equidistant now. Yet it is Tiger who bogeys the second, nerves making him prodigal.

So little separates the best player in the world from his pursuers. On the third Harrington hits a second to six feet. Woods hits his second to 25 feet. They walk away with a pair of pars. On the fourth Harrington has a god-like moment. Leaves his

Wonder drive . . . Padraig Harrington keeping good company at the US Open. Photograph: David Sleator.

drive on the right, finds the bunker with his second, makes a wonder shot with his third and putts sweetly for regulation.

'Nice par,' Tiger Woods says. Then he drops his birdie putt into the hole. It's that way right to the turn. Respectful jousting. Tiger is playing with the greater ambition; he believes he can contend. Harrington is playing with the greater patience; he knows he can consolidate and build and learn but never believes he can get to three under, which he believes would be a contending score.

Then, on the turn, they go their separate ways, Harrington down the fork of the road for ordinary but talented mortals, Woods the other way, walking on water. An array of small setbacks pins

Padraig to the ground. He bogeys the ninth and bogeys the next three holes and his face tightens. He knows he is a better player than the one this gallery is seeing now.

'I struggled with my concentration really. My tee shot on nine got the wind a little wrong. Bunker. I hit seven or eight bunkers in nine holes. Tenth? Seven iron and pulled it. Bunker. Eleven, playing to middle of green. Eye on pin and pulled it left and missed green. Twelve, down the middle going to middle of green with one eye on pin. Hit it fat to bunker. Fifteen, three wood from bunker. Sixteen, kicked left into bunker, chipped out again. Everytime I'm in there I'm chipping out and it's a straight bogey.'

Six bogeys in the last 10 holes. Not his A game. Not his B game. He adds the experience to the aggregate of all his experiences. They come to the 18th, both smiling, in the brilliant sun. Harrington surveys their shots balefully, says to the greatest player in the world, well thanks be to God they didn't cut the grass on 18 or we'd both be 50 yards off. Tiger laughs.

You said it.

And they suck in the applause. Tiger is hustled off with four policemen stuck to him. Harrington strolls towards the clubhouse and the little gaggle of media who want to hear about his day.

'My day? Well it could happen again when something is at stake and I wouldn't be so accepting of being five over on the back nine. I've familiarised myself with a situation that I hope will happen again in better circumstances. I have the experience. Next time I play with Tiger Woods I won't have seven media guys asking what I learned.'

And for Tiger Woods? He has seen that Tom Kite and Vijay Singh have already had the sort of round he was intending for himself. Some guys he couldn't pick out of a police line-up are jousting for his title but some invisible barrier of form or fortune has kept Woods from the low 60s. Ah well! One of those days, just one of those days.

One that Padraig Harrington will be nourished by. A Sunday at the US Open. Tiger Woods and half the world for company. A serious challenge for a serious player.

25 JUNE 2001

The Whole Country Has Been Warned

Keith Duggan

Gold does not rust. A timeless scene fell across Croke Park yesterday as Meath, the eternal winners, solemnly set about dousing Kildare's white fire.

They succeeded, of course. Yes, Meath won, 1-16 to 1-11.

All week, we were gripped by the rumours that their great falling, their eclipse, was imminent. The Boylan elixir, went the word, ran dry with the turn of the century. Meath, so long granite boys of summer, were running on empty. We were promised as much. Kildare – the commuter county, athletic and eager and the reigning Leinster champions – had unfinished dreams to tend to. This new time was theirs. Meath were not meant to win here. When will we learn?

They left us with the old sense of envy and wonderment yesterday. The simpler they spin it, the more profound it all appears. What is Meath? Why is Meath?

The answers were, as ever, wrapped up in the 70 minutes. To see them on the old ground, ravenous as ever, still finding a way. This time out, the Royals found daylight through a penalty. As usual, it came from nothing. Up 0–12 to 0–11 after 57 minutes, Meath were presented with a free around the 50-metre line.

Trevor Giles ambled up and held the ball in one hand, staring off into the middle distance like a man appreciating a fine view. Last year when Meath – then the All-Ireland champions – were ousted by Offaly on a dusty day in the half-constructed Croke Park, Giles famously quipped that no one would want to win an All-Ireland on a building site anyway.

The aesthetics of the stands must have been more pleasing yesterday. Giles's great radar was not as prominent as usual but one flash did it. Spying Richie Kealy on a run, he threaded a quick ball through and Kildare's nouveau defence collapsed around the wiry attacker. Penalty. Giles ambled up to the Canal End, the scene of his previous penalty woes.

'Ah yeah, the All-Ireland final in '99, I suppose, against Cork I missed one all right,' he mused quietly afterwards.

But not now. Giles hunched over the placed ball as Kildare goalkeeper Christy Byrne danced on his line as if his life depended on it. Christy was still hot-stepping when Giles drove the ball lowly, perfectly, into the corner.

'It's nice to get the odd one. If I missed today, they'd be lookin' for someone else. I suppose it was at the back of my mind. Ah, you're a great fella when you get them and when you miss you're a villain. So, it gave us a nice cushion, I suppose.'

In truth, it had looked ominous for Mick O'Dwyer's injury-ridden Kildare side before that. Padraig Brennan and Brian Lacey flickered nobly for the champions but things went against them.

Ken Doyle, the veteran in a novice Lilywhite defence, was sent off along with Paddy Reynolds on 47 minutes after the pair unwisely got into a tangle. Meath rejoiced in the newly opened land. Graham Geraghty reminded the world that he still possesses the feet of an angel, floating two beautiful points with the scores poised at 0–11 each.

Beside him, Ollie Murphy tortured Kildare's back three all afternoon, crafting four points from play. Back the field, it was equally impressive. Nigel Crawford touched the heavens from midfield. Cormac Murphy embodied all the classic Meath defensive qualities. He was hardly bettered for a ball. There was some magic with them. Ray McGee trotted in for Donal Curtis only to be shuffled off by a fussy linesman. Curtis, gladly settling into his seat, hared back on to the field and fired his only point. Seconds later, he was off again, delighted.

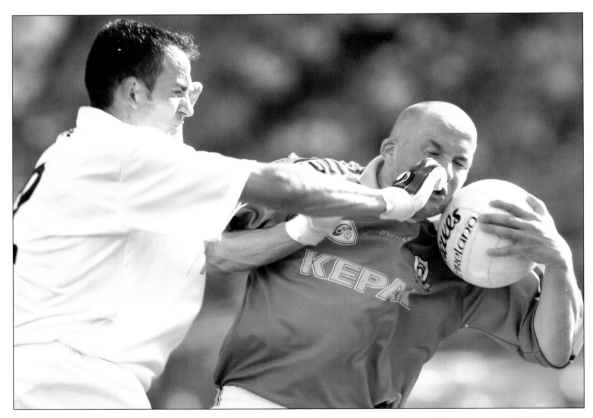

Running blind . . . Meath's Ollie Murphy and Kildare's Brian Lacey scrap it out in the Leinster Football Championship semi-final in Croke Park. Photograph: Bryan O'Brien.

In the net . . . Trevor Giles scores a crucial penalty for Meath in the Leinster Football Championship semi-final against Kildare in Croke Park. Photograph: Bryan O'Brien.

Meath's old essence was back and now the world knows it. 'Yeah, the old buzz,' said Giles. 'Certainly we finished strong and everyone was fighting very hard for the ball at the end and that's when we are at our best.

'We needed to be. If we had to blow our cover, well, that's it. At this stage, everyone knows everything about us anyway so there is no cover, really. Just good to see the old buzz is back.'

Just like that. Contented, they ambled out of the Pale and down the main road to the heartland. Another great rumble beckons now, against Dublin.

Kildare may live awhile yet. Next Saturday, they host Donegal in their backyard, the loser's consolation.

But across the country, the old fear is rising. Sean Boylan is smiling again. Meath are back. To think we believed they ever went away.

25 JUNE 2001

Aussies Try to Justify Assault

Gerry Thornley

Anger within the Lions' camp over Duncan McRae's punches and the general Australian reaction won't have subsided on seeing a screening of the game again yesterday.

'I think we know who the winner was,' quipped one of Fox TV's hilarious commentary team as Ronan O'Gara was led off with blood pouring from below his left eye, then came a shout of 'oh no' as Stuart Dickinson advocated McRae's dismissal to referee Scott Young. 'Stuart Dickinson you've had a shocker.'

Not even a close-up, slo-mo replay of McRae's estimated 11 punches swayed the commentary team. Former Wallabies Greg Martin and Phil Kearns duly weighed in with their tuppenceworth. 'I don't know what provoked Duncan McRae there and 'you don't do that without being provoked to start with.' It was a common enough theme. In the land of the blind, the one-eyed man is king. Enter Bob Dwyer.

At Saturday's post-match press conference he had begun: 'Duncan McRae has apologised. He certainly did throw a few punches but he does say he retaliated after what he felt was a swinging arm in the clean-out. Unfortunately you can only see his (O'Gara's) arm swing forward, and Duncan took offence to what he thought was a boot being lashed out. But he has apologised.' Oh well, that's okay then.

The spin doctors must have been quick into the Waratahs' dressing-room too. Dwyer revealed his boys in blue had been 'the second least penalised team in the Super 12', while he and captain Phil Waugh repeatedly cited the 60 yellow cards in this season's Super 12, of which New South Wales had received only two, one of which was for punching.

Dwyer also claimed that the game's first punch had been thrown by Danny Grewcock after 30 seconds, and 'the first penalised punch was thrown by Phil Vickery', conveniently ignoring that Tim Bowman had elbowed Grewcock literally from the kick-off to earn the game's first yellow card.

Just before they bounded out of the press-room, their haloes unmoved and pristine white, Dwyer relented a little and said: 'There is some validity in what he (McRae) says, but it doesn't really matter. Using that as an excuse is without any doubt unacceptable.' Hallelulah.

THE FINAL WHISTLE

Bullet Out of the Blue

Clubs in this country, especially in urban areas, will be familiar with the problem of encroaching golf balls. Secure your boundaries, is the byword. But what if the missiles are coming in the opposite direction?

Michigan state police were called to the Maple Leaf GC this week when a 44-year-old woman received a bullet wound in the forearm while playing the seventh hole. The errant bullet came from a nearby gun club at 8.00 p.m., two hours after the premises had closed for the day.

That was when two men entered the gun club, set up some targets and began firing a .40 calibre handgun. It seems that one bullet hit the ground and ricocheted upwards, over a tree-line and on to the golf course where the woman was standing.

'We're celebrating our 50th anniversary soon and we've never had a problem like this,' said the gun club president. 'We try to be good neighbours.' I'll bet they do. Now, what was that about being able to pick your friends….

9 JUNE 2001
Dermot Gilleece's Golfing Log

O'Gara Rex

Ronan O'Gara's nickname of 'Rog' has caused the Lions' coaching staff a few difficulties, prompting them to accidentally come up with an array of variations.

Much to the amusement of the players, Dave Alred mistakenly called him Rowan, Phil Larder splurted out Rory and Graham Henry hesitated with Roger. Armed accordingly, the players were inspired to come up with their own variations, and a small selection of these featured Rupert, Ronnie, Reginald, Ramon, Robert, Roy and Rashid. Basically anything and everything beginning with an R.

While in their hotel casino in Townsville, the players were being interviewed by somebody who claimed to be a Melbourne journalist and was doing a feature on them. When it was suggested that he should interview one of their leading players, Rex O'Kelly, 'the best player to come out of Ireland', the interloper mistakenly let on that, of course, he knew of the great Rex. So, the name that has proved the most popular and has stuck to a degree is 'Rex O'Kelly'.

18 JUNE 2001

Gerry Thornley

Rough stuff . . . David Duval of the US plays out of the rough at the 17th fairway in the final round of the British Open Championship at Royal Lytham and St Annes. He went on to win his first major, the 130th British Open Championship, with a score of 10-under-par.

J U L Y

2 0 0 1

HIGHLIGHTS

1 July: Galileo reigns supreme as the Aidan O'Brien-trained wonder horse sweeps to emphatic Irish Derby win at the Curragh. Roscommon finally reach their goal when they beat Mayo 2–10 to 1–12 to become the Connacht Senior Football champions. Tipperary take their chances in the sun and the Munster Senior Hurling Championship (Tipperary 2–16, Limerick 1–17).

7 July: Wallabies show their claws during the second Test in Melbourne (Australia – 35, The Lions – 14). Sligo add to the western saga by overcoming Kildare 0–16 to 0–15 in the third round of the All-Ireland Senior Football Championship qualifiers.

8 July: Warren Clarke stays calm to banish the demons and win the European Open at the K Club.

9 July: Goran Ivanesevic wins epic Wimbledon final against Pat Rafter.

14 July: Jaded Lions have complaints aplenty but no real excuses for losing the final game and the Test series (Australia – 29, Lions – 23).

15 July: Kerry quell rebel uprising at the Munster Senior Football Championship final at Páirc Uí Chaoimh (Kerry 0–19, Cork 1–13). Dogged Dublin lack attacking bite at Croke Park in the Leinster Senior Football Championship final and go down 0–14 to Meath's 2–11. Irish rowers strike double gold, silver at the World Cup regatta in Munich. Mika Hakkinen shows he hasn't gone away as he takes the British Grand Prix.

21 July: Major scalp from the west sends Westmeath to a new frontier as they advance to the quarter-final stage of the All-Ireland Senior Football Championship (Westmeath 1–14, Mayo 0–16).

22 July: David Duval takes major step forward to win the British Open Championship at Royal Lytham and St Annes. Australia triumph in clinical fashion at the Ashes series as England lose second Test. Galway put manager John O'Mahony through it as they progress to the quarter-finals of the All-Ireland SFC by beating Cork 1–14 to 1–10.

28 July: Galileo beats Fantastic Light into second place in the King George VI and Queen Elizabeth Diamond Stakes at Ascot.

29 July: Lance Armstrong wins third consecutive Tour de France. Wexford refuse to give up on their goal as they beat Limerick 4–10 to 2–15 in the All-Ireland SHC quarter-final at Croke Park.

2 JULY 2001

Roscommon Finally Reach Their Goal

Keith Duggan

Roscommon 2–10, Mayo 1–12

They were still sounding the car horns on the streets of Roscommon some two hours after Gerry Lohan scored the goal around which this GAA summer will revolve. They were still in disbelief. For the first time since 1991, Roscommon became Bank of Ireland Connacht champions after a match that ended as a rhapsody, as an entity beyond analysis.

Feel for Mayo. After the tears of the '90s, Pat Holmes's new side appeared to be developing into a county that had forgotten how to lose. This defeat marked a new extreme in their apparently boundless capacity for inflicting the wrath of the gods or some unseen element. Three minutes into injury-time, they were poised for a provincial championship to add to their league silver.

In hindsight, there were perhaps a number of tiny portents of the calamity that awaited them as the contest moved into those suffocating final seconds. David Nestor, Mayo's goal hero, attempted to flick a ball behind him, when cradling it might have been the better option. Mayo lost possession.

Just previously, Colm McManamon elected to thump a ball through his marker when the splendid Kieran McDonald floated free on his left. After Roscommon won the fateful sideline ball, Holmes could be observed on the sideline, desperately counselling his players to mark tight. He knew that only the threads of a lifeline remained for Roscommon.

But it was all that the home team required. Time seemed to fall into a slower motion as Roscommon worked the ball stealthily, boldly down the field. Alan Nolan's sideline kick was aided by Jonathan Dunning and then Denis Gavin, the attacking corner back was in possession and on open ground. Hyde Park froze for those seconds and what followed – his deft pass to Lohan, the shimmering finish – seemed at the same time inevitable and utterly stunning.

Fans from both sides stood trembling on the concrete bleachers as the final whistle then sounded. There was a delay between witnessing the event and actually registering what it meant. Roscommon were champions. Mayo had lost, again.

Although a classic, this match was far from pretty. The first half was a stuttering and mostly negative affair, as the counties teased each other out and stood solid by virtue of high-octane, bustling defensive units.

After the break, though, the names of summer began asserting themselves. Young Séamus O'Neill was again immense for Roscommon, toiling well with the work-thirsty Fergal O'Donnell.

Both the home corner backs excelled and as John Tobin pointed out, Roscommon has no lack of forwards. Each of the half-forward trio found the range in the first half, while Frankie Dolan and Gerry Lohan stepped up in the white hot minutes of the last period.

Mayo also had fine patches. Kieran McDonald was central in most of them and demonstrated his gliding, natural brilliance in a sustained display. The shame was that his colleagues didn't seek him out more often – his two second-half points were sublime and he also isolated Stephen Carolan with a perfect distance-pass early in the second half, a touch of brilliance that deserved a goal.

Although beaten twice, goalkeeper Peter Forde made a great stop off Nigel Dineen after 20 minutes. Trevor Mortimer was full of industry. Maurice Sheridan shook off a pair of sinful first-half misses with a worthy second half and his bravely chipped point after 52 minutes, putting Mayo 0–10 to 0–8 ahead, would have been identified as a foundation for victory on ordinary days.

But this day, of course, was not quite earthly. Despite seeing Clifford McDonald red-carded on 42 minutes, Roscommon found that deep well of resolve that has been with them all winter. Dolan and O'Neill levelled the scores. Then, with 12 minutes left, Mayo's Ray Connelly was sidelined after a scuffle that may, when examined, show the defender was harshly censured. Roscommon responded by haring through the exposed defence, John Hanley releasing Gerry Lohan, who buried the score to put them a goal clear.

From there it was a shoot-out. McDonald and Sheridan struck wonderful points to put the minimum between the teams. Holmes threw David Nestor and David Brady into the melting pot with dramatic return. With two minutes to go, Brady, the elegant Ballina leaper, ghosted on to a loose Roscommon hand-pass and broke through the last line. He freed Nestor with a precise hand-pass and watched as the forward fired low and true.

Then came the frenzied, endless added minutes and Lohan's denouement, destined for legend. Maybe Mayo play the game too nobly; so many other counties would have hacked their opponents down rather than let them build at that late stage. But those last minutes gave us sport at its most compelling.

Roscommon, then, are the first team into the All-Ireland series, the unfashionable, quiet county felling the kingpins of western football. They have a quietly serious look about them now.

Around Mayo, they will smile grimly at this. The pale joy of their league splendour will offer no consolation this week. Summer is a treacherous time and the days ahead look complicated now.

So, the first silverware of the new-look championship has been won. Roscommon are champions of Connacht for the 19th time. 2001 will be a precious date around these parts.

Croke Park beckons. There will be plenty of time for fond remembrance whenever the football is done.

ROSCOMMON: D. Thompson, D. Gavin, J. Whyte, M. Ryan, C. McDonald, F. Grehan, P. Noone, F. O'Donnell, S. O'Neill (0–2), C. Connelly (0–1), J. Hanley (0–1), S. Lohan (0–1), N. Dineen, G. Lohan (2–2), F. Dolan (0–3). Subs: G. Cox for Dineen, D. Connellan for S. Lohan, J. Dunnine for Hanley, A. Nolan for Connellan.
MAYO: P. Burke, R. Connelly, K. Cahill, G. Ruane, A. Roche, J. Nallen, N. Connelly, P. Fallon, C. McManamon (0–1), J. Gill, K. McDonald (0–4), T. Mortimer (0–1), M. Sheridan (0–4), S. Carolan (0–1), M. McNicholas (0–1). Subs: M. Moyles for Gill, D. Nestor (1–0) for Carolan, D. Brady for McNicholas.

2 JULY 2001

Munster Hurling Final Blasts Into Technicolor

Tom Humphries

Two points, the breadth of a couple of mistakes. Two points, the size of a pair of genius moments. When the dust settled at Páirc Uí Chaoimh yesterday, how you assessed the winning margin depended on where you sat and what colours mingled into the sweat which ran from your brow.

Tipperary and Limerick: not one of the most storied rivalries in the great book of hurling, but compelling nonetheless. Guaranteed. There wasn't a better sporting event anywhere this weekend. The sun shone, indeed it did more than that, and two teams under construction set about each other's reputation. It was clean, it was hard, it was surprising and it was some kind of wonderful.

Tipp, a little further along the path of perestroika and with the benefit of a race memory that expects success, but the hindrance of a populace which demands it, were the raging favourites. Talk before the game was careless among the supporters.

Hustle and muscle . . . Tipperary's Declan Ryan clashes with Limerick's Brian Geary in the Munster Senior Hurling final at Páirc Uí Chaoimh. Photograph: Eric Luke.

Tipp were looking at a favourable spread of six or seven points according to some sources. When the hurling started, though, all bets were cancelled. The teams scored five points between them in the opening five minutes. Then the pace picked up.

Performances which were huge. Ciaran Carey and Mark Foley grew into the game until they were giants of the second half. Brian O'Meara tormented Limerick all afternoon. The goalkeepers – one, Brendan Cummins, all hustle and bustle, the other, Timmy Houlihan, all shaved-head cool – were a show in themselves.

In the end Tipp prevailed; 43,500 exhaled again. After last season's grey, hurling is back in technicolor.

In the Limerick dressing-room hard truths had a literal edge. 'Tipp won the game,' said Eamonn Cregan, who sees the good side of defeat the way most people see the good side of tumours. 'It's as simple as that. We have to improve. We have to take our scores.' And he removed his baseball cap and wiped the sweat. 'How long do we have? Four weeks is it?' Four weeks indeed, before they come to Croke Park for a quarter-final engagement. Limerick have improved in quantum leaps all summer. Who knows what sort of tricks they will bring? 'We've made fantastic progress,' said Cregan. 'That's the positive side. Who would have expected that we'd be here? But maybe that's negative too. We beat Cork, beat Waterford, two points off today and people say, ah yeah you're great. We know, the lads know. We had the chances and we didn't take them. We had the ball, we were put under pressure, we put it wide. Simple.

'We have to get into a situation where we score under pressure. We have gone to a certain level. Now we have to go to the next level, then we can score more. We'll see how it goes for the next few weeks.'

As for Tipperary, they are deservedly back at the top table. The back door system hasn't taken from the lustre of winning a Munster title and the sheer joy which lapped out of their dressing-room had to be seen.

This was an epic they won yesterday, a thing of beauty and passion where they visibly grew, learning to prevail in precisely the sort of crucible where they have failed before. Some young men were lost and pulled through by the elders; some stood up and stretched their name across the southern sky. Tipp's defence was heroic, hustling and bustling Limerick into mistakes which sucked the value out of their possession. 'We did things out there today,' said Nicky English, 'which we haven't been doing. Things that come down to heart and hunger and experience.'

Weeks left. The championship rises and dies so quickly. Limerick have another month in which to find the resolve to go on. Tipp have that resolve. It was a wonderful Munster final which bestowed lots of good things on the hurling season. The old game is kicking yet.

2 JULY 2001

Roaring Lions Tear Apart the Wallabies

Gerry Thornley

Australia – 13, The Lions – 29

As has become the custom on this tour, after the hosts took exception to earlier post-match pitch invasions, there were repeated warnings at the Gabba that any spectators encroaching on to the playing surface would receive a minimum Aus$500 fine. For the first hour or so, it seemed there was a case for fining the Wallabies.

No one really knew quite what to expect, but pretty much no one expected this. Even in their most optimistic moments, the Lions may well have envisaged putting together such an all-embracing performance of their own, but not that the world champions would be so off the pace, especially their famed defence.

It was no surprise that the volume of support for the tourists was even greater than officially forecast, or that the Lions would try to take the game to the Wallabies by attacking them out wide as well as targeting the home pack in the scrums and lineout drives.

But the extent of the double whammy was still quite something and left Australia reeling.

All day long it was as if Brisbane had become a little corner of England, and Wales and Ireland and Scotland too. They had camped outside the bars, drinking and singing good-naturedly from late morning. No one needed directions to the ground: just follow the crowds.

The Gabba was awash in gold and red, but mostly red. Contrary to official forecasts of 12,000, the barmy red army must have numbered at least 20,000 of the 37,460 attendance with the help of the expatriate community. It certainly looked that way, and it sure as hell sounded that way.

Keith Wood had tried to warn the Lions' debutants of the wall of sound they would encounter, that it was greater than anything in the Six Nations. Supporters had saved, sometimes for years, for what might also be the biggest trip/holiday of their lives. Whatever, they would give it the full blast.

One local, who'd seen Aussie Rules, cricket and league at the Gabba, sitting in front of me at pitchside, said he'd never heard noise like it at the old ground.

Quite what the world champions thought of being booed on to their own turf, heaven only knows.

Then, as we suggested they might, the Lions made the bold statement of intent by moving the ball to Brian O'Driscoll with their first play for him to breach the famed golden line. To then move the recycle on to that other game-breaker, Jason Robinson, for him to transfix Chris Latham to the spot and then do his Billy Whizz around him – well, psychologically, Australia were on the back foot for the rest of a remarkable night.

When asked in a contemplative moment, in a corridor underneath, what he would savour from this game, the normally taciturn Graham Henry couldn't bottle up his immense satisfaction any longer.

'Probably the first try,' he purred. 'We took them on, got over the advantage line right away through O'Driscoll, and then scored wide out. It was a magic start. Unbelievable.'

All the coaching staff could feel reasonably well pleased – not that they'd show it too much mind.

The set-pieces were, unsurprisingly, a source of Lions' strength. The scrum was offensive (it's hard to see how the Wallabies can buy one of them in the next week) and the lineout was even better, as the Lions drove the Wallabies back.

The Lions' pack had the measure of their hosts; the only nagging doubt was that this superiority wasn't reflected on the scoreboard as Andrew Walker and Jonny Wilkinson traded penalties. But something else was happening.

The Wallabies weren't penetrating the Lions' swarming defence. The big rumblers were generally rumbled at source by excellent first-up tackling. Even when Nathan Grey or someone else might break one tackle, he was quickly smothered.

The organisation and communication must have been excellent. The numbers were always there, until the Lions lapsed into defensive mode and were reduced to 14 men with the game well won.

They'd also kept a few tricks up their sleeves, and when O'Driscoll and Robinson strutted across field, to exchange places with Wilkinson and Matt Perry to the narrower side of that 40th-minute scrum on half-way, you sensed they were up to something. The Wallabies didn't react, and O'Driscoll cut inside Stephen Larkham and Robinson provided the link for Daffyd James's try.

When O'Driscoll turned on the afterburners at the start of the second half, it was party time. All night 'Bread of Heaven', 'Molly Malone' and 'Flower of Scotland' had intermingled easily ('Swing Low'? Well, there are limits.).

Now it was time to chide the locals. 'You're not singing anymore,' echoed around the Gabba.

Viewed now, the Aussie propaganda war can almost be viewed as fear, and with good reason. They looked dangerous after multi-phases against 14 men, but otherwise they looked very patterned and certainly lacking the individualism of O'Driscoll.

There were blemishes. Scott Quinnell was the leading culprit at the breakdown, and Martin Corry was unlucky to receive the yellow card the Welshman deserved. Iain Balshaw looked ropier than Perry, but the good thing about Wilkinson's unexceptional performance is that he'll probably be exceptional next week.

SCORING SEQUENCE: 4 mins: Robinson try 0–5; 22: Walker pen 3–5; 40: James try, Wilkinson con 3–12; (half-time 3–12); 42: O'Driscoll try, Wilkinson con 3–19; 45: Wilkinson pen 3–22; 52: Quinnell try, Wilkinson con 3–29; 76: Walker try 8–29; 79: Grey try 13–29.
AUSTRALIA: C. Latham (Queensland); A. Walker (ACT), D. Herbert (Queensland), N. Grey (NSW), J. Roff (ACT); S. Larkham (ACT),

G. Gregan (ACT); N. Stiles (Queensland), J. Paul (ACT), G. Panoho (Queensland), D. Giffin (ACT), J. Eales (Queensland, capt), O. Finegan (ACT), T. Kefu (Queensland), G. Smith (ACT). Replacements: M. Burke (NSW) for Latham (half-time), M. Foley (Queensland) for Paul (56 mins), E. Flatley for Larkham (56 mins), B. Darwin (ACT) for Panoho (68 mins), M. Cockbain (Queensland) for Eales (73 mins), D. Lyons (NSW) for Finegan (83 mins).

LIONS: M. Perry (England); D. James (Wales), B. O'Driscoll (Ireland), R. Henderson (Ireland), J. Robinson (England); J. Wilkinson (England), R. Howley (Wales); T. Smith (Scotland), K. Wood (Ireland), P. Vickery (England), M. Johnson (England, capt), D. Grewcock (England), M. Corry (England), S. Quinnell (Wales), R. Hill (England). Replacements: I. Balshaw (England) for Perry (half-time), C. Charvis (Wales) for Quinnell (69 mins), G. Bulloch (Scotland) for Wood (75–82 mins), J. Leonard (England) for Smith (82 mins). Sin-binned: Corry (68–79 mins), Vickery (85–91 mins). REFEREE: Andre Watson (South Africa).

2 JULY 2001

Kinane Breaks Derby Duck in Spectacular Style

Brian O'Connor

A sweleteringly humid day at the Curragh seemed to demand peels of thunder, but instead received an equine bolt of lightning called Galileo.

A total of 13 other horses have completed the Epsom-Curragh Derby double and some of them make up the reference points we use for greatness in this sport.

But Galileo's performance yesterday was enough for even seasoned cynics to use names like Nijinsky and Troy in classical comparison to racing's newest superstar – and keep deadly straight faces while doing so.

The 4 to 11 favourite crossed the line to huge cheers from the vast crowd in a time of 2 min, 27.1 secs, a remarkable 6.8 secs faster than the mark achieved by Sinndar on similar ground last year.

Nobody, normally, can keep a straighter face than Michael Kinane, but even the joy at knocking that Irish Derby bogey on the head couldn't totally explain the wide smile and happy waves to the appreciative crowd, as Galileo paraded in front of the jubilantly packed stands.

The hungry press pack has been trying to pin down the usually stony-faced Kinane since Epsom, that Galileo is the best he has ridden in an illustrious career. Yesterday, the 42-year-old former champion jockey, seemed to give in to the inevitable.

'It is very rare that you ride a horse and feel in total control for the whole race, but this is such a

Superstar . . . Galileo, ridden by Mick Kinane, eclipses the field in the Budweiser Irish Derby at the Curragh. Photograph: Matt Kavanagh.

horse. Where others start to struggle, he still goes easily. The key is that he has such pace. It's a sign of a great horse that you can pick him out as the winner after just a furlong, and that was the case today,' said Kinane whose 17 previous Derby rides had yielded three runner-up placings and an embarrassing desertion of the subsequent 1996 winner Zagreb.

In contrast, Ireland's richest race has been relatively friendly to trainer Aidan O'Brien, who won it with Desert King in 1997. But the normally reticent master of Ballydoyle needed no prompting to eulogise Galileo.

Phrases like 'unbelievable' and 'so natural' tumbled from his mouth but as regards future plans for the colt, O'Brien played a straight bat, no doubt preferring to relish the moment.

'All options are open with this horse. He can go anywhere, from a mile to a mile and a half. The Breeders' Cup Classic is his end-of-season target, but there are a lot of options before that like the King George, the Irish Champion Stakes and the Queen Elizabeth II,' he said.

Intriguingly, O'Brien did admit to some pre-Epsom nerves about whether a horse that possesses such awesome acceleration could actually stay a mile and half.

'I wasn't sure. It was always a big doubt in my mind, but he finds it so easy. He has this gear that the others can't live with and which he can stay in easily. He grew up at Epsom but today was the first time he has turned right-handed and when they turned into the straight he didn't know Michael was pulling him up or showing him the band!' he said.

Galileo even seemed to sweat with style. The colt was awash at the start but stood still as he was wiped down and it's that sort of temperament that will help him in the challenges to come. It's unlikely that any of the horses who finished behind yesterday will be keen for another crack at him.

Morshdi, four lengths back in second, was given a 6 to 1 quote by Ladbrokes for the King George, but his rider Philip Robinson admitted: 'Mine is a serious horse but the winner is even more serious.'

Kieren Fallon blamed his number one draw for Golan's lack of spark but Niall McCullagh on the fourth, Pugin, was delighted and said: 'He's run a very honest race and looks a real Leger type who will appreciate soft ground.'

On a blue riband day for Ballydoyle, the only black type failure for the yard was Ishiguru's head defeat by the English raider, Repertory, in the Listed sprint. In contrast, Rock Of Gibraltar defeated his stable mate Hawk Wing in the Group Three Railway Stakes and Bach landed the Listed mile race.

9 JULY 2001

Clarke Stays Calm to Banish the Demons

Philip Reid at the K Club

Time, of course, is a great healer; and Darren Clarke can only but agree. Yesterday, two years on from his lowest moment on a golf course, when his friend Lee Westwood snatched this title from his grasp, the 32-year-old Ulsterman found redemption … and, by the time the glistening Smurfit European Open trophy was placed in his hands, he must have felt that a walk across the vast expanse of water that guards the 18th green would not have been beyond him.

This was a stunning victory, achieved by a man in total control of his game. A final round 66 for a 15-under-par aggregate of 273 meant he had three shots to spare over his closest pursuers — Padraig Harrington, Thomas Bjorn and Ian Woosnam — but, to everyone, the margin was even bigger than that, as Clarke clutched impending victory to his chest as a young child would do with a favourite toy.

Walking on . . . Paul Lawrie and Darren Clarke crossing a stream during the Smufit European Open Golf Championships at the K Club. Photograph: Matt Kavanagh.

No one else was going to steal it away this time. 'The best win of the lot,' remarked Clarke.

'Even better than La Costa?' – where he fended off the Tiger to win the World Matchplay last year – we queried.

'Yes. La Costa was good, fantastic. But to come along and win at home this way on this golf course gives me a high that I cannot quantify,' replied Clarke. 'To win at home is a huge thing. I've managed to win all over the world but had never managed to win in Ireland. It is a big plus for me.'

His latest success was his third of the season, but his first on the European Tour as the previous wins were fashioned in South Africa and Japan. It was the eighth win of his career in Europe

and, in becoming the first Irish player to win in Ireland since John O'Leary won the Irish Open in Portmarnock in 1982, he also ended a barren spell that had increasingly tormented home players.

In fact, one of the first people Clarke encountered in the locker-room after his winning round was O'Leary, who presented him with a pint.

'Cheers!' said O'Leary, and Clarke – forgetting about his protein rich diet that has seen him lose almost two stone in recent months – enjoyed the tipple as he savoured a win that earned him a winner's cheque for £436,096 and put him to the top of the Ryder Cup qualifying table.

All through his round, Clarke had displayed a sense of calm that his caddie, Billy Foster, reckoned he hadn't seen since that win over Tiger Woods in

In control . . . Darren Clarke sets up his putt at the 18th hole during the Smufit European Open Pro-Am at the K Club. Photograph: Matt Kavanagh.

La Costa. 'I thought he was going to win an hour before the final round the way he was swinging the club on the range,' said Foster, adding: 'It is great for him to bury the devil from two years ago.'

That was the occasion when Clarke had a course record 60 in the second round and then included a hole-in-one on the way to a third round 66, before collapsing in the final round to a 75 that allowed Westwood to sneak in.

'From as low as I was two years ago, when Lee played great in the last round and I didn't, it is great to come along and play as well as I have. My game is working in the right direction, and I am delighted to have won here at home basically,' he said.

Clarke's win – his first in Europe since his

English Open success 13 months ago – has come after an intensive tournament schedule that has seen him play eight times in nine weeks.

However, in recent months, he has changed aspects of his preparations: physiotherapist John Newtown has had him doing stretching exercises to improve his flexibility; he has started working with mental coach Jos Vanstiphout, and he has also started a diet advised to him by Ryder Cup captain Sam Torrance.

'Everything seems to have slotted into place because today I was as calm and focused on a course as I have ever been,' he insisted.

His wife, Heather, was there by the 18th to share in her husband's win. 'It's a good 'un,' she said.

'Darren loves the course, the whole place, and it just shows that if you are patient and wait, then it all comes right. Waiting is the hard part, but it is all worth it.'

Indeed, an indication of how emotional the whole win was for Clarke is that, after sinking his par putt on the last to close out the tournament, he needed time to stand by the greenside, cast his eyes out towards the fountain in the middle of the lake and simply compose himself. That's how much it all meant to him.

9 JULY 2001

Sligo Add to the Western Saga

Ian O'Riordan at Croke Park

Sligo 0–16, Kildare 0–15

In the end it wasn't about playing in Croke Park or those 26 lost years. It was about sweet football written as music for the voices of Sligo. In the end it was a sort of homecoming.

It was a rage against the machine. Against those who always say Sligo freeze on the grand stage and against all the grand hopes of Kildare.

A spontaneous, fireball victory played out as if any refusal of the heart would mean death. And so begins another tale in the year of the great western saga.

Saturday afternoon will grow dimmer in time but never will the past haunt Sligo like it did before. The only question they left unanswered then is how much further they can go this summer. Few teams could have squeezed out more energy in the allotted time.

Down a man after just nine minutes, Peter Ford asked them to jump and they said, how high? Through faultless construction and burning desire, they tore through Kildare in a way few teams have even tried.

Only a point at the finish, but whether they were three points up or three down, they never looked like losers.

Eamonn O'Hara can't quite find the words to describe it, nor is there an obvious turn of phrase for the heights of his performance. 'Well we have our own self-belief in Sligo. It doesn't get much attention in the media but we know we can compete with the best of them.

'We just kept at it the whole match, with 14 men, and still beat a team like Kildare. Hard to describe all right. But we fear nobody now.

When this draw started off everyone was looking for the likes of ourselves, the so-called weaker teams. Now who wants us? We know it will take another 70 minutes and we know what it takes to win.' O'Hara orchestrated so much of this victory, chasing down the middle of Croke Park like a wild horse and unbound by the guard of Kildare's half-backs. Dessie Sloyane and Gerry McGowan were the point-makers, smooth and consistent throughout. Others like full back Mark Cosgrove and Dara McGarty – who reappears as a substitute – and Padraig Doohan may never again see better days.

'Unbelievable.' That's the first word from Peter Ford. 'So much actually went wrong for us, losing Paul Taylor before the game and a man sent

off so soon. And we did have to change our game in the second half. We were trying to play direct but we wasted a lot of scores by kicking the ball down the middle.

'Our game would normally be more direct, but since they had the extra man we had no choice but to run at them. But sure we defended very well also. And I don't believe that philosophy that we always froze on a big day. All these players have great self-belief. They've worked awful hard and they deserve what they got.'

Neil Carew was the man sent walking nine minutes in for a collision with Padraig Brennan that no one seemed to see except the linesman and umpires. Otherwise, all the talk about Croke Park's daunting setting for the unexposed was mere media fodder.

'We came in here the night before, and that helped. We walked around a bit and we were relaxed all day coming into this. It was no big deal.'

As far as Ford is concerned, if they can repeat this performance and get some of their players back then they'll give any team a hard game. It's a statement backed up by the fact that Kildare didn't play badly. They were missing some big name players and recent training sessions resembled the battle of Wounded Knee, but the likes of Padraig Brennan, Martin Lynch and Eddie McCormack didn't do a whole lot wrong.

'We're very, very disappointed, but sure we'll have to keep going and that's it,' said Mick O'Dwyer, trying his best to draw his cunning smile. 'Sure we had a few chances to equalise at the finish and maybe we could have, but Sligo played some marvellous football. They showed great commitment the whole way through.'

But three games in three weeks? That can't be easy: 'Well the injuries were the big thing. It's not easy to replace the players of the calibre we lost. That's part and parcel of football, but I think two weeks of a break between games would give teams a chance to get injured players right. But Sligo well deserved the win. They fought and contested every ball like tigers and I tell you, it will take a good team to beat these fellows. They are no flash in the pan.'

Lady luck just ran out for Kildare. Niall Buckley pulled a hamstring on Tuesday night and Ken Doyle pulled a muscle in his back getting out of bed on Saturday morning. Also gone were Martin Ryan and Glen Ryan. But O'Dwyer tells us he'll be back again next year, and leaves us to write our headlines about Sligo.

SLIGO: J. Curran, P. Gallahger, M. Cosgrove, N. Carew, D. Durkin, M. Langan, P. Naughton, P. Durcan, K. Quinn, S. Davey (0–2), E. O'Hara (0–1), D. McGarty (0–1), D. Sloyane (0–8), J. McPartland (0–1), G. McGowan (0–2). Subs: P. Doohan (0–1) for McGarty, N. Clancy for Gallagher, D. McGarty for Durcan, K. O'Neill for McGowan, N. McGuire for Cosgrove.

KILDARE: C. Byrne, B. Lacey, C. Davey, K. Duane, J. Finn (0–1), R. Quinn, A. Rainbow (0–1), W. McCreery, R. Sweeney, E. McCormack (0–2), J. Doyle (0–1), D. Earley (0–1), P. Brennan (0–7), M. Lynch (0–2), T. Fennin, Subs: K. O'Dwyer for McCreery, G. Ware for Sweeney, D. Hughes for Finn.

10 JULY 2001

No Love Lost As Champion Holds Court

Johnny Watterson

Everybody knows Goran Ivanisevic says more than his prayers. Yesterday's entertaining, petulant, funny, offensive conference was no different as the beaming

Paradise regained . . . The Sligo bench race on to the pitch to celebrate their win over Kildare in the Senior Football Championship qualifier at Croke Park. Photograph: Eric Luke.

six foot, two inch Croatian champion arrived for his media conference.

The fourth set, during which he kicked the net and threw his racquet after his serve was broken by Pat Rafter, was the only source of his anger. A double-fault had handed his opponent the initiative, and Ivanisevic had disputed both calls – the first for a foot-fault, the second for a serve that was deemed out.

So how did he see it? 'First of all, that game I was 30-love up. Hit a great serve, he (Rafter) missed it. First foot-fault all tournament. That ugly, ugly lady. She was really ugly, very serious. I was like kind of scared. Then I hit another second serve. Huge. And that ball was on the line, not even close. And that guy, he looks like a faggot a little bit, you know. This hair all over him. I couldn't believe he did it.'

Three-times Wimbledon champion and current BBC and NBC commentator John McEnroe didn't escape Ivanisevic's casual lashings. 'I'm very disappointed, the guy who I always looked up to as my idol. Everything that he did was always perfect to me... he came to me six days ago in the locker-room. He said, "Man, you playing good. I'm really happy for you. You can do it." Then after three days, he goes and says I have one shot (a serve), I'm bad... must be he's an idiot.'

There the Ivanisevic diatribe finished. The champion looked towards a homecoming that would rival any of those organised for a successful Irish football team. 'It is so great to touch the trophy that I don't even care if I don't win another match in my life again. This is it. This is the end of the world.

'It's going to be great. I think tomorrow there is going to be at least 100,000, 150,000 people waiting for me in Split. I don't think anybody has received such a big welcome, ever. So it is one of the biggest days for Croatia, sports-wise,' said Ivanisevic.

Rafter, more reflective, looked at the massive serve that so often pulled Ivanisevic out of holes.

With Rafter 7-6 up in the fifth set and 30-love up on Ivanisevic's serve, the Croat simply launched the ball to save the game. 'It's not much fun down the other end trying to get it back. He was just serving really well when he had to. Put in a couple of really big ones, didn't allow me to do much with it. Not much fun.

'Because he put more pressure on my serve, mine was probably more likely to break down than his was,' he said.

For Ivanisevic, the two weeks have been an ongoing series of dreams mixing with reality. 'Last night I didn't sleep. I woke up at 1.30 in the morning. I thought it's 9.30 a.m., I see 1.30. Okay, let's go back to sleep – 3.30 a.m., 4 a.m. – I was so nervous. And nobody came, no angels, nobody.

'But you know, this is everything for me. My dreams came true. Whatever I do in my life, wherever I go, I'm always going to be Wimbledon champion.'

Wimbledon champion in arguably the hottest ever atmosphere on Centre Court for a final. For both players the arena, which was filled with ordinary punters who had camped out all night to get tickets, was dramatic.

'This is just too good. I don't think it's ever going to happen in the history (again). So many Australian fans, so many Croatians, it was like a football match. And it was great,' said Ivanisevic.

'It's hard to put it in perspective right now,' said Rafter. 'It was a good final, an amazing, amazing atmosphere. I don't know if Wimbledon's seen anything like it. I don't think they will again, until Tim (Henman) makes the finals.'

Unlike Rafter, who may now retire, there is no doubt that Ivanisevic will return to defend his title. A shoulder operation this year is essential to keep his career going, but on the first Monday of next year he will step out on Centre Court. 'Yeah, always wanted to see how it is when you step on court as defending champion. I want to experience that. I don't care if I win or lose but I just want

Phoenix . . . Jennifer Capriati celebrates a point during her match against America's Serena Williams at Wimbledon.

to experience it, go there and be a defending champion on that Monday, first man there.'

And how did he win it? 'I took a lot of pain killers this week, but I think I hit more aces.'

14 JULY 2001

Beijing Pummels the Opposition

Tom Humphries

It ended like one of those mismatched heavyweight fights. The great lumbering bid from Beijing connected early with a couple of haymakers, thus earning the right to set about their business for the next eight years knowing that some bitter old hack might come

and try to entertain himself by giving Beijing a medical.

Beijing, who very narrowly missed out on hosting the 2000 Games, won in the second round of voting at the International Olympic Committee (IOC) session ahead of Toronto, Paris, Istanbul and Osaka here in Moscow yesterday. Celebrations in Beijing were duly appropriate. There was western-style singing and dancing in the streets. The thin end of the wedge, some might say.

'We are very excited, very tired but very excited,' said Wang Wei, the secretary-general of the campaign. 'Our efforts have paid off. The world has come to understand Beijing and China better.

'If we build more bridges, I think we can resolve our differences. There's a lot of hard work

Playing politics . . . Chinese students celebrate after IOC President, Juan Antonio Samaranch, named Beijing as host city to the 2008 Olympic Games.

to do, but I am confident we can hold an excellent Games. I think the world will come to understand us a lot better.'

Improvements will be expected too. Amnesty International announced last week that 1,700 people had been put to death in China since April. Tibet is still occupied. Freedom of speech is still a pipe dream. And now the world will be calling with tea and cakes. Well, maybe not tea.

Tu Mingde, another key bid delegate, said he was unworried about the smoke bombs metaphorically hurled Beijing's way.

'This will help economic development and social progress in all areas, including human rights,' he said. 'We've worked hard over the last two years, just like an athlete trains hard. It was a strong campaign for us on a personal level …'

Most observers had expected a win for Beijing, but the convincing look of the result is revealing. The Chinese took 56 votes on the second round and finished it there and then. Toronto, the nearest challenger, had just 22 votes. Whatever happens, the world of sport will never be the same again. Beijing has been forgiven much by the IOC. Human rights and state-sponsored drug cheating being the major absolutions. The bid itself had fewer built facilities actually completed than any of the other four, and the environmental problems which the city suffers have been overlooked.

In return, the IOC expects. And then expects some more. Beijing plans to spend $30 billion on the Games in seven years' time. The IOC expects that its role in creating such a legacy for the future will be rewarded by an upswing in the public regard with which the committee itself is held.

Popularly depicted as grasping freeloaders, the IOC's members yearn to be regarded as world statesmen. Hence the return to playing politics. In the past these ventures into validating certain regimes in the hope that they will roll over gratefully have backfired on the IOC.

The 1936 winter and summer Games went to Germany, whose subsequent attempts to turn the world into one big team left the IOC looking foolish. The same applies to the Games which marked Juan Antonio Samaranch's ascent to the presidency of the IOC. Seven months before the Moscow Games the USSR rolled into Afghanistan. The subsequent Games were an embarrassment.

Samaranch was instrumental in this, his final political act (apart from his shameless lobbying for a Nobel prize, which will likely continue). His committee declined to embarrass him by rejecting Beijing again and, as expected, Monday's election of the successor of Juan Antonio Samaranch has been distracting the delegates all week, especially the rumours of South Korea's Kim Un Yong closing the gap on long-time favourite Jacques Rogge of Belgium.

It had been thought that a strong vote for Beijing would spell the end for Kim Un Yong and that Rogge would prevail, but the South Korean is made of tougher stuff. An anonymous fax has been floating around the IOC corridors this week promoting Kim Un Yong's idea of paying every IOC member $50,000 a year because they are Olympic diplomats and they deserve it. This (and the whisper that Kim Un Yong will bring back the trips to host sites to inspect building sites and empty fields and stay in top hotels and eat nice meals) has gone down favourably amongst the electors.

Yes. Let the decadence begin. Again.

16 JULY 2001

Jaded Lions Have Complaints Aplenty But No Real Excuses

Gerry Thornley
Australia – 29, Lions – 23

If only . . . British and Irish Lions (left to right) Rob Henderson, Keith Wood and Phil Vickery look dejected after losing the third Test match against Australia at Stadium Australia, Sydney.

In the confines of the dressing-room, the 2001 Lions were together for the last time. They were dead on their feet, experiencing probably the most bitter moment of their career, most probably. They couldn't have given any more, Donal Lenihan told them. They had coped bravely with adversity on a tough tour, the management were proud of them all. Lenihan had to quicken his sentences then, as his voice began to break under the emotional strain, and he was warmly applauded.

It's funny how the 2001 Lions seemed almost to generate more warmth when it was over than when the tour was actually taking place. Yesterday, the vast majority of the squad did what rugby tours were traditionally all about, and had a good all-day knees-up. They should have done it weeks ago. This will be a tour of what-might-have-beens.

In one sense at least there can have been no recriminations. Truly, they had given every ounce of energy available to them. As a result, it ebbed if it didn't always flow and it was compelling sport. For much of the night it was even an epic contest, the cream of the home unions going toe to toe with the world champions, a Test and 23 points apiece going into the final quarter, on the grandest of stages.

Yet you never really, really believed the miracle could happen.

And it would have been close to miraculous. At the risk of becoming a stuck record, the 11-month, seven-week tour had simply taken too much of a toll before a ball was even kicked on Saturday. It transpired, that at no point had the Lions' starting XV of last Saturday, actually trained en bloc last week, and even allowing for the fly-on-the-wall documentaries and the books which will eventually appear, it's doubtful whether we'll ever know the full extent to which they were patched up and sent out. The miracle was, they were within a converted try of stealing a series win. Of all the stats to emerge from this game and this series, perhaps the most relevant was the Lions failed to score in the final quarter, for the third Saturday running.

They simply went to the well and the well had run dry.

As they trooped out of the dressing-room corridor to the underground exit gate to their bus, the Lions understandably cut a devastated lot.

To have come this far, and in so many ways, yet to come up short must have constituted the biggest disappointment of their careers. There'll be a lot of residual anger as to why this came to pass.

For defensive coach, Phil Larder, this was a sixth losing trek to Oz in one or other of the rugby codes and it probably stank the most. 'It wouldn't be impossible', he had said, in reference to the notion of the Lions winning a series away from home at the end of a 40–50 game, 11-month season against world champions three months into their season, 'but it's like trying to do it with one hand tied behind your back'.

Martin Corry emerged and spoke in hushed, near tearful tones to a couple of us. He had been called up as a replacement, yet ultimately started in six and featured in seven of the last nine games. 'At the end you can usually say the best team won, but in this case I don't think they did.'

You could agree and disagree with this viewpoint. The better team did win on the night and over the series, but given a more level playing field you suspect the Lions would have been better.

They didn't get the rub either. For example, take last Saturday's first half when they were shunting the Wallabies toward their line, only for Paddy O'Brien's whistle to intervene because the Wallabies stood up. Then compare it with the scrum seven days beforehand, which wheeled over 180 and disintegrated before John Eales picked up in the build-up to Joe Roff's second try as Jonathan Kaplan waved play on. Utterly inconsistent.

But to a large extent you make your own luck as well. An inspired Justin Harrison began and ended the game with the first and sixth steals of Lions' lineouts. No team can cough up that much ball and win. The pressure the Lions were under at lineout had a ripple effect throughout the rest of their rugby, with the under-used Rob Henderson and Brian O'Driscoll getting precious little attacking ball.

By comparison, the Wallabies were able to launch a stunningly simple but offensive lineout variation off quick top of the line ball for George Gregan to fire the ball in front of three oncoming midfield runners; Nathan Grey taking it up, then Toutai Kefu, before Gregan put Herbert over for his crucial second try.

In all of this there was the sound of chickens coming home to roost, given the way three specialist middle-of-the-line jumpers were long since jettisoned and not even included amongst the replacements. As long as I live I'll never understand why Martyn Williams, a specialist openside, was sitting on the bench these past three Saturdays, other than to keep it warm.

Ironically, there was no bigger thorn in the Lions' side than George Smith, a groundhog cut from the David Wilson cloth, with an uncanny sixth sense for the breakdown. It was his ability to play the ball in the tackle which earned turnover penalties for Matt Burke to take it from 3–3 to 9–3.

And ultimately, the Wallabies are an utterly

cool lot. The word 'composure' has rarely been bandied about so much in post-match interviews and discussions. These Wallabies just never lose the plot. They don't have a Scott Quinnell propensity to give away a truck load of penalties, they'll patiently play aerial ping-pong all night until the opposition cracks, and imagine for a second one of their lot having a Colin Charvis-type brainstorm and throwing a defensive lineout to himself before crazily setting off on his own? Laughable all right.

Nor could you imagine the Lions closing out the game quite like the Wallabies did. No, no, the better team won on the night and over the series. It's just a shame the Lions had one hand tied behind their backs.

AUSTRALIA: M. Burke (NSW); A. Walker (ACT), D. Herbert (Queensland), N. Grey (NSW), J. Roff (ACT); E. Flatley (Queensland), G. Gregan (ACT); N. Stiles (Queensland), M. Foley (Queensland), R. Moore (NSW), J. Harrison (ACT Brumbies), J. Eales (Queensland, capt), O. Finegan (ACT), T. Kefu (Queensland), G. Smith (ACT). Replacements used: M. Cockbain (Queensland) for Finegan (76 mins), J. Holbeck (ACT) for Grey (79 mins). Replacements not used: B. Cannon, B. Darwin, D. Lyons, C. Whitaker, C. Latham.
LIONS: M. Perry (England); A. Healey (England), B. O'Driscoll (Ireland), R. Henderson (Ireland), J. Robinson (England); J. Wilkinson (England), M. Dawson (England); T. Smith (Scotland), K. Wood (Ireland), P. Vickery (England), M. Johnson (England, capt), D. Grewcock (England), M. Corry (England), S. Quinnell (Wales), N. Back (England). Replacements: C. Charvis (Wales) for Quinnell (half-time), I. Balshaw (England) for James (74 mins), D. Morris (Wales) for Smith (74 mins). Replacements not used: M. Williams (Wales), R. O'Gara (Ireland), M. Taylor (Wales). Referee: Paddy O'Brien (New Zealand).

Dogged Dublin Lack Attacking Bite

Seán Moran

Meath 2–11, Dublin 0–14

There was a beginning and an end to Meath's Bank of Ireland Leinster Football final victory. In the first five minutes Dublin missed a goal chance and Meath didn't. In the last five minutes Dublin created plenty of chances but missed them as well, and by the final whistle they were still that goal adrift.

This was a fitting illustration of the gap between the teams. Meath were clinical about taking chances despite a good collective effort from the Dublin defence.

In attack Dublin were at times hesitant, inaccurate and prone to panic. Yet they kept the match in their sights throughout yesterday's final and a little more composure might have seen them survive – particularly in the last 10 minutes when a succession of useful chances were blazed wide.

But these are the situations made for Meath. Sean Boylan's teams are remarkable for getting the best out of individuals and showcasing significant contributions from players who don't feature on the A-lists of celebrity.

Yesterday when the blue-chip duo of Ollie Murphy and Graham Geraghty managed only two scores – thanks to some tidy work by Coman Goggins and Paddy Christie – all the forwards scored from play.

Evan Kelly got three of those points, all in the first half. It was the latest significant haul for the Drumree player whose scoring contributions to the All-Ireland win two years ago were so vital and who has become such an effective presence on the wing.

Muscling in . . . Dublin's Paddy Christie gets to grips with Meath's Graham Geraghty during the Leinster Senior Football final at Croke Park. Photograph: Dara Mac Dónaill.

Similarly the half-backs – the only line on the team not to have a survivor from the 1996 All-Ireland win – played strongly as a unit, conceding little and contesting the breaks well.

Some of the established players were also prominent. Trevor Giles was as dependable as ever, working possession cleverly and posing a constant threat when he got on the ball. Full back Darren Fay was excellent and saw off the attentions of three different candidates. The biggest scalp was Ian Robertson, Dublin's most highly rated forward.

For whatever reason – and it was alien to his temperament – Robertson got involved in a niggling battle with Fay. Cue much brawling and

cantankerous clashes. When was the last time that ever benefited a full forward?

Robertson got booked and his game deteriorated. Even a move to the 40 in the second half failed to resuscitate things and he was replaced with 20 minutes of the game remaining.

Fay sailed serenely on, comfortable, marking both Jason Sherlock and Vinny Murphy and reaching the final whistle without conceding a single score. His general play and anticipation were of the highest order and in some ways they needed to be. On either side of him, both Mark O'Reilly and Cormac Murphy were troubled on a continual basis and frequently resorted to fouling as a result of which both were shown a yellow card.

Despite these rearguard difficulties, Meath held on to their early lead for the 70 or so minutes separating their first score from the final whistle. They were assisted quite generously by Dublin's incontinent sequence of wides – in the end, more than twice Meath's total.

But in fairness to Tom Carr's team, they competed all the way through and out-performed the more pessimistic pre-match expectations.

Early on, Martin Cahill suffered in a clash of heads and had to be replaced in the 12th minute. Shane Ryan came on for him and acquitted himself well, using his mobility to win a good amount of possession and move it forward.

Jonny Magee passed his fitness test to start the match, but was moved to the wing in a swap with Peadar Andrews. A bandage on his hand inhibited the regular centre-back, but he came into the action in the second half even if a series of dashes from the back largely came to nothing.

The tone for the match was set by Graham Geraghty in the fifth minute. He was the grateful recipient of a mistake by David Byrne in the Dublin goal. He spilled a dropping ball, an attempted point by Ollie Murphy, and Geraghty guided the ball into the net with his fist.

From then on, Dublin were chasing the match and although they kept the margin within two or three points – even after conceding a second goal, a great 56th-minute interchange between Richie Kealy, Giles and Nigel Nestor with Kealy finishing it – they never managed to shut the gap.

It might have been different had Sherlock done better with a goal chance in the second minute but he kicked wide.

Meath's early lead was maintained as Dublin struggled. Wayne McCarthy missed a straightforward free-kick from 30 metres and within minutes had squandered a goal opportunity after Robertson broke a ball from Sherlock to him.

It was a difficult afternoon for McCarthy. His free taking hasn't shone in the championship and

he still lacks the physical authority to impose himself on matches. Yet he persevered and saw a fair bit of ball, particularly in the second half.

Dublin's most effective forward was Des Farrell. The captain has been troubled by chronic injury problems in recent years but his reading of the game, strength on the ball and shooting have remained with him and was a constant threat.

In the semi-final against Offaly, he kick-started Dublin's scoring and yesterday he was excellent at creating space and opportunity. He kicked three points and it should have been four, but having worked himself into a great position in the 61st minute he miscalculated the shot and it blew wide.

There was something for everyone at centre-field. Meath welcomed back John McDermott and he responded with a couple of big catches and absorbed all the knocks and hits to be expected of the sector. He also lasted 70 minutes. Darren Homan played so well in the early stages that McDermott was actually moved on to him.

Ciaran Whelan sparked in the second half with surging runs and three points, including one which might have been a goal, as Dublin got a grip in the middle; but he was switched to the wing when Enda Sheehy came on as a substitute.

MEATH: C. O'Sullivan, M. O'Reilly, D. Fay, C. Murphy, H. Traynor, N. Nestor, P. Shankey, N. Crawford, J. McDermott, E. Kelly (0–3), T. Giles (0–3), R. Kealy (1–1), O. Murphy (0–1), G. Geraghty (1–0), D. Curtis (0–2). Subs: R. Magee (0–1) for Curtis.

DUBLIN: D. Byrne, M. Cahill, P. Christie, C. Goggins, P. Curran, J. Magee, P. Andrews, C. Whelan (0–3), D. Homan, S. Connell, D. Farrell (0–3), C. Moran (0–4), W. McCarthy (0–3), I. Roberton, J. Sherlock (0–1). Subs: S. Ryan for Cahill, E. Sheehy for Robertson, V. Murphy for Connell.

23 JULY 2001

Duval Takes Major Step Forward

Dermot Gilleece

Seventy-five years after the incomparable Bobby Jones had shown Americans the way here at Royal Lytham, David Duval captured the top prize of £600,000 sterling in the 130th Open Championship. But after so much promise over the preceding days, the Irish challenge faded disappointingly when Darren Clarke was forced to accept a share of third place.

Yet the Tyrone man, now top of the Ryder Cup table, felt he had much to be pleased about. 'I proved to myself that I can handle the pressure of the back nine of a major on a Sunday afternoon,' he said. 'I was very much in control until I got a couple of bad breaks on the 17th (he ran up a double-bogey). But that's links golf.'

It was also a memorable occasion for Des Smyth who, with a closing 71, realised his target of getting into the top 15, so securing an exemption for Muirfield next year – his final season before moving into senior ranks. In fact he was tied 13th, along with such notables as Colin Montgomerie and Vijay Singh.

With only a stroke separating the leading 13 players overnight, estimates varied as to how many would be involved in the inevitable play-off. Instead, we had a performance which gave a new dimension to the notion of comeback kids, as Duval swept three strokes clear for an emphatic triumph.

Down the 72nd, he was almost engulfed by the gallery. 'Even with police and the R and A around me, I got banged about a bit, but it was worth it,' he said afterwards. 'It was an unbelievable scene at

The taste of victory . . . David Duval kisses the trophy after winning the British Open Golf Championship at Royal Lytham and St Annes golf course in England.

the end of a pressure-packed round. Any minor mistake on this course is magnified, so I'm really pleased to have won here.'

Only 12 months ago, this gifted performer of serious intent was also in the last two-ball of the final day – with Tiger Woods – only to crash down the leaderboard after a closing 75 which included a wretched eight at the infamous 17th. 'I probably shouldn't have played the final round last year because of my back,' he said.

Duval went on: 'Today I played real well. I made putts. I did everything I needed to do. I worked really hard heading into the US Open last month and didn't make anything. But before coming here, I didn't hit a golf ball. I went fishing, mountain biking, riding and working out. This championship is different from the other majors. There is the history, the names on the trophies. And there is added pleasure in doing it on a golf course like this.'

He added: 'It's still a silly old game. All I tried to do today was hit it solid, move it forward and make some putts. There have been times when I've made it a lot bigger than it is. But not today. Maybe that's why I felt so good.'

Apart from the misfortune to Ian Woosnam, home supporters were understandably deflated by the muted performance of Montgomerie who, at 38, seemed set for an overdue major breakthrough. 'I just wasn't good enough on the greens,' he said. 'But the crowds have been superb, and I look forward to more of the same at Muirfield next year.'

Meanwhile, this championship will be remembered as a triumph for a strategically superb layout over modern, hi-tech equipment. 'This is the ultimate test,' said a vanquished Padraig Harrington. 'It combats technology. You are offered choices off every tee and if you decide to be brave, you'd better be straight.'

When the Open first came to Lytham in 1926, it established golf as one of the great competitive sports. The manner in which the Royal and Ancient presented this championship ensured the future of the game is in safe hands.

28 JULY 2001

Open Wounds Slow To Heal

*Colin Byrne, columnist with **The Irish Times** and caddie to Paul Lawrie, offers a fresh angle on events at Lytham and looks into the toter's routine*

Ian Woosnam crunched a six-iron 'stiff' on the first hole of his final round of the 130th British Open Championship at Royal Lytham and St Annes last Sunday. This gimmie birdie was his opening gambit in his quest for the coveted Claret Jug, he thought.

Woosnam bustled down the first hole with his inimitable busy, short steps confident that he had a short putt for a birdie; it might have been six feet, hopefully only six inches.

It had better be a short one, his caddie, Myles Byrne, thought, because what his boss assumed to be a birdie putt was going to be a bogey putt. Myles realised on his way towards the green that they had excess baggage. The charge for this particular bit of excess luggage was going to be extremely high. The figures being bandied about the world will fill sports pages for months to come and will undoubtedly rear their ugly heads intermittently for many years.

Myles was running about with some other errands that he had been asked to do, upsetting his usual pre-round routine, and he obviously didn't take heed of the extra driver – he hadn't realised Woosnam's coach had slipped it in on the practice range.

The clock was ticking and by the time the toter had unfolded the cumbersome pin sheet peculiar alone to the Open Championship, Myles had only enough time to get the yardage of 195 to

Teed off . . . Ian Woosnam and his caddie Myles Byrne stand apart after Woosman was penalised for having one club too many in his bag during the final round of the 130th Open Championship.

the pin, check the wind, which was helping off the right, and help select the club.

A rules official is with every group in the Open, and until last year the official used to always ask players and caddies in the group if they had only 14 clubs in the bag. I think it was a series of less than complimentary replies by caddies who felt insulted by being asked to check on such a basic duty that influenced the R & A to stop asking the question before the players teed off. I would imagine that there will be a revised directive for the attending officials at Muirfield next year.

Myles' world was in turmoil on the long walk down to the first green at Lytham. What was he going to do? Drop the bag and disappear into the bushes, never to be seen again? Tell his man, as he walked confidently towards an almost certain birdie and cause him to miss the putt as a result?

Brain pumping, noise, heat, vast crowds, total

confusion – what was he going to do? He wasn't going to run, he was definitely not going to cheat, and he was going to have to advise his boss before he teed off on the second that he had to add two to his score. A sphincter-tightening reality gripped Myles Byrne.

Fortunately the birdie putt was a tap in. As the duo strode to the second tee, Myles broke the news with a forewarning to Woosnam 'You're going to go ballistic.' And he did. He made a series of bogeys and obviously lost the momentum of the opening 'birdie'. The extra club almost wound up on the 1.30 train to Liverpool when Woosnam hurled it away, as the tracks were close to the second tee. The abuse was flowing.

'You just had one f★★★★★★ job to do and you couldn't even get that f★★★★★★ right,' Woosnam howled at his rodent (as we frequently refer to our colleagues, especially at times like these). Myles felt like walking away, he fiddled with his hat, he twitched, he disbelieved, he wanted to go home. But no, he couldn't, he had to go on.

He decided after the first onslaught from Woosnam that he was going to try to do the best job he possibly could for his boss for the remaining holes. By his own admission, he did an exceptional job from then on, tough as it was to bury the club incident. Smoke was billowing from the Woosnam bag in more ways than one: the porter was chewing cigarettes to calm his nerves and the player was smoking in reaction to the two-shot penalty.

Whipping boy, scapegoat and fall guy spring to mind when it comes to laying the blame on someone for a major gaffe. Ultimately the player is at fault. But the reality of today's player/caddie relationships is that there is trust placed in the caddie by the player to carry out certain basic duties. Counting the clubs before you tee off is well within the area of responsibility for the bagman. Myles Byrne feels totally responsible for the error and fully accepts the blame.

'If I am not man enough to accept the blame for this one, then at 31 years of age I will never be a man,' Myles explained to me philosophically in a bar in Stockholm last Tuesday night. He felt relatively safe from attention in central Stockholm. He was amongst colleagues who were trying to help him come to grips with the whole thing by talking it over. When I went to the bar for a round of drinks I interrupted the barman who had been engrossed in his English newspaper. It was the £220,000 sterling gaffe story that he was reading. We kept Myles away from the bar for the rest of the night.

Myles Byrne is getting a taste of the 'big time' whether he likes it or not. As he jumped from Woosnam's chauffeur-driven car at Ulna Golf Club outside Stockholm last Tuesday for the SAS International challenge match, the TV cameras were there to greet him, not his boss. As he took the golf bag from the boot, a camera was stuck in his face.

'Have you got a few words for ITN?' the reporter enquired hopefully. To which Myles replied curtly: 'Yeah, I do, and the second word is "off".'

Per-Ulrik Johansson could have been forgiven for thinking that he would have been the most famous caddie present that day. Per was caddying for his soon to be brother-in-law, Jesper Parnevik. Well, it seemed like Myles was attracting most attention. Monty walked into the room we were all assembled in before the game and jokingly called Myles a useless twit. To which he replied, at least he wasn't a fat, useless twit. The starter had to have a jab at the unfortunate duo with the 'hilarious' question, 'Did you check how many clubs you have?'

At the press conference before the game Woosnam was abrupt with the Swedish press when he answered their questions and suggested that they put the issue 'to bed'. Woosnam is visibly shaken by the whole thing. He had left the bar the previous night after just one beer; he normally likes to hang out for more than one. He threatened to whack one offending journalist over the head with the newspaper of one of the articles he read about himself. He was trying to figure out how the Chicago-based TV chat-show host got hold of his mobile phone number.

I hope for both Ian's and Myles's sake they continue their form over the next few weeks and play their way on to the Ryder Cup team and quell, to some extent, the barrage of hypothesis from those who enjoy dwelling on others' misfortune. Myles was able to put the situation in perspective when he walked off the 18th green last Sunday and looked at the row of handicapped people lined up watching the finale to the 130th Open Championship. He had recovered enough to be moved by the joy that one severely handicapped young boy had got from being given Woosnam's golf glove.

Myles has paid heavily for an error for which he accepts full responsibility. He has missed out on a very big pay day and he is being pointed at worldwide as some sort of buffoon. Nobody has looked at his performance for the remainder of the round and suggested how many good clubs he may have selected or how many good lines he read on the greens that resulted in birdies.

One thing that did work in his favour over the incident was that the hat deal he was on was based on the number of seconds he appeared on the TV screen. So when the world's TV stations were capturing one of the toughest moments of the young

Bray man's life, at least he was getting well paid for it.

Myles is coming to grips with the error he made, despite the fact that he will never forget it. I hope his boss is also dealing with the situation. The fact that Myles is still working for him would suggest that his player has forgiven him. Hopefully the press hounds will bury the unfortunate incident as quickly as the two people most directly involved with it seem to have done.

Somehow I don't think that will be the case.

THE FINAL WHISTLE

America's Grumpy Old Men are Beginning to Lose Some of their Appeal

With a reputation as a collection of grumpy old men who complain a lot and largely ignore spectators, the US Seniors Tour is going through difficult times. To which Christy O'Connor Jnr remarked with a wicked chuckle: 'I never thought I'd be missed that badly.' O'Connor, who left this week for a holiday in Spain, is making satisfactory progress from a broken left leg sustained at the end of March. To protect his top-50 status in the US, he cannot return there until next January, but he is hoping to play a few European Seniors' events towards the end of this year.

'Quite frankly I'm surprised to hear that the US Seniors is in trouble,' he added. 'In fact I thought it was extremely healthy. But I can see that it would certainly need the top stars to be competing on a regular basis.'

Where TV ratings and sponsorship were concerned, they got the wrong result in the US Senior Open at Salem last weekend when Jack Nicklaus bogeyed the 69th and 70th holes after being tied for the lead. It paved the way for victory by the low-key Bruce Fleisher, 33 years after he had captured the 1968 US Amateur.

Now in its 22nd year, the tour has record prize money of $59.2 million but the prospects of further growth are shaky, at best. Plummeting TV ratings – ESPN's ratings are half of last year's – reflect an identity crisis in a golfing world dominated by Tiger Woods.

In the Emerald Coast Classic earlier this year, barely 100,000 households bothered to tune in to watch Mike McCullough beat Andy North in a play-off. On the other hand, Woods in contention on the regular tour might bring a 5.0 rating, or 35 households for every one tuning into seniors golf.

'The ratings are much lower than anybody anticipated,' admitted Tom Kite, a supposed star of the tour. Not surprisingly, advertisers have taken note. Cadillac, once a major sponsor, have scaled back, while Callaway are reported to be watching the ratings anxiously. With no crowds and no title sponsor since a lawn fertilizer company dropped out two years ago, organisers say the Las Vegas Senior Classic will probably fold.

Though the seniors do reasonably well where there's a dearth of top-level sport, the focus has now turned to corporate entertaining to pay the bills, in the absence of cash customers. 'It's just not the same without large galleries,' said Jim Colbert. 'I think they're just starting to figure that out now.'

Perhaps O'Connor, twice a winner in the US and Senior British Open champion for the last two years, is more valued among the galleries than he might think. In the meantime, his concerns about the future are of a far more personal nature, such as having the remaining eight of an original 14 pins removed from his leg – a process he hopes will be accelerated by generous helpings of Spanish sun.

* * *

'The reality of it is that I don't draw the fans to a golf course like Trevino or Palmer or Nicklaus or Chi Chi would. People come to watch them more than they come to watch me.'

Tom Watson answering criticism about his infrequent appearances on the ailing US Seniors Tour.

7 JULY 2001

Dermot Gilleece's Golfing Log

Green with Envy

The following exchange between a visiting greenkeeper and a woman scorekeeper at this year's Volvo PGA Championship, appears in the current issue of *Greenkeeper International*.

Greenkeeper: What club are you from?

Woman scorekeeper: Wentworth.

GK: Do you live on the Estate?

WS: Yes.

GK: You don't live in one of these £3 million houses, do you?

WS: No, darling. I live in one of these £10 million houses.

21 JULY 2001

Dermot Gilleece's Golfing Log

Out of sight . . . Padraig Harrington during the Smurfit European Open golf championship at the K Club. Photograph: Frank Miller.

Bright eyed and bushy tailed … HRH Princess Haya of Jordan on Loro Piana Rock 'N' Roll, taking part in the Kerrygold Welcome Stakes on the opening day of the Kerrygold Horse Show in the RDS. Photograph: Dara Mac Dónaill.

AUGUST

2 0 0 1

HIGHLIGHTS

4 August: Dublin pull off Lazarus act during the All-Ireland SFC quarter-final at Thurles coming from eight points down with 12 minutes left to force a replay. Galway bounce back and avenge Connacht Championship defeat by beating Roscommon 0–14, 1–05 in the All-Ireland SFC quarter-final in Castlebar. England's hopes turn to dust as Australia retains the Ashes by winning the third Test of the series.

5 August: Greene lightning strikes again as Olympic champion, Maurice Greene of the United States wins the 100 metres final in a time of 9.82 seconds at the World Athletics Championships in Edmonton, Canada. A late Ollie Murphy goal denies Westmeath a famous victory in the All-Ireland SFC quarter-finals at Croke Park (Meath 2–12, Westmeath 3–9). Colin Montgomerie holds his nerve to take the crown at the Scandinavian Masters at Bareback Golf and Country Club, Malmo, Sweden.

8 August: Jones' spree for three ends in failure as Marion Jones (United States) comes second to Zhanna Pintusevich-Block of Ukraine in the 100 metres final at the IAAF World Athletics Championships in Edmonton.

9 August: Brondby take full advantage of chances and beat Shelbourne 2–0 in the UEFA Cup preliminary round first leg in Copenhagen.

11 August: Kerry leave city boys tangled up in blue at Semple Stadium as they overcome Dublin 2–12 to 1–12 in the All-Ireland SFC quarter-final replay. Meath give romance short shrift beating Westmeath 2–10 to 0–11 at Croke Park in the All-Ireland SFC quarter-final replay. Controversial Russian runner Olga Yegorova runs the gauntlet and wins the 5,000 metres final at the World Championships in Edmonton.

12 August: Old timers win a new day at Croke Park with Wexford's late charge in the All-Ireland SHC semi-final (Wexford 3–10, Tipperary 1–16). Irish golfers (Graeme McDowell and Michael Hoey) play key role as Britain and Ireland win Walker Cup on US soil. Liverpool win another trophy at the Millennium Stadium, Cardiff, where they beat Manchester United 2–1 in the FA Charity Shield.

15 August: Republic of Ireland relinquish two goal lead to draw 2–2 in International friendly with Croatia at Lansdowne Road.

18 August: Tipperary weather the storm at Croke Park winning the All-Ireland SHC semi-final replay with Wexford 3–12 to 0–10.

19 August: Champions made to suffer meltdown as Galway beat Kilkenny 2–15 to 1–13 in the All-Ireland SHC semi-final at Croke Park. A new legend in Grand Prix history as Schumacher is crowned the Formula One World Champion after winning the Hungarian Grand Prix. Major Toms (David Toms) shows great ground control to win his first major at the USPGA Championship at Duluth, Georgia.

26 August: Galway double hopes still alive as footballers turn around All-Ireland SFC semi-final at Croke Park and beat Derry 1–14 to 1–11. Irish have that golden feeling as Gearóid Towey and Tony O'Connor take Ireland's third gold medal at the World Championships in rowing at Lucerne in the Lightweight Pairs, after Sinéad Jennings and Sam Lynch won the Women's and Men's Lightweight sculls on 25 August.

29 August: Turnbull deals at silver standard as Gareth Turnbull takes silver over 1,500 metres at the 21st World University Games in Beijing.

4 AUGUST 2001

Winning Smile and a Winning Style

Dermot Gilleece talks to the ever popular Arnold Palmer about his love of golf and people – and the struggles early in his career

Arnold Palmer was about to hit shots on the practice ground at The K Club last Monday when he felt a twinge in his left shoulder. Apparently it was an ongoing problem which came as no surprise to a doctor friend who had travelled with him from the US.

On being told that medication would ease the inflammation, Palmer protested: 'I don't like pills.' 'Well then,' said the doctor, 'you're gonna have to lay off golf for a month.' After considering this for the briefest of moments, Palmer growled: 'Okay. I'll take the pills.' He looked across at me and grinned. 'There are times when I think that maybe I shouldn't play,' he conceded. 'But I can't stay away. Right now I should be reading a book or having a drink with friends or whatever, but I need to hit a few golf balls.' So he began to hit some balls.

Setting the standards ... Arnold Palmer at The K Club during his visit to inspect the development of the South Course. Photograph: Brenda Fitzsimons.

He hit another ball. 'Hell, let's talk,' he said. It had been a busy morning. In the company of Ed Seay and Harrison Minchew from his design company, he had looked over the new course at The K Club which was started earlier this year, across the Liffey from the seventh, 16th and 17th holes.

Then there was a lightning buggy trip around the existing championship layout with Michael Smurfit and director of golf Paul Crowe. The objective was to pinpoint areas of improvement in a general updating of the course but also in preparation for the Ryder Cup in 2005. I joined the entourage.

'The course is going to be in fantastic shape for the Ryder Cup,' he enthused. 'It will be so good, the players will love it. What I think is now a nice golf course will be very competitive for matchplay. It's going to be very exciting.'

There was also time for reflection on climactic events at the British Senior Open at Royal Co. Down. 'How did Jack (Nicklaus) do? Did he get close?' I explained how Nicklaus had got within two strokes of the lead before slipping away. He had, however, hit a great drive down the 18th to be within 236 yards to the front of the green. 'Oh! He drove it that far, did he?' said the other half of this legendary duo.

Estimates vary, but Palmer is acknowledged as the wealthier of the two, with a fortune of around $400 million. He will be 72 on the 10th of next month; hasn't won a major championship since 1964, nor any tournament other than the odd seniors title since 1975. Yet he can still command $90,000 for a company day and is featured by *Forbes Magazine* among the leading earners in world sport.

Against that background, it seemed odd to hear him talk of his early days of deprivation, accompanied, in the relating of one particular instance, by surprising bitterness. He was reminded of it by the fact that his first visit to this country in 1960 was also his first experience of links terrain.

'Sam Snead and I handled it fairly well, as I remember,' he said modestly of their fine Canada Cup victory at Portmarnock. 'But when you love the game as much as I did, it was a new experience which fell right into place.' Then he went on: 'I was devastated in 1954 when, after winning the US Amateur, I found I wouldn't be able to play in the British Amateur or the Walker Cup team.

'I couldn't afford it. I had no money. I had gone to Wake Forest on a full scholarship – my books, tuition and room and board. And there wasn't money for any frills.' Instead of an extended amateur career, he turned professional and joined the USPGA Tour the following year.

So, it was true that he eloped with his wife Winnie? With a conspiratorial grin, he admitted: 'I did. I met Winnie when she was a hostess at a tournament I was invited to play in the week after the Amateur. I met her on Tuesday, took her out Wednesday, Thursday, Friday and asked her to marry me on Saturday. I had a job as a manufacturer's rep, making $500 a month. But I had no money. Zero.'

How did he plan to finance a marriage? 'Well,' came the child-like reply, 'I was bold.' He explained: 'After asking her to marry me, I had to buy her a ring. And not having any money, I had to borrow from my golfing friends who were more than happy to oblige. It cost $4,000 so I was now seriously in debt.'

That was huge money then, I suggested. 'It was a nice ring,' he said, with one of those disarming smiles. And was the story about Pine Valley true? 'This is how it happened,' he went on. 'My friends then took me to Pine Valley to play golf and I won enough to pay back the money I'd borrowed. I had never played the course before, but I shot 68 on my first round and that was worth a lot. They were betting me I wouldn't break 100.'

With his eyes noticeably misting over, he then talked with moving sensitivity about his relationship with his wife, who died of cancer two years ago. 'I suppose you could describe Winnie and I as lovebirds – every minute for 45 years. Her death was terrible. She was not just a wife but she was a friend, a partner.'

I then told him about the 1994 US Open at Oakmont from where a group of visiting golf writers went to Latrobe on the Saturday of the championship. And that while playing there, Winnie arranged to have a waiter bring out drinks to the 10th tee. And how she had said to the waiter: 'Put that on my tab.' And then, almost as an after-thought, added: 'And put my tab on Arnie's tab.' He laughed heartily – 'She was great.'

He admitted at the time of her death: 'With Winnie going, I'm a bit lost right now.' But he would readily acknowledge that life goes on, and he has been helped enormously by a wonderful relationship with people.

'It started a little differently,' he continued. 'My father, Deke (a professional golfer), was a very tough task-master. He was a fighter but also a guy who could be very sentimental. He liked people and he didn't like it when others did things that weren't nice. And he drove that home to me constantly.

'Sure, you treat everyone the same as you'd like to be treated, but there was more. You had to play the whole thing out and remember it at all times. It became bred into me to the extent that I didn't have to work on it. Now, people are my life.'

His love of people has delivered one particular dividend he could never have imagined. It had its beginnings at Troon in 1962 where, in his moment of triumph in defence of the British Open, he found time to sign an autograph for a 10-year-old Glaswegian by the name of Ian Hay. It was such a charming moment that a photograph was used on the front page of a Glasgow evening newspaper.

'I have an appointment with Ian in a couple of weeks at the Mayo Clinic,' said Palmer. By an astonishing turn of events, Hay grew up to become a doctor, eventually finding his way to the famous

Mayo Clinic in Minnesota. It was there that he acted as Palmer's so-called quarter-back, 35 years after their meeting at Troon.

'When I was diagnosed with prostate cancer four years ago, my wife and daughter went with me to the Mayo Clinic and we met Ian Hay,' he explained. 'And he became my quarter-back, that's a term I use. If you go to a clinic it's nice to have a man who watches everything you do. And Ian got me to the right doctor and then watched what happened when I was there being operated on.

'That's part of why I have had so much good fortune in my life. Because I talk to people. I find if you're nice to people, it always comes back to you, one way or another.'

Palmer then talked of his close friendship with golf writer Pat Ward-Thomas of the *Guardian* and how they and their respective wives played bridge together. And how Ward-Thomas, a wartime pilot in the RAF, had flown one of Palmer's planes.

Flying, incidentally, has been a huge part of the great man's life since 1955. His current craft is a Citation 10.

Meanwhile, his love of the Ryder Cup, in which he played on six occasions from 1961 to 1973, was the last playing captain in 1963 and had the amazing record of 22 wins and two halves from 32 matches, is palpable. 'When I think about the Ryder Cup I get choked up, I like it so much,' he said.

'I think it's great in any sport that you can per-form well enough to be asked to represent your country. That was among the things I told Tiger Woods when he came to me seeking advice before he turned professional.

'I told him that because he was Tiger Woods, he was never going to be like anyone else. He would always be special. And because of having received so much, he had the responsibility to be nice to people and to treat them as he would like to be treated. And how he should act as a professional and control his emotions.

'As far as I can tell, he's heeded that advice. In

fact at this point in time I think Tiger has done a fantastic job.'

When considering Palmer's incalculable contribution to tournament golf, it seems that his legacy was already determined as far back as that fateful July day at Troon in 1962. That was when his great friend, Ward-Thomas, paid him this beautiful tribute: 'In technique, attitude and manner, he makes some of his famous rivals seem puny.

'Palmer's presence has brought greatness once more to the old Championship. It has inspired others to compete and has set a new standard which can only benefit all who follow.' And remarkably, he's still doing it.

6 AUGUST 2001

Dublin Pull Off Lazarus Act

Seán Moran

Kerry 1–14, Dublin 2–11

Semple Stadium might be unfamiliar territory for big-time football, but two Dublin goals in 10 minutes turned it into a parallel universe. With the last 12 minutes ticking away on Saturday's Bank of Ireland All-Ireland quarter-final, champions Kerry led by eight points. The lead didn't flatter them and Dublin looked every inch a team losing by eight points.

What happened next had no rational basis. Dublin scored 2–3 without reply to lead by one, and it took another legendary strike by Maurice Fitzgerald in injury-time to save the day for the All-Ireland holders.

Everyone in the ground – not least Kerry – was stunned. As comebacks go this had no origin in a slowly turning tide or some irresistible plays improvised in desperation. This was a case of two goals somehow being scored by a team that had looked dead in the water for most of the match.

Even after Fitzgerald's divine intervention, Dublin had a 45 straight in front of the posts to carry the day. Wayne McCarthy hadn't the distance into a strong wind, and both teams live to fight next Saturday at the same venue.

Despite this let-off for Kerry, there was no mistaking the players who felt they had done the better out of the deal. Dublin remained on the field to celebrate in front of the travelling Hill 16 at the Kilinan End. They mightn't have won, but after playing for the most part abysmally, they had survived, and what blue-bedecked fan would have risked even their rolled-up match programme on that barely 10 minutes previously.

There were many aspects to a sensational encounter: the strange listlessness that washed over both teams for periods; the fluid authority with which Kerry's forwards made and took chances when the humour was on them; the bizarre sequence of goal opportunities spurned by Dublin just before half-time; the hapless misfortune of Dublin for most of the match when every erratic bounce seemed to go against them; the evaporation of Kerry's challenge in the middle third of the pitch in the final quarter; a second half without a wide from Dublin. Take your pick.

Both teams have passed this way previously. Against Cork, Armagh and Galway last year, Kerry faded out of commanding positions. Dublin have revived significantly in the second half of their last three championship matches. The two habits combined yesterday to present the previously enervated attendance with a cliff-hanging denouement.

It hadn't looked remotely on the cards in the opening quarter. Dublin squandered the first four chances of the match. The first was revealing. Peadar Andrews got on the ball almost immediately and the vast expanses of the Thurles field opened up for him. Into the great blue yonder he galloped, but finding himself almost at the endline, appeared to panic.

Kerry emerged from a tentative opening to strike a serious blow in the 11th minute. Shane

Back from the brink ... Dublin's Vinnie Murphy turns to his team's supporters after scoring his goal against Kerry in the All-Ireland Senior Football Championship quarter-final. Photograph: Eric Luke.

Ryan actually shadowed Dara Cinnéide quite well and obstructed his shot, which David Byrne saved, but the rebound fell to Cinnéide who pulled the ball back for the on-coming Aodan MacGearailt, who had started the move, to clip into the net. Dublin were now chasing the match and not looking likely to catch it.

Two things were positive: the defence started gamely and continued that way. Paddy Christie and Coman Goggins in particular worked intensively to limit John Crowley and Michael Francis Russell and didn't do badly at all. Secondly, chances were being created at the other end.

But there were negatives. Russell and Crowley can be held only so tightly and chances were being wasted as soon as created. Dublin's starting forwards managed only two points between them all match.

It was another day of bitter disappointment for Ian Robertson and Colin Moran, whose injury-riddled years are climaxing in displays that do no justice to their considerable talents.

Des Farrell and Declan Darcy can win their ball but, against tight defending, lack the pace for penetration. Farrell has generally schemed his way around the problem, but he found it hard going this time and wasn't getting much support. To be fair to Darcy, his free-taking kept Dublin alive after half-time.

Jason Sherlock was the most consistent forward. His pace and hard work in showing constantly for the ball paid off. On a rough assessment, he was integrally involved in over half of Dublin's scores despite being temporarily eclipsed for periods by Eamonn Fitzmaurice.

In the first half none of this was having a major effect. Dublin managed only three points. Kerry dealt comfortably with attacks, their backs reading the clumsy intentions of Dublin's would-be playmakers and clearing the ball quickly, and without fuss. Yet clouds were gathering and if they were to end only in Dublin getting wet, signs were there that the champions were being opened up rather easily.

In the 10 minutes before half-time, three good goal chances were created. That they weren't realised had nothing to do with defensive virtuosity. Moran, finding himself in a couple of acres on the left and no one showing, reluctantly took off on a solo. As he travelled, the defence parted and a one-two with Farrell ended with him putting the ball wide of an empty target off the post. Farrell might have gone himself, but it's harsh to blame a player who sets up a team-mate with an open goal.

The captain was certainly at fault when a Ciaran Whelan run ended with Farrell blasting the ball off the underside of the bar. Two minutes later Darcy was given a difficult ball when clear inside and settled for a point but dropped that short.

Kerry led at half-time by five, 1–5 to 0–3, and went for the jugular in the third-quarter. With Darcy's unerring frees (some of the awards were a bit soft), Dublin stayed just above water and trimmed an eight-point deficit by three going into the final quarter.

Almost effortlessly, Kerry restored the margin in a few minutes and the match looked dead.

Certainly Dublin behaved that way. Farrell nearly put Declan O'Keeffe through the Kerry net in what looked like late pursuit of a dropping ball. Manager Tom Carr came on to remonstrate with referee Michael Curley over a free given against Christie for a foul on Crowley. So heated was the

exchange that even Johnny McGee decided to turn diplomat and usher his furious manager away – probably into the stand for the replay by the time the GAC are finished.

The margin stood at seven in the 63rd minute when substitute Vinnie Murphy – having taken the field in now traditional fashion like a bumper car – was picked out by Sherlock who had snapped a break from McCarthy's dropping free. Murphy's shot seemed to wrong-foot the defence and rolled into the left corner of the net.

Four minutes later the deficit was down to two when Darren Homan rose to punch another McCarthy free to the net despite O'Keeffe getting a hand to it. As time went by the one-point lead might have been enough, but a sideline ball, conceded by Byrne's poor kickout after a Crowley wide, about 45 metres out was majestically kicked over by substitute Fitzgerald.

It was reminiscent of his final score in the 1997 All-Ireland final – with added pressure – like the equaliser against Armagh last year. If that sideline score of four years ago had merely gilded the Sam Maguire, this one ensured that Kerry kept at least one hand on it.

KERRY: D. O'Keeffe, M. Lyons, S. Moynihan, M. McCarthy, T. Ó Sé, E. Fitzmaurice, T. O'Sullivan, D. Ó Sé, D. Daly, A. Mac Gearailt (1–1), E. Brosnan (0–1), N. Kennelly, M.F. Russell (0–2), D. Ó Cinéide (0–6), J. Crowley (0–3). Subs: D. Dwyer for Kennelly; M. Hassett for McCarthy; M. Fitzgerald (0–1) for Mac Gearailt; W. Kirby for Daly; D. Quill for Ó Cinnéide.
DUBLIN: D. Byrne, P. Christie, S. Ryan, C. Goggins, P. Curran, J. McGee, P. Andrews, C. Whelan (0–1), D. Homan (1–1), C. Moran, J. Sherlock (0–1), E. Sheehy, D. Darcy (0–6), I. Robertson, D. Farrell (0–1). Subs: K. Darcy for Robertson; V. Murphy (1–0) for Moran; S. Connell for Sheehy; W. McCarthy (0–1) for D. Darcy.

13 AUGUST 2001

Yegorova Runs the Gauntlet

Ian O'Riordan

A dark afternoon in Edmonton on Saturday, and the World Athletics Championships went into the cold zone. If failed drug tests and athlete protests and booing inside the Commonwealth Stadium count for anything then Olga Yegorova is seen as a cheat. And a cheat had won.

Yegorova had blown away everyone in the women's 5,000 metres final and then ran straight off the track. There was time for a brief tear, and then moments of regaining her composure before facing the waiting media:

'I would not wish on anybody, even my enemies, to live through what I had to live through the last few days,' she began.

'There were moments when I just thought I'd forget about it all, drop it all and go home. I was under a lot of strain and pressure here, but I wanted to win here for myself. It was not about money or success because I already have everything.'

Out on the track behind her echoes of disapproval competed with shouts of support for an exhausted Gabriela Szabo, who was trying to add to her 1,500 metre gold but could only manage eighth.

'For me she is not the world champion,' said the Romanian. 'I have no chance of competing against robots, but I ran to show I was not afraid of the Russian.'

The strained faces of Szabo and all the others contrasted with the ice-cool Yegorova, who had sat breathless in the bunch before delivering a lightning kick from 200 metres out. It was just like the Paris meeting last month, after which the testers discovered the magical erythropoietin – better known as EPO – was helping give Yegorova that extra gear.

Had the IAAF been serious about cleaning up their sport, Yegorova would have watched this race in Russia. But because Paris had skipped the double-checking, she was world champion and $60,000 richer. At 29, it was her first major outdoor title, adding to the world indoor title she won back in March.

Back in the mixed zone, the mixed reception continued. There were soft congratulations from the Russians and hard questions from the rest of the world, yet Yegorova stared everyone down and didn't even flinch.

'Ah, it's just a piece of metal.' That's what the tainted medal meant to her. 'If you want, I can just give it to you. Winning the world championships is not as important as life. Sport is one thing but life goes on.'

By now the Russian media were working overtime as interpreters, relaying every word from the remarkably composed athlete.

'I wouldn't say the gold medal is what you'd call the stuff of dreams. A healthy baby is the stuff of dreams. That's what's important to me. It's nice, of course, to win, don't get me wrong, but it's not what life is all about.'

What then about the booing, or the protests from Paula Radcliffe, or the claim from Szabo that Yegorova was not the true champion? The answers came with another shrug of the shoulders.

'I didn't know how the crowd was going to react. But what did you want me to do, finish second or third just to please the crowd? For me maybe 80 per cent was a distraction and 20 per cent gave me hope that everything would be fine.

'And I've nothing against the protest or whatever because that's their right. And I wish Paula Radcliffe her health and happiness. Maybe it's their personal choice but I do not consider myself guilty. You can't accuse one of something they have not done.'

Later still, as the three medal winners sat in the formal press conference, the hard questions

Horsing around ... A horse waits his turn at the Kerrygold Horse Show at the RDS. Photograph: Eric Luke.

continued. Spain's Marta Dominguez and Ethiopia's Ayelech Worku, who took silver and bronze, were nothing more than a side show.

Why didn't we see a lap of honour? 'I'm sorry, I forgot.' How do you explain the positive test in Paris? 'That's up to the doping committee, I don't have the authority. Of course I condemn the use of drugs because it's not good for the health.'

A lot of short answers then, yet she was happy to talk about her training, and how the harder work at altitude and increased mileage had helped improve her time over 5,000 metres by over 40 seconds last year. All observed solely by her coach and husband Nikolay Anisimov.

And though her fellow Russian athletes had offered support throughout the week, only one man, Valentin Balakhnichev, president of the federation, actually fought for her.

For Jos Hermens, manager of Szabo and many other leading athletes in Edmonton, the situation was sad but not without its cause: 'Athletics is still going through some growing pains. I hope we can win a few battles like this one, but I don't know if we will ever win the war.'

16 AUGUST 2001

Chequered Past Revisits Ireland

Emmet Malone

Republic of Ireland – 2, Croatia – 2

There was a sense of dèja vu about it all. The 2–2 draw was a repeat of the first-ever encounter between these two sides here at Lansdowne Road five years ago, the 93rd-minute Davor Suker strike a more painful reminder of Ireland's late slip-up during the last European Championship qualifying campaign.

But if last night was a dry run for those amongst Mick McCarthy's squad who needed to prove themselves ahead of the visit of the Dutch next month then the manager can't have been at all displeased, even after some sloppiness late on allowed the Croatians to come from two down and gain an unlikely draw.

Before the flood of substitutions rendered the match almost meaningless, the Irish looked superior in just about every department. Steve Staunton and Richard Dunne coping admirably in central defence, Damien Duff and Robbie Keane both looking sharp and fit after their summer's rest.

Those were the areas that McCarthy had wanted to be impressed by – and he must have been. After that the fact that the result stretched the Republic's unbeaten run to 13 matches can have been nothing more than a pleasant bonus.

Ireland's passing through the opening 20 minutes suggested that they were capable of opening up the Croatian defence, but even then the ease with which they did it for the opening goal was surprising.

Robbie Keane, as he did so often through the game, got involved in the move early on, picking up the ball outside the box before quickly feeding it short to Roy Keane a few yards away.

Quickly, the Manchester United skipper slipped the ball diagonally towards Duff. He, in turn, looked to have been mistaken in not having a crack at goal first time but the 22-year-old clearly knew what he was at, dragging the ball back a couple of yards before driving it back across the goal and into the top left corner.

It was the Dubliner's first goal for his country in 21 games but, more promisingly from McCarthy's point of view, his first in two starts as a striker. Whether the partnership worked that well overall was another thing, though, for the tendency of one or other of the front men to drop deep towards midfield repeatedly left the Irish short of bodies in the Croatian box.

Still, the pair both had a good night with each troubling the visiting side's accomplished three man defence.

On a couple of occasions Keane, in particular, won possession from decidedly unpromising positions. The pair's link-up play with their team-mates out on the flanks was good too, but while Mark Kennedy posed a threat that he occasionally delivered on from the left, Stephen Reid, though he did little wrong, played as if still a little dumbstruck by the pace of the events that had resulted in him wearing the number seven.

Not so Clinton Morrison, the Crystal Palace striker who it is hard to imagine being lost for words. Barely on to the pitch for his first senior cap, the 22-year-old announced his arrival by first beating Dario Simic for pace as the pair hurtled down the right-hand touchline and then, with the corner flag approaching fast, managing to get in a fine cross for Connolly, who was only prevented from getting in a shot by the very close marking of Tudor.

He gave Connolly an even better chance 20 minutes later when Steve Finnan started the process of getting the ball down the right flank and Morrison's quick thinking set the Wimbledon striker well clear of the Croatian defence.

At the Morrison stage of his own international career, Connolly would surely have slipped the ball away in the one-on-one that ensued. Instead his head went down and the ball was driven low and well to the right of the right-hand post.

If his confidence in front of goal has seemed questionable for a while now at this level, Connolly still looked very comfortable as he pushed the ball around for others last night and it was his movement and through ball that provided the opening for Ireland's second goal of the night.

Sun set … Ireland play Croatia in a friendly match at Lansdowne Road. Photograph: Jason South.

Jason McAteer should have been the one to benefit, but the 30-year-old midfielder's shot was well stopped by Stipe Pletikosa. To the dismay of the Croatian goalkeeper, the ball ran straight into the path of the oncoming Morrison.

With the game looking won it was perhaps understandable that the defence would ease up a little over the closing stages, although even when Davor Vuginec quickly pulled one back for the Croatians with a long-range header, anything other than an Irish win seemed unlikely.

As the game entered its closing stages, though, McCarthy had made all nine of his permitted changes and Kevin Kilbane was now playing at left back while John O'Shea was in alongside the impressive Steve Staunton in the centre.

Richard Dunne, having performed well during the first half, had gone off at the break, leaving his manager, one suspects, in less doubt than ever about the ability of his starting partnership to cope against the Dutch.

Only once had they really been caught out during the half but even on that occasion, Alen Boksic had been on the receiving end of what looked a harsh off-side decision and Dunne never had to begin what would have been a hopeless chase.

As the second half's chopping and changing kicked in, however, and the game became more open generally, there were bound to be some misunderstandings around the Irish area.

In fact, there were a few and Davor Suker should have capitalised on one, when he volleyed wildly over from 12 yards having been left entirely unmarked. Just as he had done late in injury time the last time these two sides met in Zagreb almost two years ago, though, the 33-year-old managed to score with the game deep into injury time.

A Robert Prosinecki corner from the right was handled by the night's third Irish debutant, John O'Shea, and the former West Ham striker made it 44 goals in 63 internationals from the penalty spot.

REPUBLIC OF IRELAND: Given (Newcastle United); Kelly (Leeds United), Dunne (Manchester City), Staunton (Aston Villa), Harte (Leeds United); Reid (Millwall), Keane (Manchester United), Carsley (Coventry City), Kennedy (Wolves); Keane (Leeds United), Duff (Blackburn Rovers). Subs: A. Kelly for S. Given (half-time), A. O'Brien for R. Dunne (half-time), J. McAteer for R. Keane (half-time), S. Finnan for S. Reid (half-time), K. Kilbane for M. Kennedy (half-time), C. Morrison for R. Keane (52 mins), D. Connolly for D. Duff (52 mins), S. McPhail for I. Harte (60 mins), J. O'Shea for G. Kelly (82 mins).
CROATIA: Pletoikosa; R. Kovac, Tudor, Simic; Stanic, N. Kovac, Soldo, Rapaic, Jarni; Balaban, Boksic. Subs: I. Biscan for M. Stanic (half-time), B. Zivkovic for M. Rapaic (half-time), V. Vugrinec for B. Balaban (half-time), D. Saric for R. Jarni (60 mins), S. Thomas for Z. Soldo (74 mins), D. Suker for A. Boksic (74 mins), R. Prosineski for S. Simic (74 mins), N. Bejelica for N. Kovac (82 mins).
REFEREE: A. Schluchter (Switzerland).

18 AUGUST 2001

Glamour Pays, Glamour Costs

Tom Humphries finds the English game and its television partners ever more voracious in their appetite to get our money

The bigger English football gets, the further away from us it goes. The English game has consciously been trying to shed its working class base for the past decade and the trend for the next few years will be even more exclusionary as pay-per-view television finds a more refined method of getting your money into football's bulging pocket. If it's still your money they are after. One suspects that football would like its games to be occasions where the

Cornered... The Croation defence in control from this corner in their 2–2 draw with the Republic of Ireland at Lansdowne Road. Photograph: Jason South.

upper middle classes gather to applaud the athletic deeds of millionaires.

It would be reassuring to think that while your favourites are driving past you in their sports cars, on their way home to their grand-gated communities, that there was at least some fairness or inherent wisdom in the manner in which your money gets spent once you hand it over. There's not.

Football takes it and spends it like a ruined addict. According to the sober people at Deloitte-Touche, after transfer costs, profits on sale of players and finance costs, English clubs' overall pre-tax loss more than doubled to £145 million in the 1999/2000 season. The Premier League recorded a £34.5 million pre-tax loss (a significant deterioration against a £13.7 million profit in 1998/99) while the combined losses of the Football League Clubs worsened from £75.3 million to £110.1 million.

Which is where you and your working wage come in. TV (which you pay for, both directly and indirectly) has kicked in £2 billion worth of current deals but it won't be enough.

'Even', say Deloitte-Touche, 'if the whole of the extra £85 million or so that Football League Clubs will receive from TV and Internet deals in the 2001/02 season was to flow through to "the bottom line" − i.e. with no wage increases at all − the 72 clubs would still have to find another c. £30 million to "balance the books". The "Supporter/Investor" or "Benefactor" has a role that is far from over.'

The outlook is equally bleak for the Premiership where wages are running out of control and large transfer fees are running to Italy and Spain.

Your role as supporter/investor will be to pay more and to pay it more often because football isn't going to stop spending. Transfer spending went to a record £340 million last year with 53 per cent going to clubs outside England. In the absence of any salary cap scheme wages continue to spiral. Over the 1999/00 season, total wages costs increased to £747 million (69 per cent of income) from £620 million the year before, 65 per cent of income. Roy Keane's rumoured £52,000-a-week deal doesn't even sound unlikely now and how quaint is it to think back a few years to Pierre Van Hooijdonk's outrage at being paid £7,000-a-week, an allowance for a homeless person as he saw it. So true, Pierre.

The Premier League salary bill increased by 20 per cent compared to a growth rate of 28 per cent in 1998/99. Over the same period Division One saw the biggest hike with wages bill up by 35 per cent. Division Two remained static, although the make-up of the clubs in these divisions is the likely reason for these very different effects. In the five years since 1995/96, all the divisions' annual wages growth rates exceed the rates of income growth. Now seven out of every 10 clubs have a total wage bill in excess of 70 per cent of their income: 70 per cent is the dividing line between comfort and concern. Only three clubs – Leeds United, Watford and Manchester United – have wages: turnover ratios below 50 per cent.

Incredibly, 16 clubs across the four leagues have total club wage bills that exceed 100 per cent of their turnover. In Division One, from where the promised land of Premiership excess is clearly visible, over a third of clubs pay wages that exceed 100 per cent of income. That's just so they can get to the Premiership and spend further beyond their means.

Premier League clubs generated 15 per cent more income in 1999/2000, bringing the total to £772 million. Between them the remaining 72 Football League clubs generated just £306 million. The rich keep spending more without actually getting richer. The Premiership clubs shared out almost £600 million more than their Division One counterparts. Average club income in 1999/2000

season for the Premier League was £38.6 million, Division One £7.7 million, Division Two £3.3 million and Division Three £1.7 million.

Up to the mid-80s clubs had two traditional sources of revenue – gate receipts and transfer income. If enough of you failed to turn up, they sold your favourite players. All changed there. Income now comes from different sources. Sometimes you hardly notice you're handing your money over at all. In 1999, Manchester United's gate receipts accounted for just 38 per cent of turnover after a season of full houses. 'MUFC' is now a global logo and commodity which earns well over £20 million per annum from merchandising (your money), £17 million from sponsorship and £7 million from conferences and catering (that's £7 million from match day catering, events, conferences, weddings, etc. – your money again).

It's up to you, of course. You can stay home, put your feet up. There is more football than ever on television, much more. Back in the days of 'Match of the Day' and Sunday's post-prandial 'Big Match', football got less than 13 hours a month screen time divided almost equally between ITV and the Beeb. Now you can watch football for 421 hours a month if you had the time. And if you had the time you almost certainly wouldn't have the money. Seventy-three per cent of that is on satellite, which will cost you installation fees plus a minimum of Stg£60 if you wish to purchase a 40-game Premiership season ticket. Sky had sold 100,000 such packages before the league season began.

The other pay-per-view options currently available are from Telewest (£8 per game) and ITV Sport channel at £9.99 a month. Ticket prices continue to rise. A seat at a Premiership game can cost you anything from a low of £16 at Fulham and Leicester to a high of £40 at Chelsea. A recent study put the cost of a trip to a Premiership match for a family of four at £200, including tickets, public transport, programme and four drinks and four burgers, purchased at the ground.

And it's getting worse. The digital era will personalise packages for your taste and for your budget. You'll soon be used to the direct debit drip drip being an integral part of your footballing experience. Roy Keane thought that the prawn sandwich brigade were killing the atmosphere? Well, the league has found that season ticket holders earning more than £30,000 a year are the most desirable but the least committed and bother to turn up for only half the games they pay for.

Ain't seen nothing yet, Roy.

20 AUGUST 2001

ITV Unveil Après Match of the Day

Mary Hannigan

'Better for you, better for all of us,' promised Des Lynam at the unveiling on Saturday evening of the most expensive football transfer of the year, 'The Premiership' (BBC to ITV, £183 million on a three-year contract). By the time he said goodnight, 75 minutes later (23ish if you didn't count the ads), it was achingly apparent: Des Lynam is not a man of his word.

And speaking of words, Dustin the Turkey has one for stuff like ITV's 'The Premiership': brutal. He usually uses it as a term of abuse for boy bands, but no boy band I've ever heard irritated as much as this dross. Apart, maybe, from Milli Vanilli. Between ourselves, there were times when a plaintive cry of 'Bring Back Brian Moore and "The Big Match" (or even Bob Wilson)' filled the air, it was that dire.

When Ally McCoist declared, after watching Arsenal's win over Middlesbrough, that 'as 4–0s go that was never a 4–0', a comment (his most cogent of the evening) that had Tel Venables' shoulders vibrating in hilarity and Des's eyebrows rotating in mirth, something else was clear: ITV's revolutionary coverage of English football involves transforming it in to a cross between 'The Jimmy Tarbuck Half Hour' and 'Stars In Your Eyes'.

It also involves them confidently pitching their football against the likes of the celebrity version of 'The Weakest Link' on the other side because they reckon, like Anne Robinson's party, it's showbiz.

And it involves them attempting to convince us that the game of Association Football was invented on the day ITV won the rights to show us 'The Premiership' (see Des's opening speech on Saturday evening). Sky Sports tried this tactic when it started out all those years ago but lads, like football, we weren't born yesterday.

Yes, 'Match of the Day' devotees (the bulk of them born pre-1970) feared the worst when the contract was lost to ITV but if Saturday is anything to go by their worst fears weren't worst enough.

Des? The game of football, as opposed to all the stuff that clings to it, ISN'T, despite what you've been hinting in all your pre-launch interviews, showbiz, even if all its accessories are.

The only pure, uncontaminated part of it left is that 90-minute bit played on grass, the bit that's sandwiched between all the glitz. The rest of it can be a laugh, no harm in that, but that 90-minute bit is simple, beautiful and occasionally sublime and merits intelligent, insightful and honest analysis, not the 'entertaining', hyped-up twaddle ITV, evidently, seems intent on dishing up.

A case in point. Liverpool ground out a 2–1 win over West Ham on Saturday in a less than convincing display, but they stuck at it and got their points.

A season or two ago they would have drawn, lost maybe. The ITV pundits dismissed the performance as poor, largely, one assumed, because it wasn't entertaining enough (low showbiz factor).

Over on RTÉ John Giles was thoroughly impressed, largely because he has the wit to know that if Liverpool are to be serious title contenders this season that's precisely the kind of scruffy (copyright: Mark Lawrenson) win they NEED to grind out. Scruffy = midweek points away to

Don't bring me down … Leinster's Leo Cullen is tackled by Martin Ridley, Ebbw Vale, in their opening Celtic League game at Donnybrook. Photograph: Joe St Leger.

Southampton = prizes = genuine stab at Premiership title. But doesn't necessarily = £183 million worth of entertainment. But don't tell ITV.

Back on ITV they had Andy Townsend sitting in their 'on-site tactics truck' (he had a pen in his hand so this hinted that we might get some analysis – we were wrong) asking Middlesbrough's Ugo Ehiogu (conceded penalty and sent off in 4–0 defeat, apart from that he'd had a good day) where it had all gone wrong. Ugo wasn't sure, but he thought the ref had something to do with it.

Andy nodded.

Then we returned to the studio to be told by Des that 'this season Tel's going all tech, he's on Prozone – not to be confused with what he's on'.

Tel's shoulders re-vibrated. 'How do you know what I'm sitting on,' he asked, lifting himself from his chair. Ally chortled, Des guffawed, the rest of us wailed:

'Alan Hansen, Gary Lineker, Trevor Brooking, Mark Lawrenson: – MISS YOU LOTS.'

Prozone? An aerial view of a Subbuteo table populated by football-jersey-wearing ants replicating footballers running around in circles in the course of a game.

Unless your name is David Ginola, in which case you'll be the stationary ant hugging the left touchline. Tel will study these ants for the season and share his conclusions with us. Gimmick-a-rama? Don't need it lads, football's grand as it is – after all it was the planet's most loved sport long before ITV brought us footballing ants and on-site tactics trucks.

RTÉ? Your 11th-hour decision to run, after all,

with 'Premiership' will, one suspects, be greatly rewarded in a Saturday evening telly-football-ratings-battle kind of way. Especially if The Dunph carries on describing players like Liverpool's Danny Murphy as 'a donkey, but a good donkey'. Note: a good donkey, but not a great donkey.

Can you imagine Tel, Des or Ally labelling Danny Boy as a donkey? No. They'd compare him, straight-faced, with Edgar Davids, because they know they'll never beat the game show on the other side in the ratings war if all they can promise us is edited highlights of a Scouser hee-hawing while he tracks back. That's hardly showbiz Cecil.

The Dunph's opening howarya in Network Two's 'Premiership' on Saturday resembled a kind of a state-of-the-nation address, or a late 1970s Minister for Finance's grave budgetary 'tighten-yer-belts-lads' televised lecture to the people, but then he got chatting with Gilesie and he chilled out.

'Now John', he said, 'it's a long time since you were lying awake in bed at night …' Gilesie flinched, looking acutely uncomfortable and you suddenly realised that the Après Match Gilesie is more Gilesie than Gilesie himself.

'Mother of Jeeesus, what's he about to say to me,' said Gilesie's face.

'Since you were lying awake in bed at night dreaming about the new season – do you still get excited about it?' – the Dunph enquired. Gilesie's sigh of relief was so cavernous it resulted in a tidal wave lapping Western Samoa's shores.

'Yes, I get a little buzz when the new season starts,' he admitted. Note: a LITTLE buzz. Not a big buzz worth £183 million, or even a good donkey of a buzz worth a free transfer to Rushden and Diamonds. A little restrained, calm, hype-free, controlled buzz which explains why, in the absence of Hansen and Lawrenson from televised Premiership duty this season, Gilesie is our only hope of a helping of sanity in the midst of on-site tactics trucks and aerial views of footballing ants.

Hurling Shocked Into Life

Tom Humphries

So, hurling has kept all its surprises till the closing paragraphs of a prosaic season. This weather-abused weekend was the first which hurling has had to itself all summer and the games provided controversy and shock rather than beauty, and two refereeing performances each as odd as the other in their own ways.

On Saturday Tipperary prevailed against Wexford in a game which was strangled in infancy by over-zealous refereeing. Tipperary's Brian O'Meara and Wexford's Liam Dunne were sent to the line by Pat Horan for the sort of argy bargy fun that normally merits a finger wagging or a name taking. Minutes later Wexford's Mitch Jordan joined them. A promising, absorbing game fizzled and died.

Wexford kept going, but in the drizzle against a Tipp team relocating their confidence they always had too far to go and too little time to get there. Tipp return to the All-Ireland then.

Yesterday was Kilkenny and Galway's big day out. Or not. An air of fatalism hung over this one all week like a brooding storm trough. Galway received 8,000 tickets and declined to take any more, thanks. Travelling to Dublin to see the team beaten is another supposedly fun thing which Galway people have sworn off.

Kilkenny people made up some of the slack. Last chance to rub the chins and appraise the form before the coronation next month.

Afterwards, Galway's manager Noel Lane must have been speaking tongue-in-cheek when he said that he and his team were a little insulted not to have been given a chance. They got to Croke Park under cover of darkness and that suited them perfectly.

Ball control ... Galway's Kevin Broderick gets away from Kilkenny's Philip Larkin in their All-Ireland Hurling semi-final, which Galway won. Photograph: Jason South.

Kilkenny were thoroughly ambushed yesterday. Ambushed, disarmed and disbanded.

The teams started off like a couple of weasels involved in a blood feud and suddenly snared in a bag. John Power broke his stick before the throw-in as the blows went in early and often. Fortunately, the rules which apply on Saturdays in Croke Park are suspended on Sunday when the referee must have the strong stomach of an emergency room orderly.

It was a game of unfaltering ugliness, redeemed from ignominy only by the surprise result left in its wash, by Kevin Broderick's sublimely cheeky late point and by the engineered quality of Eugene Cloonan's play.

Cloonan had 2–9 of his team's total yesterday and those who bent an ear to his faultless modesty afterwards left with the impression that it was the luckiest 2–9 anyone scored in Croke Park for a long time.

'Our second goal? Ah it was a lucky ball that came in high. I just got a boot to it. I suppose you take the chances; you need the breaks if you are going to beat Kilkenny. I always said we wouldn't give up like we did other years. The first (goal) was lucky, I hit the free a bit short, the sun caught (Kilkenny goalkeeper) James McGarry, it was a lucky goal. We tried as hard the other years, but we just got the breaks today.'

For Kilkenny, the All-Ireland champions and

the team who promised to rule the hurling decade to come, it was a sorry way to say goodbye. Their full-forward line, touted as perhaps the best ever, were limited to one point from play. Autopsy reports will suggest that they were starved of decent ball.

Kilkenny generally suffered in front of the goal, with Galway players throwing themselves again and again into their paths. In midfield and in the half-back line Kilkenny were filleted clean. Galway's young midfield pairing of Richie Murray and David Tierney aged about 10 years in the course of the match.

The win was achieved with just 14 men. After several extraordinary outbreaks of bad temper and bile a player was finally sent off on the half hour. Given what had gone before and what came afterwards Greg Kennedy was perhaps a little unlucky, but by then referee Pat O'Connor had gotten over the fear that daylight would fade his cards. So when D.J. Carey slipped with a freshly-booked Kennedy in the vicinity the red card was snapped out pronto.

On Saturday, at the time of the double sending off, Tipp would have accepted the loss of Brian O'Meara once it came with the loss of Liam Dunne for Wexford. To see Mitch Jordan go as well, minutes later, was a bonus which altered the character of the game.

Kennedy's dismissal had a less dramatic effect on proceedings. Galway for one, are the fittest hurling team around. Making up the space wasn't going to be a problem. Galway brought on Brian Higgins who hurled very well. Kilkenny, for all their wiles, didn't appear to know how to use the extra man.

'It maybe worked to our benefit,' said Galway trainer Mike McNamara. 'They were lost with the extra man. They tried using the spare man in a couple of places, sort of 'if that doesn't work try this'. And we had our defence packed, it was pure naked fear!

High and mighty ... David Tierney of Galway towers over John Power on Galway's way to an upset win against Kilkenny. Photograph: Jason South.

'Today was the challenge nobody relished, but any team would prefer Kilkenny in a semi-final rather than a final. We were able to remain more low key. Incredible pressure will come on in the final.'

Too true. Tipp and Galway have never held each other in fond regard. Next month's is a final both teams reckon they can win. The race to claim the mantle of underdogs begins today.

27 AUGUST 2001

Irish Have That Golden Feeling

Liam Gorman

They don't make many weekends like this, but they should, they should. With 400 metres left in the final of the men's lightweight pair yesterday here in Lucerne we knew it was just too much to ask. A third goal medal at the World Championships, it just never happens Irish teams.

But the two men on the water, Tony O'Connor (32) and Gearoid Towey (24) had different ideas. They had come from behind to lead

by a tiny margin, but as the Netherlands crew pushed hard, it was nerve wracking to watch. With an assurance and determination which has marked out Irish teams here, however, O'Connor and Towey pushed harder still and even a late sprint by Italy, who had led in the early stages, could not deny them their gold. The Italians finished third.

When Saturday's other Irish gold medallists, lightweight scullers Sam Lynch and Sinead Jennings, launched themselves into the water beside the winning boat, some of the crowd seemed bemused.

But the support of the team members for each other has been admirable. Lynch had made a point on Saturday of asserting that the pair was bound for gold, and Jennings and O'Connor are an even

Golden moments … Sinead Jennings and Sam Lynch of Ireland with their gold medals after winning their individual lightweight single sculls races at the World Rowing Championships at Lucerne, Switzerland.

closer team, as they are engaged. 'Don't lose the gold,' somebody shouted as Jennings, medal around her neck, bobbed up beside the boat. 'Don't lose the ring on your finger,' quipped O'Connor.

Echoing the philosophy Lynch had expressed the day before, O'Connor said that the pair believed they could win, they just had to do it on the day. Towey, close to physical collapse immediately after climbing out of the boat, pointed out that they had been 'racing the same crews all year'. They knew they could beat them.

For O'Connor this was a case of long threatening coming at last. He first competed at the World Championships in 1993, and with Neville Maxwell he holds two bronze and two silver medals for the lightweight pair, the first bronze won in America in 1994.

'If you keep working hard it is going to pay off some day. That's what I have been telling myself for the past 17 years now!

'I have four medals but no gold — until now,' added the qualified teacher and full-time oarsman. 'I had a good partner today. But I've had a good partner before. I suppose we had the luck.'

But luck had little to do with this wonderful performance by the Irish team at this beautiful course, a Mecca for rowers, and bathed in sunshine over the weekend. Gold was what the Irish team sought, as team manager Mick O'Callaghan stated with no apologies, and it was duly landed.

The impressively large Irish crowd saw our first gold since Niall O'Toole won the lightweight single in 1991 in Vienna. And our first women's gold medal, the first sweep (non-sculling) medal. Ireland were joint third in the medal table with Australia, behind Germany and Britain.

Yet it was the manner of the wins which made the greatest impression: Jennings (24), in only her 10th major championships, let the twice World Champion Pia Vogel (32) and Holland's Mirjam Ter Beek swap the lead through almost three-quarters of the race, taking over at 1,500 metres and holding off a late push by the Dutch woman to win.

It went, said the Donegal woman, as planned, to 'take the first 500 steady' and row through the leaders. 'With 750 to go I was in control, I knew I could do it,' she told the press.

Lynch (25) also showed the sort of top-of-the-world coolness which is unusual in an Irish sportsperson. He knew Jennings had won the race immediately before his, and turned this to good effect. 'At the start of my race, just before he said "go", I heard the result of the lightweight single … and I just said "okay, it's down to me now to make it through".' Like Jennings he let others, in this case Frenchman Frederic Dufour, take the early lead, but by 1,250 metres the Limerickman was in control. And what a sight it was to see him, with a strike rate well below his opponents, stretch out that lead and hold off a late push by Italy's Stefano Basalini.

Despite never having to fully extend himself he was little over two seconds outside world record pace; he would also have been fourth in the heavyweight single scull, which saw a win for another small country, as Norway's Olaf Tufte took gold.

But the early part of the A finals session on Saturday belonged to Ireland. Two attempts, two gold medals. It was good to be in Lucerne this weekend.

In fact they were the first two awards ceremonies of the day, as Britain's James Cracknell and Matthew Pinsent had won the first race of the day, the coxed pair, with cox Neil Chugani, and had their medal ceremony deferred until later, because they had the little matter of making history by winning the coxless pair.

Both races had close, exciting finishes and to see the open emotion shown by Cracknell afterwards and the calm analysis of Pinsent as he sweated profusely when talking to the media only minutes after the second win was to realise how admirable rowers can be: they don't do this for the money, rather the chance of glory and testing themselves to the limit.

Ekaterina Karsten of Belarus tried to match the feat in the double and single scull, but had to settle for two bronzes. The British added a third title at the end of the day when their coxless four won, allowing Britain to top the table on their own – leaving Ireland and Germany joint second with two titles.

Britain had a less satisfactory day yesterday, with both eights doing badly. Australia won the women's eights and surprise packets Romania the men's, with Croatia second. Germany won the overall prize, with Italy second and Britain third. Ireland were ninth.

In one of the first races on Saturday, Padraic Hussey could finish only fifth in the C final of the

men's single sculls. The race was dominated by Britain's Matthew Wells, who won impressively, while Hussey became involved in a dogfight a few hundred metres from the finish with American Timothy Whitney and Italy's Marco Ragazzi to avoid last place. The Irishman avoided sixth at the expense of the Italian.

Yesterday started with some gutsy performances by two crews who were also sent here for development purposes: the young lightweight four, whose average age is just 20, finished second in the C final by .27 of a second after pushing the eventual winners, South Africa, hard in the closing stages, and the lightweight quadruple scull were also second home in their B final, after upping the ante in the closing stages against the Netherlands.

THE FINAL WHISTLE

Sykes Strikes Back

This being a time for thoughts of hotter, sunnier climes, I'm reminded of the delightful story Peter Alliss tells about Eric Sykes, Jimmy Tarbuck, Sean Connery et al, on a golfing holiday in Marbella. And how, while they were taking a sauna, Tarbuck decided to take a rise out of fellow comedian Sykes, who was often ribbed about his deafness.

Seeing Sykes approaching, Tarbuck suggested that by way of switching things around, they should all pretend to be unable to hear anything he might say. So, when greeted with a hearty 'Good morning' from Sykes, they made no reply.

Unperturbed, he sat down in the sauna and looked around at the others. 'Well, I don't feel too bad considering,' Sykes went on. 'I must confess I had one or two brandies and a couple of big cigars last night.' Still no response. And still he persevered: 'How long are we going to stay in here? Will we play nine or 18 holes before lunch? What's happening?' Not a word.

As the minutes ticked by, however, Sykes twigged they were up to something. Whereupon he suddenly looked up and said: 'Can anyone tell me what time this train gets into Calcutta?'

11 AUGUST 2001
Dermot Gilleece

Whatever Happened To ... Stade De France?

The venue for the 1998 World Cup final was turned into a giant, artificial beach during the summer, complete with palm trees, deck-chairs and a giant pool for swimming and windsurfing. The beach was lined with palm, olive and bamboo trees to give it the feel of the Côte d'Azur, all designed to make stay-at-home Parisians feel like they were really away. And you were thinking Stadium Ireland wouldn't be used in the summer.

20 AUGUST 2001
Mary Hannigan

Top Five Summer Injuries

(1) Kieran Durkan (Rochdale) – ended up with a blistered groin after team-mate Richard Green spilt a mug of hot tea over his privates.

(2) Peter Canero (Kilmarnock) – needed several stitches in his arms and legs after falling through a glass-cased gaming machine in Magalluf. San Miguel, eh?

(3) Carlo Cudicini (Chelsea) – needed surgery on his knee which he tweaked when the dog he was walking suddenly pulled on his lead. Mortified. Why didn't he just tell the club he did it in the gym?

(4) Lars-Gunnar Carlstrand (Elfsborg) – a Newfoundland-German Shepherd cross (a dog, to you and me) shaped up to have a scrap with Carlstrand's Rottweiler, Ted, but the Swede decided to take on the mongrel himself and ended up being bitten (twice) on the leg. Missed Elfsborg's next game. Ted was last seen filing his nails.

(5) Florentin Petre (Dinamo Bucharest) – suffered an electric shock when he got his fishing line entangled in an overhead power cable and sustained severe burns to his head and body. Onefootball.com quoted a family member saying he had 'blood gushing from his eyes and foam bubbling at his mouth, while the ground he had been standing on was left scorched'. The poor lad's still recovering.

20 AUGUST 2001

Mary Hannigan

Splashing out ... Robert Egan and Mandy Egan from Worcester Canoe Club, England, in the Senior Racing Kayak Doubles class, try to avoid a capsized kayak while taking part in the Jameson Liffey Descent at Straffan Bridge, Co. Kildare. Photograph: Dara Mac Mónaill.

SEPTEMBER

2 0 0 1

HIGHLIGHTS

1 Sept: Heart and courage prevail as plucky Republic of Ireland shock Holland in their World Cup Group Two qualifier at Lansdowne Road. Jason McAteer's goal guarantees the Republic at least a place in the World Cup play-offs. England dream of days just like this – England 5, Germany 1 – in the World Cup Qualifier/Group 9 at the Olympic Stadium, Munich. North steal point on the road and draw 1–1 with Denmark in the World Cup Qualifier/Group Three tie in Copenhagen. Poland (Group Five) become the first team from the European zone to qualify for the World Cup 2002, joining hosts South Korea and Japan, champions France and five African qualifiers.

2 Sept: Regal Meath steamroll the Kerry champions and tear down the Kingdom 2–14 to 0–5 in the All-Ireland SFC semi-final at Croke Park. Padraig Harrington pipped again as American John Daly equals a European Tour record at the BMW International Open in Munich.

5 Sept: Spain (Group 7) and Sweden (Group 4) are the second and third teams from the European zone to qualify for the World Cup 2002 finals in Japan/South Korea. Argentina topped the South America Group to qualify for the 2002 World Cup finals by beating Brazil 2–1 in Buenos Aires while Costa Rica qualified by beating the United States in the CONCACAF group.

8 Sept: Fantastic Light edges ahead of Galileo to win the Irish Champion Stakes at Leopardstown in a thrilling finish. Venus Williams outshines sister Serena 6–2, 6–4 to capture the women's title at the US Open in New York.

9 Sept: Tipperary prove team spirit counts in becoming All-Ireland Hurling champions at Croke Park. (Tipperary 2–18, Galway 2–15.) Cork crush Galway's dream of three-in-a-row All-Ireland Minor Hurling Championships 2–10 to 1–08 at Croke Park. Australia's Lleyton Hewitt brushes past American Pete Sampras to capture his first Grand Slam singles title 7–6 (7/4), 6–1, 6–1 at the US Open in New York.

15 Sept: St Leger glory as Vinnie Roe lands the Jefferson Smurfit Memorial Irish St Leger at the Curragh.

16 Sept: The decision to postpone the Ryder Cup to September 2002 due to the terrorist attack on America is met with sadness and understanding. Limerick taken to the limit in late scare at the All-Ireland Under-21 Championship final at Thurles (Limerick 0–17, Wexford 2–10). Tipperary romp to third in-a-row All-Ireland senior camogie title at Croke Park beating Kilkenny 4–13 to 1–6. Connacht reveal a cutting edge beating Caerphilly 62–0 and join Leinster, Ulster and Munster in the quarter-finals of the Celtic League.

22 Sept: Ireland's very bad day at the office leaves the Irish rugby team baffled, embarrassed and hammered 32–10 by Scotland in the Six Nations Championship at Murrayfield.

23 Sept: Meath are the victims as Galway turn it on in the All-Ireland Senior Football Championship final at Croke Park (Galway 0–17, Meath 0–8). Tyrone eventually release their grip and allow Dublin salvage a replay in the All-Ireland Minor Football final at Croke Park (Tyrone 0–15, Dublin 1–12).

I SEPTEMBER 2001

Fascinating Story of How the Ryder Cup was Won Last Time Out

Dermot Gilleece

Called 'Inside Golf's Greatest Comeback', it is unquestionably the most fascinating fly-on-the-wall story to have been written about the Ryder Cup. Apart from several of the world's leading players, the cast includes the former Governor of Texas, George W. Bush, who has since become the President of the United States.

In compiling the piece for their current issue, *Golf Digest* spoke to 37 key figures: all 11 surviving members of the victorious 1999 US Ryder Cup team (Payne Stewart has since died), European skipper Mark James and members of his team, players' wives and caddies, US skipper Ben Crenshaw and his assistants Bruce Lietzke and Bill Rogers and George W. himself.

Among the issues confronted is a highly controversial situation in Andrew Coltart's clash with Tiger Woods, when the Scot's drive off the ninth tee couldn't be found. 'A marshal was standing on it [Coltart's ball], no question of it,' the player's caddie, Ricci Roberts insists, two years on.

Roberts went on: 'He [the marshal] was right behind me. He goes "Uh, there's a ball here. Titleist with a blue dot". He was standing on it the whole time. The ball's 10 or 15 feet off the fairway, at least 15 yards from where we'd been looking. The ball is embedded and there's a footprint around the ball, so you tell me.' Woods, who went three up there, eventually won by 3 and 2.

Crenshaw's wife, Julie, described the scene on the Saturday night when the American team faced a four-point deficit entering the final day's singles. 'We watched the video, then Governor Bush came in,' she said. 'Ben had planned the Alamo speech [in 1836 Alamo commander William Barret Travis famously refused to surrender] three months before the Ryder Cup. We had no idea it would be so appropriate.'

President Bush recalled: 'I walked in the room and was surprised by the relaxed atmosphere of the players. As I read Travis's famous letter, the room was silent, the players and wives seemed to listen to every word. I finished with the "victory or death", wished them God-speed, told them the country was pulling for them, and immediately left the room.'

He went on: 'I wasn't sure of the effect. Who knew what would happen? One man did: Ben Crenshaw. He never lost faith.'

Eventually, we get to the 17th on Sunday afternoon. Firstly, we have an explanation from Padraig Harrington as to his play of the hole against Mark O'Meara. 'I wasn't pacing yardage at all. I went up to have a look at the surface. I couldn't live with myself if I didn't check the condition of the green. If that cost me the match, what would I think afterwards. What? I was too lazy to walk 90 yards.'

Minutes later, Justin Leonard sank the decisive putt from all of 50 feet. Hal Sutton recalled: 'The main thing I remember is when the putt got to the top of the hill, I thought "My God, hit the hole" because it was going eight feet past.'

The vanquished Jose-Maria Olazabal's memory of the incident is: 'Okay, he's got a good line, but if it doesn't go in, he's going to have a tricky putt coming back. When I saw the ball going in, the whole picture changed.'

Phil Mickelson: 'I turned and grabbed [wife] Amy's face and said "We won!" I felt a little awkward about seeing guys go on the green. Fortunately it didn't last longer than a few seconds, but it did seem weird to celebrate a win when it wasn't exactly over yet.' Stirring stuff.

A Top-Class Double Bill

Tom Humphries

The dinky little bandroom in the corner of Lansdowne Road is sardine tin full for this one. In fairness, double bills don't come much better. Mick McCarthy in triumph, coming to slay his detractors. Louis van Gaal in defeat, coming to be barbecued with an apple in his mouth

Mick McCarthy first. He arrives wreathed in laurels, festooned by well-wishers. We hacks come wearing sackcloth and ashes. We must render unto Caesar the tributes that are due to Caesar. It has always been easier to bury him than to praise him, though, and our questions can't rise to the occasion. We, the folks who latch onto the negative, who never accentuate the affirmative, who sometimes mess with mister-in-between.

Good as you'd hoped for Mick? We ask as if we were in the aftermath of a salvaged draw.

'Yes', he says, 'as good as I'd hoped for. Having 10 men for 25 minutes made it better and sweeter. A famous victory, hard earned, by a very honest bunch of fellas.'

Our instincts are to rake over the low points of course. We can't help it. That's the kind of animals we are. We could ask if this was vindication, we could ask how he felt when the goal went in, when the final whistle blew, what words he has said in the hap hap happy dressing room. But we follow with: How did you feel when Gary Kelly was sent off?

'Great,' he says (and pauses while we laugh). 'I knew we were on top and with 10 men we could take the game to them.'

Vindication … Ireland's Jason McAteer scores the only goal of the match against Holland at Lansdowne Road. Photograph: Brenda Fitzsimons.

There is another pause while we reflect on the banality of our ways.

'I can't answer that. I'm not trying to be funny. I thought let's get a striker off, let's get another defender. Let's keep it. We'll take nil nil now. Then to go on and win it was something else. I'm delighted for Jason McAteer. Epitomised the spirit.'

We go from bad to worse of course. We knock McCarthy out with the dumbest question of the afternoon. One that we could ask Louis van Gaal later but don't. Instead it gets blurted out here.

'Mick, what did you think of the ref overall?'

'I thought the ref was fine [exasperated pause] … I really find that an incredible question. We've just had a fantastic performance, we've beaten a fantastic team with 10 men and you ask me about the ref. It disappoints me that I didn't get a better question.'

Us too, but we are a limited side playing in conditions we aren't used to. We recover ground with a gentle question. Is this the best win? In the world?

'The current win is always the best. I think it's 14 unbeaten now. That number 13 had a nasty ring to it when I came in here the last day. But look, five regular first teamers out, one sent off. It's been one of the best wins and one of the most significant.' We're going well. We ask basically the same questions again. Is this the most significant win? In the world? Ever?

'It means the plan has worked.' He says: 'I took the two games Holland and Portugal away and everyone thought I should be in a strait-jacket and carted off to some mental institution.' (No, no, we never thought that.) 'We caught them at the right time, we got good results. I'd have taken four draws against the big teams and beaten everyone else. I think that would have been a great achievement. We've gone one step better; it's a sign we have grown up and perhaps can win it. We did ride our luck but we earned it.'

We know the routine now. Stan and Duffer? Best players in the world, Mick? Best ever?

'I agree. I think Stan, what he has achieved in the game – I've just done a real selling job for Jason McAteer, on telly, perhaps I should do one for Stan now – lads like that who play so well in international football, don't go knocking the current managers, there are players who I haven't picked today and you're all going [switches to using moany child's voice to depict media] why haven't you picked him, why haven't you picked him. But when two players of that quality are available and can't find teams, well.'

And the plan Mick? It worked!

'Leaving Niall out. It was the thing to do. Stam and Hofland would have preferred Niall. I know playing against little fellas it's a pain in the backside them chasing up the side of you all the time twisting and turning. If I'm not sat here with a win it would look like a gamble that failed but it paid off.'

Louis van Gaal arrives looking like a schoolboy about to knock on the head brother's door wherein he will be asked to hold out each hand in turn and take six belts of a leather strap. We ask Mick to be magnanimous about the Dutch.

'I have to say it's a shame they're not going to the World Cup,' says Mick. 'I wasn't going to just let him [Louis] go and he knows that. We came and we did battle and it was a terrific game. The World Cup will be less for the Dutch not being there, but if we are going instead, I'm not going to be sad. It would be nice if we were all going. But for now I'm going to be professional. We have got to win again and if we do we have a chance of winning this group. Another job to do. I'll leave you.'

And the table is left to Louis van Gaal. 'We started well for the first 20 minutes, we created two open chances, one for Kluivert, one for Zenden. We played the game we wanted to play but after that we went along with the Irish. We looked for the long ball instead of the free man in midfield.'

Which is fine but he starts to ramble. 'But the

pitch was wet and very smooth an hour before the match, but due to the wind it dried out which made it more difficult for us in midfield to pass the ball along. This may sound an exaggeration but it was very important for us.'

He follows up with a long pre-emptive explanation of why he took the best player on the pitch off.

'When Ireland scored the goal I thought it was their only chance in the match, but at that time we were worn out, we were broken. Melchiot and Stam started playing away from their position. And with Van Hooijdonk and Nistelrooy and Kluivert up front, it became crowded, which is why I brought on Van Bronkhurst for Overmars, although I thought Overmars was the best player on the pitch today. In the last minutes all our men were up front on the penalty box. It was too crowded.'

Did you believe it was a penalty Louis, when Given brought down van Nistelrooy? 'No, it's too cheap an excuse. A referee can blow or he cannot. Today he did not.'

Poor man. He looks, in his own words, worn out and broken, but he knows the truth of it all. A World Cup without the Dutch will be a smaller, less colourful experience. And Louis has only himself to blame.

3 SEPTEMBER 2001

Meath Hordes Tear Down Kingdom

Seán Moran

Meath 2-14, Kerry 0-5

There's unlikely to be big consumer demand in Kerry for the fetching new jerseys worn by the county footballers yesterday. The gulf between the sides, rather than the similarity of their colours, became the more pressing problem for the All-Ireland champions, as their predecessors ate them without salt, in this extraordinary Bank of Ireland football semi-final at Croke Park.

Long before half-time, Kerry had been entangled in the razor wire of their opponents' unforgiving ambitions. The deposed champions have enough quality footballers to recapture their titles, but there was a heavy sense of the epochal, as the most successful county of the modern age went head-to-head with the old aristocracy and destroyed them.

The whole match had an air of the surreal. It wasn't a fair reflection of the teams' respective capabilities, but that Kerry should prove so lifeless, in the face of what was presumably an anticipated onslaught, suggested that the past 12 months had taken an enormous amount out of the champions. Two replays and all that surviving on their nerves a year ago, combined with the difficulty encountered in putting away Dublin, all falls into a sort of retrospective context.

From the start yesterday, Kerry were flat and unable to meet the challenge. And what a challenge it was. Throughout his 19 years in charge of Meath, Sean Boylan has consistently sent out teams that did themselves more than justice on big days. Last year's flat line against Offaly was one of the exceptions but, even then, those 12 months of enforced idleness clearly left the Leinster champions hungry as prairie dogs.

All of the expected pivotal clashes around the field went Meath's way. In the battle of the highly-rated full-forward lines, the balance tilted so decisively that the Leinster champions didn't even have to reach for plan B. Mark O'Reilly took John Crowley's season of deadly accomplishment and left it strewn in tatters, at one stage even winning a ball in the air despite his height disadvantage.

In fairness to the Glenflesk corner forward, he rarely got serviceable ball, and apart from a gutsy point before half-time, he was unable to kick-start his game.

Tattered dreams ... Kerry's Mossy Lyons tries to hold on to Evan Kelly as Meath thrash Kerry in the All-Ireland Football semi-final. Photograph: Jason South.

If Meath never had recourse to plan B, Kerry just didn't seem to have any plan. They were stricken by the loss of three wing backs: Tomás Ó Sé was suspended and his replacement, Mike Hassett, and Tom O'Sullivan had to leave injured before the first half was over. Even by then, however, the trend was hardening against the champions.

With O'Reilly sticking to Crowley, and Cormac Murphy battling with unexpected success against Michael Frank Russell, Kerry's big guns were spiked. In the middle, Darren Fay had a magnificent match, seeing off several opponents and dominating so comprehensively in the second half that he was hardly challenged under – let alone beaten to – a single ball.

At the far end it was a different story. One of the strongest characteristics of the Ollie Murphy – Graham Geraghty combination, according to as shrewd a judge of Meath football as Matt Kerrigan,

is the pair's unshakeable self-belief. They aren't fazed by losing ball, even 50–50 ball, because they know – in the improbable vernacular of Mills and Boon – that every now and then the right one will come along.

In the first half Seamus Moynihan and Michael McCarthy won a number of outstanding possessions. Yet Murphy kicked three points from play, and with the first ball that suited Geraghty he was gone like a shot and drew a good save from Declan O'Keeffe.

It was expected that between the 40s Meath would have an edge, but not that they would swamp Kerry. With John McDermott asserting himself here and showing remarkable stamina in roaming the field, the champions had no answers in the battle cockpit.

The fluid mobility with which Meath get numbers back, or into attack, alternately frustrated

Kerry and cut them to ribbons. In the early stages, the winners didn't look entirely at ease with the swathes they were slicing through the middle of their opponents' defence. More than once, players fouled the ball or seemed daunted by the competing options of possible goals and certain points.

Eventually, they realised that it was really happening for them and started to take the points. Evan Kelly had a marvellous first half, covering back and bursting forward, making the explosive penetrations that were ultimately to overwhelm Kerry.

On a day when they needed to be twice as forceful as usual, the champions' half forwards weren't able to raise their game at all.

There was a good bit of switching, but nothing loosened the stranglehold that Meath had taken on the game.

On 35 minutes, the first major incision was made. Hank Traynor – one of a splendid half-back line with Donal Curtis and especially Nigel Nestor who swarmed around their opponents and then into attack in almost ceaseless motion – carried the ball up to Kelly. His short kick found Murphy, whose quick transfer sent Geraghty in on goal. He drew the last defender and placed McDermott, who finished to the net.

There was a brief flurry from Kerry to cut the margin to five at half-time, just about enough to convince the optimistic that it wasn't quite all over yet. But the truth was that had Meath not wasted good goal chances they would have been out of sight.

The match was formally put to bed, by a relentless blast of six unanswered points just after half-time, as Trevor Giles moved out of the shadows of a quiet first half. Kerry managed a single point in the entire second period, from substitute Declan Quill in the 63rd minute. By the end of the third quarter, Kerry had fielded all five replacements but their last cards were played to no improved effect.

It's not just that Meath don't lose big leads. They protect and extend them when on top – as

Offaly found within a couple of weeks of their League title three years ago. Murphy was careless in stepping into the square; otherwise there would have been another goal in the 45th minute. It came in the end when substitute John Cullinane got onto a breaking ball from a free in the 66th minute.

The remaining action saw Eamon Fitzmaurice get the line for a second yellow card for a foul on the rampant Geraghty, and Murphy kick the resulting free. By then, Kerry fans had been leaving for fully 20 minutes. They know their football down there.

MEATH: C. O'Sullivan, M. O'Reilly, D. Fay, C. Murphy, D. Curtis, H. Traynor (0–1), N. Nestor (0–1), N. Crawford, J. McDermott (1–0), E. Kelly (0–2), R. Kealy (0–1), T. Giles (0–1), O. Murphy (0–4), G. Geraghty (0–1), R. Magee (0–3). Subs: J. Cullinane (1–0) for Magee; P. Reynolds for Curtis; M. O'Dowd for Kelly; J. Devine for Kealy.
KERRY: D. O'Keeffe, M. Lyons, S. Monyihan, M. McCarthy, M. Hassett, E. Fitzmaurice, T. O'Sullivan, D. Ó Sé, D. Daly, E. Brosnan (0–1), N. Kennelly, A. MacGearailt, M.F. Russell (0–1), D. Ó Cinnéide (0–1), J. Crowley (0–1). Subs: T. Griffin for Hassett; M. Fitzgerald for O'Sullivan; W. Kirby for Ó Cinnéide; J. McGlynn for Daly; D Quill (0-1) for Mac Gearailt.

Galileo Is Ready to Join Greats

Brian O'Connor finds conflicting views about Galileo's ability

It's all set up. The grass is in wonderful nick, a huge worldwide TV audience are frothing at the mouth, and a mano-a-mano scrap in sport's best tradition is almost certain: Galileo versus Fantastic Light. It's not so much top as

Superstars ... Fantastic Light ridden by Frankie Dettori (right) edges ahead of Galileo ridden by Mick Kinane to win the Irish Champion Stakes at Leopardstown. Photograph: Matt Kavanagh.

double top. In fact, all it's missing is the best horse in Europe.

Oh dear, always the bitter word from the spoilsports. There we go turning Galileo into some sort of high-trotting über-hero, and then a handicapper goes and pees on the parade, tries to tell us the best ever isn't even the best this year.

Sakhee is the best horse in Europe, probably the world, right now, and that's official. The Godolphin colt's seven-length demolition of the field at York means he is rated at 131, a pound ahead of Galileo, which means at the moment the handicappers reckon Sakhee would beat Galileo by almost three-quarters of a length if they clashed.

In fact, Sakhee was so good at York there is a growing suspicion that 131 could be a little conservative. In fact, it could also be resolutely argued

that Sheikh Mohammed is sending the reserve team for today's big clash.

Now, now, all you Galileo fans, there is no need to spit the dummy out. Everyone knows the handicapper's opinion is just an opinion, but since it is the official one, and it's presumed to be devoid of wishful thinking, it's usually best to pay attention to it and try to get some focus on this phenomenon called Galileo.

To very many, after all, this horse is the latest successor to Sea Bird, Nijinksy and all the other evocative names of the past. Unbeaten, perfectly bred and supposedly blessed with the sort of talent that turns even the most flint-hearted at Coolmore into giggling groupies, he has already exhausted most of the media superlatives allocated to racing for a year.

Fanciful headlines announcing Galileo as the first $100 million horse must be like mother's milk to the always publicity conscious Coolmore team. There is also their repeatedly stated belief that Galileo will be even better over shorter trips, which suggests freakish ability but also a long-term view to that all-important stallion career.

But all this adulation presumes a once-in-a-lifetime talent, and while that talent may yet unfold today, or in the Queen Elizabeth II Stakes, or on dirt in New York, nothing we have seen yet from Galileo has shaken the resolutely objective from their view that while he is good, he ain't that good.

'Galileo's winning performance in the King George was well up to King George standard but it was nothing exceptional. To rank him with the greats, he has to go beyond that,' says Ireland's handicapper, Gary O'Gorman.

'He is quite a charismatic horse who won the Derby easily and showed fighting qualities at Ascot. He is also beautifully bred, so you can't crab him,' allows O'Gorman, who nevertheless returns to the 130 mark Galileo earned by his two-length defeat of Fantastic Light in the King George.

'Even allowing for Fantastic Light improving a few pounds this season, you still have to look back at the King George last year and how easily Montjeu beat him. Hightori [third to Galileo in the King George] was also murdered by Sinndar in the Arc last year,' he says.

Sinndar's trainer, John Oxx, points to similarities with his Arc-winning champion in the

High jump … Frankie Dettori leaps from Fantastic Light after his victory at Leopardstown. Photograph: Matt Kavanagh.

uncomplicated nature of both horses and the flexibility which that allows tactically. He also feels today's mile and a quarter should not be a problem to Galileo.

'Just because very good horses don't run over a certain distance doesn't mean they can't win over it if they are tried,' he says.

However, Galileo will have to improve dramatically for the drop in trip if he is to achieve officially what he already appears to have in reputation and value. Another two-length victory after another slug-out with Fantastic Light will tell us nothing we don't already know except an admirable versatility in terms of trip.

But what is fascinating about today's race is the chance that Galileo could indeed hammer Fantastic Light & Co. to smithereens and put in the sort of performance that will leave no one in doubt about his place among the great names.

'If you look at a horse like Commanche Run [1995 Champion Stakes winner] you can see that class can get you home over longer distances,' O'Gorman acknowledges.

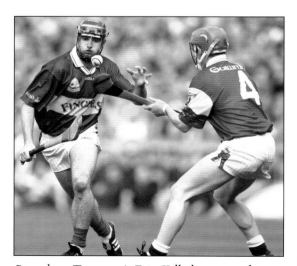

Rugged ... Tipperary's Eoin Kelly keeps control despite pressure from Ollie Canning of Galway during the All-Ireland Hurling final at Croke Park. Photograph: Frank Miller.

'But I am also coming round to the view that Fantastic Light could be better over 10 furlongs. I'm not particularly convinced he ran as well in the King George as he did at Royal Ascot. It should be an intriguing race,' he adds.

And there is nothing bitter about that word. Intriguing fits just right.

10 SEPTEMBER 2001

Right and Fitting that Tipperary Are Crowned as Champions

Tom Humphries sums up an All-Ireland final that was rugged rather than beautiful

So here's where the story ends. A great lurching twister of a season blew itself out at Croke Park yesterday. When it counted Tipperary were the only team still standing. Yes, Tipperary, the old bluebloods of hurling. They took their 25th title with a margin of three points and none has been harder fought or better deserved.

They left behind them a bewildered Galway team. Last month, Galway – young, brash and very wound up – came to town and handed Kilkenny a lesson in hurling. It seemed like an arrival. Yesterday they showed the same fight, but not the same finesse, and while Tipperary picked points from long distance, Galway huffed and puffed. It looked like an eviction.

That Tipperary should be crowned champions at the end of a solid and sometimes spectacular summer of hurling is right and fitting. They have hurled hardest, they have hurled the most often and they have hurled best. No backdoors. No easy passage. No excuses necessary.

Furthermore they have the keenest moral claim to an All-Ireland title. While other teams are coming slowly or have peaked or are rebuilding, Tipp are that ripe blend of experienced hands and young swashbucklers. They have served their time under a manager who has learned his trade quickly but sometimes painfully.

It's been 10 years! A decade during which five other hurling counties have divvied out the good times while Tipp took their beatings and learned their lessons. Yesterday at Croke Park they took the lead in the second minute and never let it go again. Heroes emerged all over the pitch, a pitch it should be said which disintegrated badly as the afternoon progressed. Croke Park will be blessed with a new surface next summer. Not before time.

Anyway, the early business was brisk and uncompromising but if Kilkenny had been surprised by Galway's physical exuberance in last

months' semi-final, well Tipperary were well prepared for it. Matched physically, Galway didn't look so gifted or so lithe. The scores came dropping slowly.

'It was tough around midfield all right,' said Tipp captain Tommy Dunne afterwards. 'There were a lot of hits going in but it was fair and sporting, that should be said after all the publicity there has been about sendings off.'

It was rugged rather than beautiful but still there were moments of genius amid the granite shoulder challenges. Tommy Dunne scored some sublime points; young Mark O'Leary, of Kilruane outside Nenagh, popped up for two goals, one in each half. Even Declan Ryan, written off by many as being slow and needing more space than a cruise ship requires to turn in, found the time to revel. In the

Shocking youth … Feargal Healy of Galway slams his side's second goal past Tipperary keeper Brendan Cummins during the All-Ireland Hurling final at Croke Park. Photograph: Frank Miller.

first half he caught Brendan Cummins' puck-out and handpassed to Eoin Kelly to rifle home. In the second half Ryan plundered everything while younger players swang from him and bounced off him. Tipp's sole link with the good times enjoyed himself.

Tipperary led by two points at half-time but went to their teabreak with the sobering knowledge that Galway had scored the last four points of the half and would be playing with the wind after the intermission. They needed something by way of a statement of intent and three minutes into the half it came via Mark O'Leary's second goal of the game.

After that, Galway went hunting for goals and got a decent one. If Tipp lived dangerously at times towards the finish, that was because nobody expects to get through an All-Ireland final any other way.

'If you are going to win an All-Ireland', said Brendan Cummins, Tipp's goalkeeper, 'you need a little luck. I remember in 1997 saving a ball and Jamesie O'Connor hit it over the bar. There's nothing you can do about luck.'

Still Tipperary never looked threatened by anything which might prove fatal. Their defending was as it has been most of the year – hard, honest and smart. There were bone shaking challenges, last-second clearances and courageous blocks but nothing which smacked of despair or desperation. Theirs was a win founded on conviction.

That self-belief flowed from the top downwards. Manager Nicky English, who was once merely a beloved son of the county, has evolved into the sort of man whose very heartbeat seems somehow linked to that of his county. He spoke afterwards of what this meant.

'It means I'm out of the hole. You take a job like this and you are in a hole from the beginning. People around me, people close to me, when this job came up, they all said don't take it but I couldn't stop myself taking it. I love Tipperary and the Tipperary hurling jersey so much. I'm very good at digging holes for myself in life anyway. This feels like I've got out of one.'

For Galway the end was disappointing, but it has been a year of marked progress culminating in a return to the big dance. Manager Noel Lane looked to his team and their shocking, indecent youth and said they would be back. 'No complaints, we were beaten by a good team on the day. We have the young players and it will stand them. Galway will be back.' That's the plan anyway.

Forty years ago a Tipperary team captained by a Toomevara man, Matt Hassett, won an All-Ireland to add to the league title, a feat they were to repeat twice more within four years. If Tipp, with Tommy Dunne in the vanguard, are on the cusp of another such era, Galway might have to wait and wait.

17 SEPTEMBER 2001

Harrington Says Decision Was Right and Proper

Philip Reid

Padraig Harrington was in the gym when the news came. It didn't come as any great surprise, though. And the decision to postpone the Ryder Cup for a year – until September 2002, with the same teams as those originally due to do battle at The Belfry next week – was one with which the Dubliner fully concurred.

'When you look at the bigger picture, I believe that the decision to postpone it for a year is probably the right one,' remarked Harrington, who had spent much of the past golfing year ensuring that his name would be on the team-sheet.

'The Ryder Cup is a big event, it is not just like another golf tournament. But when you compare it with what happened in America last week, then it is not the most important thing in the world. As a mark of respect, it is probably correct that it is postponed.'

Rather than reopening the whole qualifying

process, Harrington also felt that it was only right and fitting that the players who had qualified for the event this time round should be the ones selected to play in next year's rescheduled meeting, 'especially for the likes of Paul [McGinley] and Phillip [Price] who have qualified and who would be competing in the Ryder Cup for the first time.'

Harrington added: 'I think that postponing the matches for a year is the best thing for everyone. What's a year? We can wait … If it had gone ahead next week, I am sure that a lot of players would not have been focussed, and that would not have been right because it is a really big occasion.

'As a European player, I am 100 per cent behind the decision taken by the Americans. It was totally their call and this whole tragedy affects them a whole lot more than it affects any of us. Over the past week, I have seen just how much pressure they have all been under.'

This is the first time since 1975 – when Christy O'Connor Jnr, Eamonn Darcy and John O'Leary were on a team under the old Britian and Ireland selection – that three Irishmen had qualified to play under the European team set-up.

For Darren Clarke (who played at Valderrama in 1997 and Brookline in 1999), who led the European qualifying, it would have been a third appearance, while for Harrington (who made his debut in Brookline), and who was second in the qualifying table, it would have been a second appearance. McGinley, who qualified in seventh position in the European table, was due to make his debut in the competition.

Harrington, Clarke and McGinley all arrived back in London on Saturday from the US, where they were in St Louis for the American Express World Strokeplay championship which was cancelled because of the atrocities in New York, Washington and Pennsylvania, on a chartered flight and had expected to hear news of the Cup's postponement.

Ryder Cup rookie Pierre Fulke also felt the move to postpone the matches was 'the only deci-sion that could have been taken.'

Fulke, who was also on that chartered plane that brought the European-based players back from St Louis, added: 'Everybody's gut feeling after Tuesday was that the Ryder Cup would be in danger, and you have to understand the American players who did not want to travel, and it is the only decision.

'From a personal point of view, if they had cancelled it, it would have been a disappointment. But it has only been postponed and so we will still be Ryder Cup players next year. On the way back from the States, all the European team agreed that we wanted the match to go ahead, but the decision has basically been made by the US team.

'We don't know what is going to happen. It could be World War III or something, so I think it is a very good decision.'

Meanwhile, former Ryder Cup player Christy O'Connor Jnr, who is one of those with his hat in the ring for the captaincy in 2005 when it will be played at The K Club, remarked: 'The main think-ing would be that the Americans wouldn't have the Ryder Cup on their minds. They would not feel they were giving 100 per cent and, with the Ryder Cup, you need 100 per cent. But I am delighted that they haven't cancelled it.'

17 SEPTEMBER 2001

The Best Revenge Is Living A Good Life

Tom Humphries

So, six days now, stuck in this airless space, and the mind begins to stray from the blackly riveting images with which TV desensitises us. There remains the amputee's sharp sense of grief and loss; a part of us is gone. New York belongs to all of us, and those shareholding nations who built it, loved it, lived in it or just dreamed of it, now mourn the place and its children.

Lately, though, grief is accompanied by thudding dread as we watch America choose a spot at which it may perpetrate reciprocal atrocities. This will be one-sided and it will be awful, another Hiroshima (100,000 civilians), Nagasaki (60,000), Laos (350,000) or Cambodia (600,000). Bracing oneself against mendacity doesn't feel like appropriate mourning.

We've been here before, pre-Gulf War. It is a commonplace in this solemn time to denounce sport as 'trivial', to say that all this death has 'put sport in perspective'. And it is hard to argue in the face of grief. When David Duval asks if 'we're supposed to be golfing?' at The Belfry while funerals proceed in his homeland, he comes across again as unselfish and decent.

And perhaps sport isn't anything profound. We take some of it (winning, losing, Beckham) too seriously, while not taking the heart of it (the rules, the spirit and the ability to live with both) seriously enough. Yet, I stand with sport right now. It is nothing trivial. It better frames our perspective on life than mass destruction does.

All the abuse runs the other way. The theft of sports' phrases to inadequately describe war's horror is a real rape of the language. Those peasants upon whom bombs will rain, they will be in the strike zone as Bush quarterbacks the latest drive and they near endgame.

These people who will appropriate the language and the morality of our times in the coming weeks, all those ghouls whose deadening expertise we haven't been faced with since the Gulf War, these are the people who need perspective, these are the truly dysfunctional.

Sport is a distraction, dreamtime, folly. It's what keeps the lines from our face, the heaviness from our hearts. It's what bonds us and lets us identify with one another.

It is the best of us, too, a shared joy which lets us identify and mingle with each other. A year ago exactly we were in Sydney. Sure, sure, there's plenty that's phoney and counterfeit about Olympism, but for those few weeks as we bobbed about under the Harbour Bridge and around the Opera House (architectural icons, it's poignant to reflect, matched only perhaps by the erased Towers of Manhattan), everyone was friends, everyone was united, and as the world gathered to watch on TV it was with happy anticipation. Call me sentimental, but …

At this point there will be groans from the flinthearts who elbow their way to the front at a time like this. Get real, Pollyanna, they will say. People who can be serious (bullish even) about war wonder how we who love it can take sport so seriously. They are mystified by how we can engage emotionally with the outcome of a football game, be disappointed by a race, connect with a horse; they wonder how Michelle de Bruin's sins can make us cry while Roy Keane just makes us smile and shake our heads.

Well, we wonder how they can take war so lightly. There's something wrong with them, not with us. Some malfunction in their cobwebbed brains. Sport has more to do with the investigation of human possibility than war does. Sport has more to do with life.

There are times when we belittle sport by partaking in it wantonly or by pimping it to the panjandrums in blazers to have their way with. I can't imagine a Chinese Olympics unless that country's human rights record changes. I couldn't imagine us playing football against Yugoslavia while that country slaughtered Kosovans. But I can imagine sport in New York again. The joyful, resilient defiance of it. I can imagine it and wish for it, because that will be the victory of civilised people.

Lean-shanked men leaping for basketballs on the blacktopped, chainlinked courts that punctuate the city. The greedy cadences of hustlers scalping tickets outside Madison Square Garden as the pulse of excitement builds. Scuffling studs on Roosevelt Island amid the babble of tongues which sound-track the soccer leagues that grip the city, every colour and creed and belief playing the beautiful game on those little aprons of grass.

Simple stuff. Couples skating at the Rockefeller Centre, fathers playing catch with their sons in Central Park while joggers pound the pathway around the reservoir. New York is a city made for distraction and enjoyment. Not war.

Right now, when simple justice is wilfully confused with revenge, we are asked to stand back and get our sense of perspective right. Well, nobody has felt any better when George W. Bush has executed troubled kids in Texas, and they won't feel any better when they obliterate the enfeebled people of Kabul or Baghdad or wherever. There won't be closure, there is no such thing. No victims will be restored to us.

There is justice. There are rules. Sport, incidentally, strives to teach us about both; what is being talked about just now seeks to ignore both, despite our having built a civilisation upon them.

Then there is the best revenge: the living of happy and good lives, the busy trails of soccer moms and little league baseball coaches, the sight of peewees skating after pucks on frozen ponds, grown men playing touch football on sunny afternoons. The best revenge is people doing what they do best, living full lives.

That's what was taken away last Tuesday morning, that vision of sunlit moments and coiled energy which Manhattan, in particular, and the American dream in general offers us all. And that is what must be restored.

As America prepared to exfoliate the spore of its foreign policy, they played football in England this weekend and we played camogie in Croke Park and enjoyed sports in a thousand other places. With respectful distance, that is the most fitting style of mourning for a city of such unbounded gaiety and energy.

Ireland's Very Bad Day at the Office

Gerry Thornley

Scotland 32, Ireland 10

In the pantheon of Irish duds, this latest offering is right up there. Comparable in many ways with the Twickenham debacle of two seasons ago, and with any of the previous eight on the spin in Murrayfield, we presumed days like this were a thing of the past. Oh fools that we are.

Recalling the more recent Murrayfield horror shows of four and two years ago, when Ireland lost by 38–10 and 30–13, at least Ireland threw an illusory blow or two before subsiding. At least there was the opening seven-point salvo and the continuing excellence two years ago of Dion O'Cuinneagain. There wasn't even that here. By the time an abject Ireland threw a punch, they were already on their knees.

The contest ended pretty much with the kick-off, when no Irish forward was remotely near enough to field Gregor Townsend's steepling kick. What made this particularly galling was that the team and its supporters had rightly travelled in expectation as much as hope. Therein, of course, lies the rub to a degree.

For Warren Gatland and the rest of the management team this was a bad day at the office. During the week Eddie O'Sullivan had described the half-dozen changes to the previous Championship outing against France and the attempt to imbue the team with more pace and flair as a caculated gamble. In pretty much all instances, the gambles failed.

Prized amongst these was assuredly the decision to pick Guy Easterby and drop Peter Stringer. As much in his stature and his size, Stringer had become something of a lucky totem for this team, debuting in the rejuvenatory win over Scotland 18 months ago and only being on the losing team in three of his 11 test starts, without ever really letting Ireland down. A fear had been that Easterby would overplay his hand and – compounding a delivery to Ronan O'Gara that was significantly more ponderous than Stringer's quicksilver service – that he did.

The management had to be taken at their word in the selection of both Easterbys, based on a few outings in the Celtic League for Llanelli, and the younger Simon struggled too. He hardly counted at the breakdown or on the gainline, and even his agility and soft hands at the tail of the line failed to provide the line-out service that was the main set-piece plank for Ireland two seasons ago.

However, in their hasty desire to revive the well-balanced and mightily successful back-row of

that campaign by recalling the Llanelli back-rower at the expense of Alan Quinlan or Eric Miller, the management erred. Clearly the younger Easterby hadn't enough rugby under his belt after virtually missing all of last season.

Nor did the selection of Shane Horgan ahead of Kevin Maggs stand up too well either, though arguably Mike Mullins is more dynamic and creative than either of them just now. Why even his once suspect defence might have shored Ireland's porous midfield here (Townsend, John Leslie, James McLaren and Glenn Metcalfe punching the holes that led to their first three tries), while all the talk of this being a form selection never particularly tallied with the selection of Jeremy Davidson ahead of Gary Longwell and Mick Galwey especially.

No doubt all of this will have completed many self-fulfilling prophecies down Munster way, yet

Days like this ... Ireland Captain, Keith Wood, is tackled by Scotland's Simon Taylor (left), John Leslie and Gregor Townsend (ground) at Murrayfield. Photograph: Dara Mac Dónaill.

Crushing defeat … Brian O'Driscoll, Ireland, is tackled by Scotland's James Mc Laren (right) and John Leslie at Murrayfield. Photograph: Dara Mac Dónaill.

talk of a player here or there, or even three or four brings to mind thoughts of the *Titanic* and deck chairs. Most likely even Gailimh would have gone down with this ship, perhaps for good. Hell, for that matter, even John Eales might have gone down.

Perhaps this Ireland aren't as good as we or they thought they are, but for all Scotland's in-yer-face, pressure defence, their spoiling at the breakdown and their competetiveness on the Irish throw, the hosts can't suddenly be that good. This was a scrappy match riddled with mistakes and Scotland won in a canter. They were a decidedly moderate outfit last season and even allowing for the flawed flair Gregor Townsend gives them at out-half, they can't have become technically superior collectively or in most of the 15 head-to-heads. Not to this extent anyhow.

Nor, you'd have thought, can Scotland be physically in better shape even if, puzzlingly, they looked stronger and more explosive in contact across the gain line and in terms of stamina too, judging by way the Irish jerseys went hiding all over the pitch for Anderew Henderson's try. As Irish bodies struggled to the breakdown when Denis Hickie broke out to half-way, as no-one failed to fill in at scrum-half when the ball came out, and as so few had the will or the legs to react when Metcalfe chased Townsend's ensuing punt downfield, this looked like a return to the bad old amateur days of yore.

Yet whatever mistakes were made selectorially or in the physical preparation of the side, it's hard to credit that Scotland could be this much better technically or physically. No, no, no, thus one can only deduce that the team weren't mentally

215

switched on anything like they should have been, that they themselves and the management pressed the wrong buttons.

The tactical gambit of slowing down the arrival of Ireland's forwards to the line-outs, ostensibly to disguise the intended target of delivery, certainly didn't fool the Scots. As faulty as Keith Wood's throws were, so too were the calls after freeing up one of the jumpers, which instead repeatedly found Scott Murray and co. Coupled with the repeated decision to kick penalties for touch and ponderously at that, not to mention that Scottish forwards persistently hit the rucks harder all afternoon, it meant that only one team were playing with any tempo.

If pretty much all the pre-match concerns came to the surface, so too did a good few more besides. It's hard to recall Wood, twice stumbling before contact, having such an ineffective game. As heavily marked as two years ago here, at least Wood looked fit then. In a rudderless display, focussing in on the Irish huddle after Scotland's killer third try through Leslie, there was a lot of blowing but very little talking. Nor did any of the leaders rise to the challenge, for Anthony Foley was curiously anonymous and Ronan O'Gara had his worst game for Ireland and probably his worst representative game ever. Compounding the problems inside by taking on the ball too much himself and ineffectually, so Ireland struggled for width. The Munstermen weren't immune from the malaise either.

As one player, whose viewpoint is usually succinct and to the point, conceded afterwards, 'Mentally we weren't right. We were over-confident. It's that old bloody favouritism tag again.' Pretty pathetic in this day and age really. You'd have thought that in 2001 and in the sixth year of professionalism, Ireland had moved on from that. Clearly not. And after this, you wonder if they ever will.

SCORING SEQUENCE: 24 mins: Pountney try, Townsend con 7–0; 33 mins: Paterson pen 10–0; 38 mins: Smith try, Paterson con 17–0; (half-time 17–0); 50 mins: O'Gara pen 17–3; 58 mins: Leslie try, Paterson con 24–3; 67 mins: Paterson pen 27–3; 78 mins: Henderson try, Pasterson con 32–3; 85 mins: Dempsey try, Humphreys con 32–10.

SCOTLAND: G. Metcalfe (Glasgow); J. Steel (Glasgow), J. McLaren (Glasgow), J. Leslie (Northampton), C. Paterson (Edinburgh); G. Townsend (Castres), B. Redpath (Sale); T. Smith (Northampton), G. Bulloch (Glasgow), M. Stewart (Northampton), J. White (Glasgow), S. Murray (Saracens), G. Simpson (Glasgow), S. Taylor (Edinburgh), B. Pountney (Edinburgh). Replacements: G. Graham (Newcastle) for Stewart (64 mins), A. Henderson (Glasgow) for Leslie (64 mins), S. Grimes for White (72 mins), J. Petrie (Glasgow) for Simpson (76 mins), A. Nicol (Glasgow) for Redpath (79 mins), D. Hodge (Edinburgh) for Townsend (79 mins), S. Scott (Edinburgh) for Bulloch (79 mins).

IRELAND: G. Dempsey (Terenure College and Leinster); G. Murphy (Leicester), B. O'Driscoll (Blackrock College and Leinster), S. Horgan (Lansdowne and Leinster), D. Hickie (St Mary's College and Leinster); R. O'Gara (Cork Constitution and Munster), G. Easterby (Llanelli); P. Clohessy (Young Munster and Munster), K. Wood (Harlequins, capt), J. Hayes (Shannon and Munster), J. Davidson (Dungannon and Ulster), M. O'Kelly (St Mary's College and Leinster), S. Easterby (Llanelli), A. Foley (Shannon and Munster), K. Dawson (London Irish). Replacements: K. Maggs (Bath) for Murphy (23 mins), E. Byrne (St Mary's College and Leinster) for Hayes (35 mins), P. Stringer (Shannon and Munster) for G. Easterby (54 mins), D. Wallace (Garryowen) for Foley (64 mins), D. Humphreys (Dungannon and Ulster) for O'Gara (64 mins), G. Longwell (Ballymena and Ulster) for Davidson (75 mins).
REFEREE: C. White (England).

Top score … Padhraic Joyce, Galway, breaks from Darren Fay, Meath, during the All-Ireland Football final at Croke Park. Photograph: Dara Mac Dónaill.

24 SEPTEMBER 2001

Meath the Victims as Galway Turn it On

Seán Moran

Galway 0–17, Meath 0–8

As you do unto others, so shall it be done unto you. The matador sound effects with which Meath supporters had taunted Kerry a brief three weeks previously were turned against them yesterday as a stylish and convincing Galway team elegantly played down the clock after an extraordinary end to what has been an historic Bank of Ireland football championship.

There were exceptional performances all over the field but the headliners were Declan Meehan, who gave a live-wire display at wing back, Kevin Walsh, masterful at centrefield, and Padhraic Joyce who was at his most cutting with 10 points, five of them from play in a coruscating second half.

Galway thus became the first team to win the championship after availing of the qualifier system introduced this year – albeit that it wasn't the first time the county has won the title after losing a match. They were awarded the All-Ireland 76 years ago after a committee room wrangle had disqualified all the provincial champions, but we can safely assume that this year's win counts as one of the most satisfying of the nine the county has now won.

'It was sweet, all right,' said Galway manager John O'Mahony more than once in the dressing-room aftermath. And so it must have been. The team were distant outsiders going into the match – the bookmakers' odds exaggerating the difference between the teams but reflecting the general assumption that Meath would win.

The two areas where Galway were likely to make an impact, centrefield and the half forwards, both came through for them in emphatic style and to add to Meath's problems, their own half forwards experienced terrible difficulties for much of the 70 minutes. With the middle two thirds of the field a hostile environment, their hitherto sparkling inside forwards were starved of possession and their full backs were subject to intolerable pressures.

Worse was to come for the Leinster champions. In the space of seven minutes, their leading forward, Ollie Murphy, had to be substituted with a broken finger and wing back Nigel Nestor was sent off for a second yellow card.

The Meath legend is built on such adversity but not this time. The match had been too tight before the scales lurched for such blows not to have a massive impact, but even before these incidents the match had been slipping alarmingly away from the favourites.

Clawing something from the direst circumstances has been a characteristic of the team, but that is because performance levels have been lifted. Yesterday that did not happen, as all of their major players chose the same time to bottom out and for the first time in Seán Boylan's distinguished, 19-year tenure as manager, his team collectively failed to rise to the occasion.

Of them all, it was ironically John McDermott – who had had to be tempted out of retirement earlier this year – who performed nearest to his best. He worked hard at centrefield and then got forward in the desperate attempts to turn the match. One of these provided a pivotal moment when substitute Niall Kelly – who can evidently kick like a mule – drove in a long ball which broke for McDermott.

On being challenged he toppled over. Television pictures suggest that this may have had little to do with the challenge but, in any case, referee Michael Collins awarded the penalty. In some

ways you might be justified for putting your house on Trevor Giles in such a situation. His well-earned reputation for stepping forward when the need is greatest supports such faith. But on the other hand he has missed a penalty in an All-Ireland before, two years ago, albeit with less fatal consequences.

Whether Michael Donnellan's advice to Galway keeper Alan Keane had an effect or not, Giles sent the kick wide – his attempt to place it inside the left post failing narrowly. There was 11 minutes left on the clock at that stage and had the kick been converted, it would have cut the margin to two. Instead Galway powered on and added another four unanswered points to their winning margin. The error was in keeping with Giles's day. Strongly favoured to exercise a decisive influence for at least some of the match, he found himself in the company of a man in the hottest of form. Few would have doubted Tomás Mannion's football ability, but keeping track of Meath's playmaker was a tough challenge. He met it head on and with the defensive alignment cleverly configured to protect his lack of pace, Mannion controlled the middle of his defence.

On his flanks, Declan Meehan rampaged up and down the right whereas Seán de Paor curbed his adventuring a little. The result was an optimising of the half-back effort. They continually held off their men with the odd exception of Evan Kelly's forward runs, some of which would normally have been points but in the desperate circumstances obtaining were frequently the prelude to some doomed attempt on goal.

Meehan was exceptional, particularly in the first half and might have had a goal in the 67th minute but coolly opted to guarantee a point and push the margin out a little further.

McDermott's display in the centre was in something of a vacuum, as his opponent Kevin Walsh was the dominant figure there. His fully-fit availability to the team has been in many ways the

Victory … Galway captain, Gary Fahey, hoists the Sam Maguire aloft after Galway beat Meath in the Al-Ireland Football final at Croke Park. Photograph: Matt Kavanagh.

most important aspect of the team's successes. He had, according to O'Mahony, been going very well in training over the past two weeks and it showed.

Yesterday he worked tirelessly, got onto a great deal of ball and moved it fluently.

In full cry Galway were an awesome sight. It's one football has become accustomed to in recent years but yesterday they rode out the difficult period and never looked back when the pendulum began to swing their way.

More than anyone could have anticipated, Meath seemed flat – as if their semi-final blitzing of Kerry had taken too much out of them.

When difficulties arose, they had none of the leadership figures they needed – or that Galway had in abundance. Jarlath Fallon, after an injury-disrupted season to test the stoicism of Job, was busy and useful even if not at the top of his game. His words of encouragement in the dressing-room lifted the players and on the field he led by example.

Galway's bad patch came in the first half and even then, it wasn't without its redeeming features. They created a great deal of chances but failed to take them – often in the most demoralising of ways.

Padhraic Joyce gave no hint of what was to come with a couple of ghastly wides and at half-time the level scoring, 0–6 each, seemed to favour Meath because less effort had been expended in their accumulation.

Neither Graham Geraghty nor Murphy were hacking up, but there was nothing too strange about that. One assumed that the chances would come and both of them looked sufficiently sharp to make the necessary incisions when the right ball was directed into them.

Nothing was coming easy however. Kieran Fitzgerald franked a great debut year with a great covering and pacy clearances while the Fahey brothers patiently stuck to their task. Until Meath were in a position to create a decent supply to their top guns, the Galway full backs weren't going to give away anything cheaply.

Meath will see the turning point as Murphy's departure. He was replaced by wing back Paddy Reynolds. In the absence of convincing forward cover on the bench, the question suddenly arose: how were they going to get scores? Slowly and bleakly the answer became apparent. They weren't.

Michael Donnellan made the switch from centrefield in the 31st minute but struggled to hit the rhythms that normally drive his game, but others up front set the agenda. Derek Savage's swift elusiveness turned Meath inside out while Padhraic Joyce's four-minute salvo of three points from play demoralised Meath and put the match beyond the reach of all but the most remarkable comebacks.

And on this occasion, even Meath hadn't an answer.

GALWAY: A. Keane, K. Fitzgerald, G. Fahey, R. Fahey, D. Meehan (0–1), T. Mannion, S. de Paor, K. Walsh, M. Donnellan (0–1), J. Bergin (0–2), P. Clancy (0–2), J. Fallon (0–1), P. Joyce (0–10), D. Savage, T. Joyce. Subs: A. Kerins for Bergin; K. Comer for T. Joyce.
MEATH: C. Sullivan, M. O'Reilly, D. Fay, C. Murphy, D. Curtis, H. Traynor, N. Nestor, N. Crawford (0–1), J. McDermott (0–1), E. Kelly (0–1), T. Giles (0–1), R. Kealy, O. Murphy (0–1), G. Geraghty, R. Magee (0–2). Subs: P. Reynolds for O. Murphy; J. Cullinane (0–1) for Kealy; N. Kelly for C. Murphy; A. Kenny for Magee.

24 SEPTEMBER 2001

O'Mahony A True Western Hero

Tom Humphries

Suddenly it was over. When the longest season in Gaelic football history shuddered to a finish yesterday it was fitting that it was a team which took the scenic route who were still standing. Galway climbed highest, marched longest, and overcame the most.

This was the most quixotic of recent All-Ireland wins, a romantic defiance of the odds and an outcome that none among the attendance of 70,482 would have guessed at if surveyed during the intermission.

It's the tallest of tales really. Galway almost sundered themselves with infighting in May. They lost to Roscommon on the first weekend in June. Put themselves back together to beat Wicklow four weekends later and then continued the healing with an extraordinary series of wins against Armagh, Cork, Roscommon, Derry and now Meath.

Along the way they kept tilting at windmills until they rediscovered the zestful attacking football which brought them success after the long hunger back in 1998.

They played their way through therapy and meanwhile drew on some old fashioned motivational tools.

'The media made a great job of us,' said totemic midfielder Kevin Walsh. 'It's been very easy to pick up one or two papers and shove it in front of a few fellas' faces. It's motivation in itself,

Champion boss … John O'Mahony, Galway manager, celebrates after his team beat Meath in the All-Ireland Football Final at Croke Park. Photograph: Dara Mac Dónaill.

they were more or less saying we were flukey to be there, the last year or two. So it's sweet.'

Sweet but nourishing.

It has been a long and strange summer for Galway and yesterday's final made an unlikely end to their adventure. The third quarter of the game had an almost surreal quality to it as Meath began shipping water fore and aft while Galway serenely picked off their points.

Imagine this. In a 20-minute spell Meath lose Ollie Murphy when the player of the championship thus far broke his finger. Then Nigel Nestor gets sent off for a second yellow card before Trevor Giles misses a penalty.

Yet if Meath needed any more proof of the old saw which warns that just because your wife dies it doesn't mean you're house can't burn down, they had only to gaze at Padhraic Joyce.

While calamity was piled upon disaster, Joyce was at the other end putting together a sequence wherein he scored eight Galway points in a row as part of a scoring performance to stand with those of Galway elders like Seán Purcell and Frankie Stockwell.

The victory represents a remarkable triumph for Galway's manager John O'Mahony, a schoolteacher from Ballaghdereen, who has now taken Galway to wins and one beaten final appearance in four seasons in charge. In his two winning appearances as a Galway manager he has outsmarted no less than Mick O'Dwyer and Seán Boylan on All-Ireland final day.

At times this year he has looked drained and tired by the job, but yesterday took the lines from his face.

He now stands among the greatest Gaelic football managers of modern times, his work with Galway, Leitrim and Mayo having almost single-handedly raised the stock of Connacht football. Yesterday, his use of the extra man – rotating the task among three players after Nigel Nestor was dismissed – frustrated a Meath team who have often taken inspiration from such setbacks in the past.

'It was a great feeling,' he said afterwards. 'We had something to prove. Take a guy like Padhraic Joyce, a lot of assessments are made on players after five minutes. Players like Padhraic Joyce shouldn't always have to be proving themselves. He was written off, but in many ways this whole team was written off.'

As for Joyce himself he finished the game (and any arguments there ever were about his ability) with 10 points to his credit, half of them from play. He finishes the season as the championship's top scorer by some distance, averaging just short of seven points per game. His rise to eminence reflects also a change in the power centre of the Galway side since 1998. If that All-Ireland represented a triumph for the elder core of the team, this victory was brought about by the succeeding generation.

If they have been written off in the past 12 months, the epicentre of the disillusion has been Galway itself, where the fractiousness of the team's early season was keenly parsed and analysed.

Trouble presents opportunity, of course, and management and players alike jumped at the chance to come to Croke Park in the underdog role, having watched Meath dice the All-Ireland champions Kerry into small pieces a few weeks ago.

As John O'Mahony arrived in from the jungle of well-wishers and hangers-on on the Croke Park field, he met his counterpart Seán Boylan outside the door of the Galway dressingroom. Boylan had already visited the Galway team to give them the benediction of gracious words. 'I missed you again Seán,' said O'Mahony. 'Well done, fella', said Boylan as the two embraced, 'have a great night.'

They were quick words exchanged between equals. As O'Mahony disappeared to join his team, Boylan paused to reflect on a bizarre afternoon of football.

'It was all to play for. In the second half they went up a gear and we just weren't able to do it. We just weren't able to respond. It didn't happen today. We honour Galway and give them full credit.

'There would be no excuses. Nigel going off was significant, Ollie going off was significant but there's days that those things will go for ya and there's days they won't; there's no excuses.

'On a day like today when they were the ones who took the game to us, raised it to a higher level than we could get to, we'd no answer. Doesn't happen to us often and I'm sorry for the lads but Galway went through the pain of losing last year and they've come back. I'm delighted for John O'Mahony.'

And with that Boylan disappeared down the cool corridor to immerse himself in the silence of his team, to check that Ollie Murphy had gotten away to hospital, that the detritus of yet another campaign was put away.

For Galway this epic season will never be put to bed. The team of 1998 have often heard it said on nights when drink has been taken and talk has been loose that they 'only' beat Kildare four years ago. After a run this summer which took them far and wide and gave them a fixture list from hell, they are the worthiest of champions.

Last words in the Galway dressingroom went to their captain Gary Fahey: 'Every player in our team lifted themselves today. To watch it was unbelievable. At the end, with the crowd cheering the passes and us so far ahead, well, I don't know. You could never write a script for a game like that.'

24 SEPTEMBER 2001

Lockerroom: GAA Versus Soccer No Contest

Tom Humphries

In a spirit of peace and understanding some reasons why the GAA season just finished will once again put the Premiership in the ha'penny place.

1. No diving for penalties. No diving.

2. Indeed the general ethos of love and tenderness which pervades the GAA. If the media can forgive the Galway hurlers their press night then anybody can forgive anything. Getting a one-on-one chat with Osama bin Laden would be less trouble than getting some face time with a Galway hurler.

3. The paranoia of GAA managers has gloriously exceeded that of their Premiership counterparts. It was a GAA manager who once said, 'No comment and I don't want to be quoted as saying that', but at the time that was just a flash in the pan. Standards have risen across the board.

4. Seán Boylan.

5. Spare a thought for the Croke Park Residents, who unaccustomed to our ways didn't notice a big stadium beside their house when they moved in … They are still awaiting a reply to the stern letter they sent to the Black and Tans regarding the dreadful racket on Bloody Sunday.

6. GAA fashion has at last moved on. So long mired in the millinery department, from where hats of finest crepe paper and cheapest fake fur dyed in the county colours were foisted on us, the GAA afficionado now just stretches the county jersey over his gut or her bust. A small price to pay for dignity.

7. At the risk of a stern letter from Joe Lennon, let us say that the tackle in Gaelic football remains as yet a nebulous and poorly defined thing, a subtlety appreciated by followers of the game and envied by those lamenting the passing of the tackle from Premiership life entirely.

8. The fact that my seven-year-old could wander over to Johnny Magee of Dublin while he was practising free kicks in Parnell Park. Instead of calling security he bent and had a chat, signed a programme, endured her asking 'which one are you' and then went back to his free kicks. That doesn't happen at Manchester United.

9. Maurice Fitzgerald's equalising sideline kick against Dublin in Thurles.

10. Breakthrough in physics. The greatest recorded rate of deceleration in history was established by a GAA team this year. The Kilkenny hurlers awoke one Sunday morning as perhaps the best team in history and went to bed that night wondering if they'd get any All Stars. Ladies and gentlemen, nobody has gone backwards faster or further than these brave men.

11. The unbearability of life since England hammered Germany, is the apocalypse upon us?

12. Limerick's hurling renaissance.

13. Because the GAA is still a world where you can ask a player if his family were GAA oriented, and he will say yes his uncle played for Galway, and you will ask what his name was, and he will say blankly, Uncle Frank.

14. Eamon Coleman.

15. Razzmatazz. We ain't got it.

16. Post Taylor report. I don't think there is anywhere in the Premiership where one can feel the pure claustrophobia, the groin in buttock intimacy with strangers, the airless, breathless fear that one can experience in the tunnel under the stand in Páirc Uí Chaoimh.

17. The smell of fried onions.

18. Kevin Broderick's point.

19. Vinnie Murphy's entrances.

20. Peter Canavan's exits.

21. Yerra ye're only a back-door team. Only innate contrarians like the Gaels could yearn for years for a system which allows their team more than one match a year and then when it arrives christen it the back-door system and use the term as a weapon of derision.

22. Isn't Richard Dunne really a soccer player trapped in the body of a junior B full back? Or a tree?

Striking out … Deirdre Hughes of Tipperary hits the ball toward the Kilkenny goal during the All-Ireland Camogie final at Croke Park. Tipperay beat Kilkenny 4–13 to 1–6. Photograph: Cyril Byren

23. David Bloody Beckham. Imagine if GAA players chose to name their children after where they were conceived. What's the Irish for Mondeo? Primera?

24. The Westmeath footballers.

25. Larry O' Gorman interviews. The only white man in Wexford to call everyone else brother. Big ups to Larry and his posse.

26. GAA players don't pull their jerseys over their faces while celebrating a goal. What's all that about?

27. The strange odyssey of the Cork minor hurlers.

28. The evangelisation of Mullinahone

29. Fowler and Houllier. Fowlier and Houller. Howler and Foullier. Who really cares if they've fallen out, there's always a millionaire replacement for either of them waiting in the wings.

30. John O'Mahony and Mickileen Donnellan.

That matters.

31. Micheal Ó Muircheartaigh.

32. ITV's Coverage. Premiership Lite for the Ibiza set.

33. Only the GAA offers the chance to interview players while they completely embalm themselves in Wild Mist spray-on deodorant.

34. Social mobility. Westmeath will win an All-Ireland before West Ham cease to be mid-table purveyors of fancy football.

35. All Star controversies still to come!

36. The thought that this could be the last Premiership season before England win the World Cup and oppress us all with it.

37. Killarney on a summer's day. If you are reading this Frank Murphy, Killarney on a summer's day is nice.

38. Frank Murphy. The comb-over who rules the world.

39. The wonder of the new timing systems and substitution boards.
40. Linesmen who show same to all parts of the ground except the press box.
41. Journalists who see that there is one minute of injury time to be played and turn to each other in hilarious unison and say 'look they're substituting the goalie'.
42. Sligo's groovy new shirts.
43. The admirable conservatism of GAA haircuts.
44. Kieran McDonald's haircut.
45. Meath comebacks.
46. The word 'sliotar'.
47. The word 'schelping. As in Paidi's 'there was grand shhhcelping out there today'.
48. Sky Sport/Pay Per View/MUTV.
49. It just is.

THE FINAL WHISTLE

Granny Who?

We loved Onefootball.com's story last week on Gillingham striker Marlon King's efforts to prove he is eligible to play for the Republic of Ireland through his maternal grandmother … 'even though he does not know her name, where she is from, or whether she is still alive'.

'My grandmother's name is Joyce, but I don't know her surname and I don't know where she is from in Ireland. I met her once but I don't know if she is still alive,' said King.

A close family, then.

10 SEPTEMBER 2001
Planet Football Mary Hannigan

Keen on Keane

Sven-Goran Eriksson and Giovanni Trapattoni, the coaches of England and Italy respectively, were interviewed on Italian television last week about their teams' World Cup prospects. Trapattoni was highly complimentary about the English team, prompting the interviewer to ask him which English player he would most like in his side. 'Roy Keane of Manchester United,' he replied, instantly. Yep, he did.

17 SEPTEMBER 2001
Planet Football Mary Hannigan

When First-Class Tournaments Only Count

Like the individual who has had quite a remarkable hole in one, it is easy to imagine Jason Bohn thinking he had shattered all records when carding a spectacular 58 to win the Bayer Championship on the Canadian Tour last weekend. After all, the best that has been managed on the USPGA Tour are 59s by Al Geiberger, Chip Beck and David Duval.

But the official records apply only to 'first class professional tournaments' and I'm afraid the Bayer Championship doesn't fit that category. Meanwhile, as far back as January 1956, English Ryder Cup player Harry Weetman carded a 58 on the 6,171-yard Crohan Hurst Course in Croyden, Surrey.

The all-time record, however, is attributed to Alfred Edward Smith (1903–1985) who had a round of 55 (15 under par) on his 4,248-yard home course on 1 January 1936. His card read: Out – 423, 424, 343 = 29; In – 233, 332, 546 = 26. Incidentally, nine holes in 25 (433, 233, 142) was recorded by Bill Burke in a round of 57 on the 6,389-yard par-71 Normandie course in St Louis, Missouri on 20 May 1970. So there.

22 SEPTEMBER 2001
Dermot Gilleece's Golfing Log

SELECTED 2001 SPORTS RESULTS

ATHLETICS

WORLD ATHLETICS CHAMPIONSHIPS, EDMONTON, CANADA

100 METRES — Men

1	Greene Maurice	USA	9.82
2	Montgomery Tim	USA	9.85
3	Williams Bernard	USA	9.94

200 METRES — Men

1	Kedéri Konstadínos	GRE	20.04
2	Williams Christopher	JAM	20.20
3	Collins Kim	SKN	20.20

400 METRES — Men

1	Moncur Avard	BAH	44.64
2	Schultz Ingo	GER	44.87
3	Haughton Gregory	JAM	44.98
	Coman Tomas	IRL	45.90
	(6th in heat, failed to progress)		

800 METRES — Men

1	Bucher André	SUI	1:43.70
2	Bungei Wilfred	KEN	1:44.55
3	Czapiewski Pawel	POL	1:44.63
	Caulfield Daniel	IRL	1:47.23
	(4th in heat, failed to progress)		

1500 METRES — Men

1	El Guerrouj Hicham	MAR	3:30.68
2	Lagat Bernard	KEN	3:31.10
3	Maazouzi Driss	FRA	3:31.54
	Nolan James	IRL	3:42.84
	(10th in heat, failed to progress)		

5000 METRES — Men

1	Limo Richard	KEN	13:00.77
2	Saïdi-Sief Ali	ALG	13:02.16
3	Wolde Million	ETH	13:03.47
	Carroll Mark	IRL	13:37:27
	(10th in heat, failed to progress)		

10000 METRES — Men

1	Kamathi Charles	KEN	27:53.25
2	Mezgebu Assefa	ETH	27:53.97
3	Gebrselassie Haile	ETH	27:54.41

MARATHON — Men

1	Abera Gezahegne	ETH	2:12.42
2	Biwott Simon	KEN	2:12.43
3	Baldini Stefano	ITA	2:13.18

3000 METRES STEEPLECHASE — Men

1	Kosgei Reuben	KEN	8:15.16
2	Ezzine Ali	MAR	8:16.21
3	Barmasai Bernard	KEN	8:16.59

110 METRES HURDLES — Men

1	Johnson Allen	USA	13.04
2	García Anier	CUB	13.07
3	Dorival Dudley	HAI	13.25
	Coghlan Peter	IRL	13.61
	(5th in semi-final, failed to advance)		

400 METRES HURDLES — Men

1	Sánchez Felix	DOM	47.49
2	Mori Fabrizio	ITA	47.54
3	Tamesue Dai	JPN	47.89

HIGH JUMP — Men

1	Buss Martin	GER	2.36
2	Voronin Vyacheslav	RUS	2.33
3	Rybakov Yaroslav	RUS	2.33

POLE VAULT — Men

1	Markov Dmitri	AUS	6.05
2	Averbukh Aleksandr	ISR	5.85
3	Hysong Nick	USA	5.85

LONG JUMP — Men

1	Pedroso Iván	CUB	8.40
2	Stringfellow Savante	USA	8.24
3	Calado Carlos	POR	8.21

TRIPLE JUMP — Men

1	Edwards Jonathan	GBR	17.92
2	Olsson Christian	SWE	17.47
3	Spasovkhodskiy Igor	RUS	17.44

SHOT PUTT — Men

1	Godina John	USA	21.87
2	Nelson Adam	USA	21.24
3	Harju Arsi	FIN	20.93

DISCUS THROW — Men

1	Riedel Lars	GER	69.72
2	Alekna Virgilijus	LTU	69.40
3	Möllenbeck Michael	GER	67.61

HAMMER THROW — Men

1	Ziółkowski Szymon	POL	83.38
2	Murofushi Kojl	JPN	82.92
3	Konovalov Ilya	RUS	80.27

JAVELIN THROW — Men

1	Zelezny Jan	CZE	92.80
2	Parviainen Aki	FIN	91.31
3	Gatsioúdis Konstadinós	GRE	89.95
	McHugh Terry	IRL	75.49
	(11th in qualifying group, failed to progress		

20 KILOMETRES WALK — Men

1	Rasskazov Roman	RUS	1:20.31
2	Markov Ilya	RUS	1:20.33
3	Burayev Viktor	RUS	1:20.36
14	Heffernan Robert	IRL	1:25.02

50 KILOMETRES WALK — Men

1	Korzenlowski Robert	POL	3:42.08
2	García Jesús Angel	ESP	3:43.07
3	Hernandez Edgar	MEX	3:46.12
28	Costin Jamie	IRL	4:11.58

4 X 100 METRES — Men

1	United States	USA	37.96
2	South Africa	RSA	38.47
3	Trinidad and Tobago	TRI	38.58

4 X 400 METRES — Men

1	United States	USA	2:57.54
2	Bahamas	BAH	2:58.19
3	Jamaica	JAM	2:58.39
	Ireland	IRL	3:04.26
	(Rob Daly, Tom Comyns, Paul McKee, Tomas Coman, 7th in heat, new national record)		

1500 METRES WHEELCHAIR — Men

1	Gordian Aaron	MEX	3:08.04
2	Adams Jeff	CAN	3:08.13
3	Mendoza Saul	MEX	3:08.16

DECATHLON — Men

1	Dvorák Tomás	CZE	8902
2	Nool Erki	EST	8815
3	Macey Dean	GBR	8603

100 METRES — Women

1	Pintusevich-Block Zhanna	UKR	10.82
2	Jones Marion	USA	10.85
3	Thánou Ekateríni	GRE	10.91

200 METRES — Women

1	Jones Marion	USA	22.39
2	Ferguson Debbie	BAH	22.52
3	White Kelli	USA	22.56
	Reilly Sarah	IRL	23.24
	(3rd in heat 23.02 new national record; 6th in semi-final, failed to progress)		

400 METRES — Women

1	Mbacke Thiam Amy	SEN	49.86
2	Fenton Lorraine	JAM	49.88
3	Guevara Ana	MEX	49.97
	Shinkins Karen	IRL	51.66
	(6th in semi-final, failed to progress)		

800 METRES — Women

1	Mutola Maria de Lourdes	MOZ	1:57.17
2	Graf Stephanie	AUT	1:57.20
3	Vriesde Letitia	SUR	1:57.35

1500 METRES — Women

1	Szabo Gabriela	ROM	4:00.57
2	Szekely Violeta	ROM	4:01.70
3	Gorelova Natalya	RUS	4:02.40

5000 METRES — Women

1	Yegorova Olga	RUS	15:03.39
2	Domínguez Marta	ESP	15:06.59
3	Worku Ayelech	ETH	15:10.17
	Dennehy-Willis Breda	IRL	15:26.97
	(10th in heat, failed to progress)		
	McCambridge Maria	IRL	16:04.49
	(17th in heat, failed to progress)		
	English Una	IRL	16:26.15
	(18th in heat, failed to progress)		

10000 METRES — Women

1	Tulu Derartu	ETH	31:48.81
2	Adere Berhane	ETH	31:48.85
3	Wami Gete	ETH	31:49.98

MARATHON — Women

1	Simon Lidia	ROM	2:26.01
2	Tosa Reiko	JPN	2:26.06
3	Zakharova Svetlana	RUS	2:26.18
39	Duffy Teresa	IRL	2:43.33

100 METRES HURDLES — Women

1	Kirkland Anjanette	USA	12.42
2	Devers Gail	USA	12.54
3	Shishigina Olga	KAZ	12.58

400 METRES HURDLES — Women

1	Bidouane Nezha	MAR	53.34
2	Nosova Yuliya	RUS	54.27
3	Pernía Daimí	CUB	54.51

HIGH JUMP — Women

1	Cloete Hestrie	RSA	2.00
2	Babakova Inha	UKR	2.00
3	Bergqvist Kajsa	SWE	1.97

POLE VAULT — Women

1	Dragila Stacy	USA	4.75
2	Feofanova Svetlana	RUS	4.75
3	Pyrek Monika	POL	4.55

LONG JUMP — Women

1	May Fiona	ITA	7.02
2	Kotova Tatyana	RSU	7.01
3	Montalvo Niurka	ESP	6.88

TRIPLE JUMP — Women

1	Lebedeva Tatyana	RUS	15.25
2	Mbango Etone Françoise	CMR	14.60
3	Marinova Tereza	BUL	14.58

SHOT PUTT — Women

1	Korolchik Yanina	BLR	20.61
2	Kleinert-Schmitt Nadine	GER	19.86
3	Pavlysh Vita	UKR	19.41

DISCUS THROW — Women

1	Sadova Natalya	RUS	68.57
2	Zvereva Ellina	BLR	67.10
3	Grasu Nicoleta	ROM	66.24

HAMMER THROW — Women

1	Moreno Ylpsi	CUB	70.65
2	Kuzenkova Olga	RUS	70.61
3	Eagles Bronwyn	AUS	68.87

JAVELIN THROW — Women

1	Menéndez Osleidys	CUB	69.53
2	Manjani-Tzelíli Miréla	GRE	65.78
3	Bisset Sonia	CUB	64.69

20 KILOMETRES WALK — Women

1	Ivanova Olimpiada	RUS	1:27.48
2	Tsybulskaya Valentina	BLR	1:28.49
3	Perrone Elisabetta	ITA	1:28.56
13	Loughnane Olive	IRL	1:35.24
	O'Sullivan Gillian	IRL	
	(Disqualified for three fouls)		

4 X 100 METRES — Women

1	Unites States	USA	41.71
2	Germany	GER	42.32
3	France	FRA	42.39

4 X 400 METRES — Women

1	Jamaica	JAM	3:20.65
2	Germany	GER	3:21.97
3	Russia	RUS	3:24.92

800 METRES WHEELCHAIR — Women

1	Sauvage Louise	AUS	1:56.86
2	Hernandez Ariadne	MEX	1:56.99
3	Tsuchido Wakako	JPN	1:57.35

HEPTATHLON

1	Prokhorova Yelena	RUS	6694
2	Sazanovich Natalya	BLR	6539
3	Burrell Shelia	USA	6472

FORMULA ONE GRAND PRIX

4 March	Australian	Melbourne
1. M. Schumacher	GER	Ferrari
2. D. Coulthard	BRIT	McLaren Mercedes
3. R. Barrichello	BRA	Ferrari
5. H.-H. Frentzen	GER	Jordan Honda
J. Trulli	ITA	Jordan Honda
(did not finish)		

18 March	Malaysian	Kuala Lumpur
1. M. Schumacher	GER	Ferrari
2. R. Barrichello	BRA	Ferrari
3. D. Coulthard	BRIT	McLaren Mercedes
4. H.-H. Frentzen	GER	Jordan Honda
8. J. Trulli	ITA	Jordan Honda

1 April	**Brazilian**	**Interlagos**
1. D. Coulthard	BRIT	McLaren Mercedes
2. M. Schumacher	GER	Ferrari
3. N. Heidfeld	GER	Sauber-Petronas
5. J. Trulli	ITA	Jordan Honda
H.-H. Frentzen	GER	Jordan Honda
(did not finish)		

15 April	**San Marino Imola**	
1. R. Schumacher	GER	Williams BMW
2. D. Coulthard	BRIT	McLaren Mercedes
3. R. Barrichello	BRA	Ferrari
5. J. Trulli	ITA	Jordan Honda
6. H.-H. Frentzen	GER	Jordan Honda

29 April	**Spanish**	**Barcelona**
1. M. Schumacher	GER	Ferrari
2. J.P. Montoya	COL	Williams BMW
3. J. Villeneuve	CAN	BAR Honda
4. J. Trulli	ITA	Jordan Honda
H.-H .Frentzen	GER	Jordan Honda
(did not finish)		

13 May	**Austrian**	**A-1 Ring**
1. D. Coulthard	BRIT	McLaren Mercedes
2. M. Schumacher	GER	Ferrari
3. R. Barrichello	BRA	Ferrari
H.-H. Frentzen	GER	Jordan Honda
(did not finish)		
J. Trulli (disqualified)	ITA	Jordan Honda

27 May	**Monaco**	**Monaco**
1. M. Schumacher	GER	Ferrari
2. R. Barrichello	BRA	Ferrari
3. E. Irvine	NIRE	Jaguar Racing
H.H. Frentzen	GER	Jordan Honda
(did not finish)		
J. Trulli	ITA	Jordan Honda
(did not finish)		

10 June	**Canadian**	**Montreal**
1. R. Schumacher	GER	Williams BMW
2. M. Schumacher	GER	Ferrari
3. M. Hakkinen	FIN	McLaren Mercedes
7. R. Zonta	BRA	Jordan
J. Trulli	ITA	Jordan Honda
(did not finish)		

24 June	**European**	**Nürburgring**
1. M. Schumacher	GER	Ferrari
2. J.P. Montoya	COL	Williams BMW
3. D. Coulthard	BRIT	McLaren Mercedes
H.-H. Frentzen	GER	Jordan Honda
(did not finish)		
J. Trulli	ITA	Jordan Honda
(did not finish)		

1 July	**French**	**Magny Cours**
1. M. Schumacher	GER	Ferrari
2. R. Schumacher	GER	Williams BMW
3. R. Barrichello	BRA	Ferrari
5. J. Trulli	ITA	Jordan Honda
8. H.-H. Frentzen	GER	Jordan Honda

15 July	**British**	**Silverstone**
1. M. Hakkinen	FIN	McLaren Mercedes
2. M. Schumacher	GER	Ferrari
3. R. Barrichello	BRA	Ferrari
7. H.-H. Frentzen	GER	Jordan Honda
J. Trulli	ITA	Jordan Honda
(did not finish)		

29 July	**German**	
1. R. Schumacher	GER	Williams BMW
3. R. Barrichello	BRA	Ferrari
3. J. Villeneuve	CAN	BAR Honda
J. Trulli	ITA	Jordan Honda
(did not finish)		
R. Zonta	BRA	Jordan Honda
(did not finish)		

19 August	Hungarian	Budapest
1. M. Schumacher	GER	Ferrari
2. R. Barrichello	BRA	Ferrari
3. D. Coulthard	BRIT	McLaren Mercedes
10. J. Alesi	FRA	Jordan Honda
J. Trulli	ITA	Jordan Honda
(did not finish)		

2 September	Belgian	Spa Francorchamps
1. M. Schumacher	GER	Ferrari
2. D. Coulthard	BRIT	McLaren Mercedes
3. G. Fischella	ITA	Bennetton Renault

6. J. Alesi	FRA	Jordan Honda
J. Trulli	ITA	Jordan Honda
(did not finish)		

16 September	Italian	Monza
1. J.P. Montoya	COL	Williams BMW
2. R. Barrichello	BRA	Ferrari
3. R. Schumacher	GER	Williams BMW
8. J. Alesi	FRA	Jordan Honda
J. Trulli	ITA	Jordan Honda
(did not finish)		

GAELIC FOOTBALL

Provincial Championship Ulster
Preliminaries

Donegal	1–16	Fermanagh	2–13

Replay

Fermanagh	1–09	Donegal	0–11

Quarter-finals

Armagh	1–9	Tyrone	1–14
Cavan	1–14	Down	2–10
Antrim	0–9	Derry	1–11
Fermanagh	0–14	Monaghan	2–10

Semi-finals

Derry	0–14	Tyrone	3–07
Cavan	0–13	Monaghan	0–11

Final

Cavan	1–11	Tyrone	1–13

Provincial Championship Leinster
Preliminaries

Longford	1–11	Louth	1–09
Laois	0–18	Wexford	0–14
Carlow	1–09	Wicklow	2–06

Replay

Carlow	0–09	Wicklow	0–08

Quarter-finals

Laois	0–12	Offaly	1–13
Dublin	2–19	Longford	1–13
Carlow	1–11	Kildare	0–19
Meath	2–12	Westmeath	1–14

Semi-finals

Dublin	1–12	Offaly	0–13
Kildare	1–11	Meath	1–16

Final

Dublin	0–14	Meath	2–11

Provincial Championship Connacht
Preliminaries

New York	1–09	Roscommon	3–13

First Round

Galway	3–24	Leitrim	3–05

Semi-finals

Roscommon	2–12	Galway	0–14
Mayo	1–12	Sligo	1–11

Final

Roscommon	2–10	Mayo	1–12

Provincial Championship Munster

First Round
Cork	3–16	Waterford	1–07
Kerry	3–17	Tipperary	1–04

Semi-finals
Kerry	1–15	Limerick	0–10
Clare	1–10	Cork	2–11

Final
Cork	1–13	Kerry	0–19

All-Ireland Championship Qualifiers

Round 1
(involving teams beaten at first round stage in the provincial championships)

Louth	0–13	Tipperary	1–08
Antrim	0–13	Leitrim	1–08
Armagh	1–13	Down	2-04
Carlow	3–11	Waterford	1–10
Westmeath	1–19	Wexford	1–19
Longford	0–11	Wicklow	1–14

Replay
Westmeath	1–15	Wexford	1–08
Donegal	0–15	Fermanagh	1–06

Round 2
(involving winning teams from qualifing round 1 versus teams beaten at the stage in the provincial championships)

Antrim	0–07	Derry	0–10
Carlow	2–07	Sligo	2–14
Limerick	0–07	Westmeath	0–17
Louth	0–12	Offaly	1–08
Wicklow	1–09	Galway	3–12
Kildare	1–17	Donegal	1–16
Monaghan	0–10	Armagh	2–12
Laois	0–13	Clare	1–08

Round 3
(involving winning teams from qualifier round 2)

Galway	0–13	Armagh	0–12
Sligo	0–16	Kildare	0–15
Laois	0–08	Derry	1–08
Louth	0–13	Westmeath	1–13

Round 4
(involving winning teams from qualifier round 3 and beaten provincial finalists)

Westmeath	1–14	Mayo	0–16
Galway	1–14	Cork	1–10
Sligo	0–12	Dublin	3–17
Derry	1–14	Cavan	2–07

Quarter-finals
Kerry	1–14	Dublin	2–11
Galway	0–14	Roscommon	1–05
Derry	1–09	Tyrone	0–07
Meath	2–12	Westmeath	3–09

Replays
Kerry	2–12	Dublin	1–12
Meath	2–10	Westmeath	0–11

Semi-finals
Galway	1–14	Derry	1–11
Kerry	0–5	Meath	2–14

Final
Galway	0–17	Meath	0–8

All-Ireland Minor Final
Tyrone	0–15	Dublin	1–12

Replay
Tyrone	2–11	Dublin	0–6

All-Ireland Club Final
Crossmolina	0–16	Nemo Rangers	1–12

All-Ireland Colleges Final
St Patrick's Navan	2–10	St Jarlath's Tuam	2–08

National League

Division One
Semi-finals
Mayo	0–16	Roscommon	1–10
Galway	2–12	Sligo	0–11

Final
Mayo	0–13	Galway	0–12

National League

Division Two
Final
Westmeath	2–11	Cork	2–13

HURLING

Provincial Championship Ulster

Preliminaries

Down	1–16	New York	2–12

Semi-finals

Derry	1–24	London	0–12
Antrim	1–10	Down	2–14

Final

Derry	1–17	Down	3–10

Provincial Championship Leinster

Preliminaries

Carlow	2–13	Westmeath	0–14
Kildare	5–11	Wicklow	2–16
Meath	2–25	Kildare	2–24
Laois	2–17	Carlow	1–04
Laois	3–16	Meath	1–07

Quarter-finals

Dublin	2–11	Laois	1–15

Semi-finals

Laois	0–10	Wexford	0–17
Kilkenny	3–21	Offaly	0–18

Final

Wexford	0–12	Kilkenny	2–19

Provincial Championship Munster

Preliminaries

Cork	1–15	Limerick	1–16

Semi-finals

Tipperary	0–15	Clare	0–14
Waterford	2–14	Limerick	4–11

Final

Tipperary	2–16	Limerick	1–17

All-Ireland Championship

Quarter-final

Galway	4–23	Derry	1–11
Wexford	4–10	Limerick	2–15

Semi-final

Tipperary	1–16	Wexford	3–10

Replay

Tipperary	3–12	Wexford	0–10
Galway	2–15	Kilkenny	1–13

Final

Tipperary	2–18	Galway	2–15

All-Ireland Minor Final

Cork	2–10	Galway	1–08

All-Ireland Under 21 Final

Limerick	0–17	Wexford	2–10

All-Ireland Senior Camogie Final

Tipperary	4–13	Kilkenny	1–06

All-Ireland Junior Camogie Final

Tipperary	4–16	Offaly	1–07

All-Ireland Club Hurling Final

St Mary's Athenry	3–24	Graigue-Ballycallan	2–19

All-Ireland Colleges Final

St Colman's		Gort	
Fermoy	2–10	CS	2–07

National Hurling League

Semi-finals

Tipperary	2–19	Galway	1–15
Clare	2–21	Kilkenny	3–08

Final

Tipperary	1–19	Clare	0–17

GOLF PROFESSIONAL

US MASTERS

272	T. Woods	70	66	68	68
274	D. Duval	71	66	70	67
275	P. Mickelson	67	69	69	70
284	D. Clarke	72	67	72	73
287	P. Harrington	75	69	72	71

US OPEN

276	R. Goosen	66	70	69	71
276	M. Brooks	72	64	70	70
	(Goosen won play-off)				
277	S. Cink	69	69	67	72
278	R. Mediate	71	68	67	72
288	D. Clarke	74	71	71	72
288	P. Harrington	73	70	71	74

BRITISH OPEN

274	D. Duval (US)	69	73	65	67
277	N. Fasth ((Swd)	69	69	72	67
278	E. Els (SA)	71	71	67	69
278	D. Clarke (NI)	70	69	69	70
278	M.A. Jimenez (Spa)	69	72	67	70
278	I. Woosnam (Wal)	72	68	67	71
278	B. Langer (Ger)	71	69	67	71
278	B. Mayfair (US)	69	72	67	70
280	D. Smyth (Ire)	74	65	70	71
286	P. Harrington (Ire)	75	66	74	71
289	P. McGinley (Ire)	69	72	72	76

USPGA CHAMPIONSHIP

265	D. Toms	66	65	65	69
266	P. Mickelson	66	66	66	68
268	S. Lowery	67	67	66	68
278	P. McGinley	68	72	71	67

IRISH OPEN

266	C. Montgomerie	63	69	68	66
271	N. Fasth	68	71	69	63
271	P. Harrington	67	72	68	64
271	D. Clarke	70	72	65	64
273	T. Bjorn	66	69	72	66

EUROPEAN OPEN

273	D. Clarke	68	68	71	66
276	T. Bjorn	73	71	65	67
276	I. Woosnam	69	66	73	68
276	P. Harrington	70	67	69	70
277	M. Movland	70	71	68	68

IRISH SENIORS OPEN

207	S. Ebihara	65	71	71
208	S. Owen	68	65	75
209	D. Durnian	71	67	71
209	B. Gallacher	69	68	72

IRISH WOMEN'S OPEN

200	R. Carriedo	68	66	66
201	S. Gustafson	69	67	65
202	L. Davies	70	67	65
202	A. Sanchez	66	68	68

AMATEUR GOLF – MEN

IRISH CLOSE CHAMPIONSHIP

G. McNeill (Waterford) bt S. Browne (Hermitage) at 20th

IRISH AMATEUR OPEN

277	R. McEvoy (England)	69	67	68	73
277	M. Hoey (Shandon Park)	70	69	71	67

(McEvoy won on 3rd play-off hole)

IRISH SENIORS AMATEUR OPEN

153	D. Jackson (Clandeboye)	77	76
154	D. White (Moate)	77	77

WEST OF IRELAND CHAMPIONSHIP

M. McDermott (Stackstown) bt M. Hoey (Shandon Park) 2 and 1

EAST OF IRELAND CHAMPIONSHIP

283	K. Kearney (Roscommon)	72	74	65	72
287	M. McDermott (Stackstown)	74	68	72	73
287	P. Murray (Kinsale)	72	68	77	70

SOUTH OF IRELAND CHAMPIONSHIP

J. Kehoe (UCD/Birr) bt S. Browne (Hermitage) 6 and 4

NORTH OF IRELAND CHAMPIONSHIP

S. Paul (Tandragee) bt G. McDowell (Rathmore) 2 and 1

AMATEUR GOLF – WOMEN

IRISH LADIES CLOSE

A. Coffey (Warrenpoint) bt C. Coughlan (Cork) 4 and 3

IRISH LADIES AMATUER OPEN

214	A. Laing (Vale of Leven)	71	70	73
218	V. Laing (Mussleborough)	72	72	74

NATIONAL HUNT RACES

AIG EUROPE CHAMPION HURDLE (Grade 1)

£66,500. Abt 2m. Leopardstown, 21 January 2001

1 Istrabraq (b'g by Sadler's Wells – Betty's Secret) J.P. McManus 9 11-10 (4/11 fav) C.F. Swan

2 Mantles Prince 7 11-10 (1/1) N. Williamson

3 Penny Rich 7 11-10 (50/1) D.J. Casey

Trainer: A.P. O'Brien

Distance: 4½l, 2l.

HENNESSY COGNAC GOLD CUP (Grade 1)

£65,450. Abt 3m. Leopardstown, 4 February 2001

1 Florida Pearl (b'g by Floriday Son – Ice Pearl) Mrs Violet O'Leary 9 12-0 (5/4 fav) R. Johnson

2 Alexander Banquet 8 12-0 (20/1) B.J. Geraghty

3 Doran's Pride 12 12-0 (11/1) P.G. Hourigan

Trainer: W.P. Mullins

Distance: 2l, 9l.

MARTELL GRAND NATIONAL CHASE (Grade 3) (Class A)

4m 4f Showcase Handicap Chase, Aintree, 7 April 2001

1 Red Marauder (ch'g by Gunner B – Cover Your Money) N.B. Mason 10–11 (33/1) R. Guest

2 Smarty 10–0 (16/1) T.J. Murphy

3 Blowing Wind 10–9 16/1 A.P. McCoy

4 Papillon 11–5 14/1 R. Walsh

Trainer: N.B. Mason

Distance: Dist, dist

POWERS GOLD LABEL IRISH GRAND NATIONAL (Grade A)

£81,500. 3m abt 5f. Fairyhouse, 6 May 2001

1 David's Lad (b'g by Yashgan – Cool Nora) Edie Joe's Racing Syndicate 7 10–0 (10/1) T.J. Murphy

2 Rathbawn Prince 9 10–13 (25/1) K.A. Kelly

3 Sheltering 9 10–1 (9/1) N. Williamson

4 King's Valley 10–0 (14/1) P. Carberry

Trainer: A.J. Martin

Distance: 1½l, 11l, sht hd.

FLAT RACING

SAGITTA 2,000 GUINEAS STAKES (SHOWCASE RACE) (Group 1)

£291,900 1m. Newmarket, 5 May 2001

1 Golan (bc Spectrum – Highland Gift) Lord Weinstock 9–0 (11/1) K. Fallon

2 Tamburlaine 9–0 (12/1) R. Hughes

3 Frenchman's Bay 9–0 (14/1) Pat Eddery

Trainer: Sir M. Stoute

Distance: 1½l, nk

SAGITTA 1,000 GUINEAS STAKES (SHOWCASE RACE) (Group 1)

£276,900 1m. Newmarket, 6 May 2001

1 Ameerat (b f Mark Of Esteem – Walimu) Sheik Ahmed Al Maktoum 9–0 (11/1) P. Robinson

2 Muwakleh 9–0 (13/2) L. Dettori

3 Toroca 9–0 (10/1) M.J. Kinane

Trainer: M.A. Jarvis

Distance: nk, 1½l

ENTENMANN'S IRISH 2,000 GUINEAS (Group 1)

£126,675 1m. Curragh, 26 May 2001

1 Black Minnaloushe (b'c Storm Cat – Coral Dance) Mrs J. Magnier 9–0 (20/1) J.P. Murtagh

2 Mozart (20/1) J.A. Heffernan

3 Minardi (2/1) M.J. Kinane

Trainer: A.P. O'Brien

Distance: 2l, ¾l

ENTENMANN'S IRISH 1,000 GUINEAS (Group 1)

£126,675 1m. Curragh, 27 May 2001

1 Imagine (b'f by Sadler's Wells – Doff The Derby) Mrs J. Magnier 9–0 (16/1) J.A. Heffernan

2 Crystal Music 9–0 (9/2 fav) L. Dettori

3 Toroca 9–0 (11/2) M.J. Kinane

Trainer: A.P. O'Brien

Distance: 2l, 2l.

VODAFONE DERBY STAKES (3–Y–O Group 1)

£580,000 1m 4f 10yds. Epsom, 9 June 2001

1 Galileo (b'c Saddler's Wells – Urban Sea) Mrs J. Magnier 9–0 (11/4 jt fav) M.J. Kinane

2 Golan 9–0 (11/4 jt fav) P. Eddery

3 Tobougg 9–0 (9/1) F. Dettori

Trainer: A.P. O'Brien

Distance: 3½l, NK

BUDWEISER IRISH DERBY (Group 1)

£510,865. 1m abt 4f. Curragh, 1 July 2001

1 Galileo (b'c by Sadler's Wells – Urban Sea) Mrs J. Magnier 9–0 (4/11fav) M.J. Kinane

2 Morshdi 9–0 (20/1) P. Robinson

3 Golan 9–0 (4/1) K. Fallon

Trainer: A.P. O'Brien

Distance: 4l, 4l.

KING GEORGE VI AND QUEEN ELIZABETH DIAMOND STAKES (Group 1)

£712,950.00 1m 4f. Ascot, 28 July 2001

1 Galileo (b'c by Sadler's Wells – Urban Sea) Mrs J. Magnier 8–9 (1/2) M.J. Kinane
2 Fantastic Light 9–7 (7/2) L. Dettori
3 Hightori 9–7 (22/1) G. Mosse

Trainer: A.P. O'Brien

Distance: 2l, 1l.

IRELAND THE FOOD ISLAND CHAMPION STAKES (Group 1)

£825,000.00 1m 2f. Leopardstown, 8 September 2001

1. Fantastic Light (b'h by Rahy – Jood) Godolphin 9–7 (9/4) L. Dettori
2. Gallileo 8–11 (4/11 fav) M.J. Kinane
3. Bachb 9–4 (20/1) J.A. Hoffeman

Trainer: Saeed Bin Suroor

Distance: Hd, 6l

RUGBY

SIX NATIONS CHAMPIONSHIP

Italy	22	Ireland	41
Wales	15	England	44
France	16	Scotland	6
Ireland	22	France	15
England	80	Italy	23
Scotland	28	Wales	28
Italy	19	France	30
England	43	Scotland	3
France	35	Wales	43
Scotland	23	Italy	19
Italy	23	Wales	33
England	48	France	19
Ireland	10	Scotland	32

LIONS TOUR OF AUSTRALIA

Lions	116	Western Australia	10
Lions	83	Queensland Presidents XV	6
Lions	42	Queensland Reds	8
Lions	25	Australia A	28
Lions	41	NSW Waraths	24
Lions	46	NSW Country	3
Lions	29	Australia	13
Lions	30	ACT Brumbies	28
Lions	14	Australia	35
Lions	23	Australia	29

EUROPEAN CUP

Leicester	34	Stade Francais	30

EUROPEAN SHIELD

Harlequins	42	Narbonne	33

ALL IRELAND LEAGUE

	Winners	Runners-up
Division 1	Dungannon	Cork Constitution
Division 2	UCD	Carlow
Division 3	Thomond	Barnhall

LEINSTER SCHOOLS SENIOR CUP FINAL

Terenure College	21	Blackrock College	19

MUNSTER SCHOOLS SENIOR CUP FINAL

Rockwell College	17	St Munchin's College	5

ULSTER SCHOOLS SENIOR CUP FINAL

Methodist	15	RBAI	10

CONNACHT SCHOOLS SENIOR CUP FINAL

Garbally College	13	Portumna CS	12

SOCCER

WORLD CUP QUALIFYING Group 2

2001 RESULTS

Cyprus	0	Rep of Ireland	4
Andorra	0	Rep of Ireland	3
Rep of Ireland	3	Andorra	1
Rep of Ireland	1	Portugal	1
Rep of Ireland	1	Holland	0
Rep of Ireland	4	Cyprus	0

FRIENDLY INTERNATIONAL

Rep of Ireland	2	Croatia	2

NATIONAL LEAGUE

Premier Division – Bohemians

Runners-up Shelbourne

First Division – Dundalk

Runners-up Monaghan

FAI CUP FINAL

Bohemians	1	Longford Town	0

LEAGUE CUP FINAL

St Patrick's Athletic	3	UCD	1
UCD	2	St Patrick's Athletic	2

(St Patrick's Athletic win 5-3 on aggregate)

IRISH CUP FINAL

Glentoran	1	Linfield	0

IRISH LEAGUE –

Linfield

Runners-up Glenavon

ENGLAND

Premiership: Manchester Utd. Runners-up: Arsenal

Relegated: Manchester City, Coventry, Bradford

Division One: Fulham. Runners-up: Blackburn

Play-off final: Bolton 3, Preston 0

Division Two: Millwall. Runners-up: Rotherham

Play-off final: Reading 2, Walsall 3

Division Three: Brighton. Runners-up: Cardiff

Play-off final: Blackpool 4, Leyton Orient 2

FA CUP FINAL

Liverpool	2	Arsenal	1

LEAGUE CUP FINAL

Liverpool	1	Birmingham	1

(Liverpool won 5–4 on penalties)

SCOTLAND

Premier League: Celtic. Runners-up: Rangers

First Division: Livingston. Runners-up: Ayr

Second Division: Patrick. Runners-up: Arbroath

Third Division: Hamilton. Runners-up: Cowdenbath

SCOTTISH CUP FINAL

Celtic	3	Hibernian	0

LEAGUE CUP FINAL

Celtic	3	Kilmarnock	0

CHAMPIONS LEAGUE FINAL

Bayern Munich	1	Valencia	1

(Bayern won 5-4 on penalties)

UEFA CUP FINAL

Liverpool	5	Alaves	4

TENNIS

AUSTRALIAN OPEN, MELBOURNE, 15-28 JANUARY 2001

Men's Singles Semi-Finals

Andre Agassi USA (6) bt. Patrick Rafter AUS (12) 7–5, 2–6, 6–7 (5-7), 6–2, 6–3.

Arnaud Clement FRA (15) bt. Sebastien Grosjean FRA (16) 5–7, 2–6, 7–6 (7-4), 7–5, 6–2.

Men's Singles Final

Andre Agassi USA (6) bt. Arnaud Clement FRA (15) 6–4, 6–2, 6–2.

Women's Singles Semi-Finals

Martina Hingis SUI (1) bt. Venus Williams USA (3) 6–1, 6–1.

Jennifer Capriati USA (12) bt. Lindsay Davenport USA (2) 6–3, 6–4.

Women's Singles Final

Jennifer Capriati USA (12) bt. Martina Hingis SUI (1) 6–4, 6–3.

Men's Doubles Semi-Finals

Jonas Bjorkman SWE and Todd Woodbridge AUS (4) bt. Wayne Arthurs AUS and Nehad Zimonjic YUG (1) 4–6, 6–0, 6–2.

Byron Black ZIM and David Prinosil GER (14) bt. Justin Gimelstob and Scott Humphries USA (15) 7–6 (7-2) 6–1.

Men's Doubles Final

Jonas Bjorkman SWE and Todd Woodbridge AUS (4) bt. Byron Black ZIM and David Prinosil GER (14) 6 and 1, 5–7, 6–4, 6–4.

Women's Doubles Semi-Finals

Serena Williams and Venus Williams USA bt. Martina Hingis and Monica Seles USA 7–5, 6–2.

Lindsay Davenport and Corina Morariu USA (7) bt. Nicole Arendt USA and Ai Sugiyama JPN (2) 7–5, 6–2.

Women's Doubles Final

Serena Williams and Venus Williams USA bt. Lindsay Davenport and Corina Morariu USA (7) 6–2, 4–6, 6–4.

Mixed Doubles Semi-Finals

Ellis Ferreira RSA and Corina Morariu USA (3) bt. Robbie Koenig RSA and Meghann Shaughnessy USA 6–4, 7–5.

Joshua Eagle AUS and Barbara Schett AUT (4) bt. Todd Woodbridge and Rennae Stubbs AUS (1) 6–2, 7–6 (7–5).

Mixed Doubles Final

Ellis Ferreira RSA and Corina Morariu USA (3) bt. Joshua Eagle AUS and Barbara Schett AUT (4) 6–1, 6–3.

FRENCH OPEN, ROLAND GARROS, PARIS, 28 May–10 June 2001

Men's Singles Semi-finals

Gustavo Kuerten BRA (1) bt. Juan Carlos Ferrero SPA (4) 6–4, 6–4, 6–3

Alex Corretja SPA (13) bt. Sebastien Grosjean FRA (10) 7–6, 6–4, 6–4

Men's Singles Final

Gustavo Kuerten BRA (1) bt. Alex Corretja SPA (13) 6–7, 7–5, 6–2, 6–0

Women's Singles Semi-finals

Jennifer Capriati USA (4) def Martina Hingis SUI (1) 6–4, 6–3

Kim Clijsters BEL (12) bt. Justine Henin BEL (14) 2–6, 7–5, 6–3

Women's Singles Final

Jennifer Capriati USA (4) bt. Kim Clijsters BEL (12) 1–6, 6–4, 12–10

Men's Doubles Semi-finals

Petr Pala and Pavel Vizner (13) CZE bt. Arnaud Clement and Nicolas Escude FRA 7–5, 6–4

Mahesh Bhupathi IND and Leander Paes IND bt. Michael Hill AUS (11) and Jeff Tarango USA (11) 6–3, 3–6, 6–4

Men's Doubles Final

Mahesh Bhupathi and Leander Paes (Ind) bt. Petr Pala and Pavel Vizner CZH (13) 7–6, 6–3

Women's Doubles Semi-finals

Virginia Ruano-Pascual SPA and Paola Suarez (2) ARG bt. Justine Henin BEL and Elena Tatarkova UKR 6–2, 6–0

Jelena Dokic YUG and Conchita Martinez (16) SPA bt. Lisa Raymond USA and Rennae Stubbs (1), AUS 7–5, 6–2

Women's Doubles Final

Virginia Ruano Pascual SPA and Paola Suarez (Arg) (2) bt. Jelena Dokic YUG and Conchita Martinez SPA (16) 6–2, 6–1

Mixed Doubles Semi-finals

Paola Suarez ARG and Jaime Oncins BRA bt. Elena Likhovtseva, RUS and Mahesh Bhupathi IND 7–5, 4–6, 6–2

Mixed Doubles Final

Virginia Ruano-Pascual and Tomas Carbonell SPA bt. Paola Suarez (Arg) Jaime Oncins, Brazil 7–5, 63

ALL-ENGLAND CHAMPIONSHIPS, WIMBLEDON, 25 June–8 July 2001

Men's Singles Semi-finals

Goran Ivanisevic CRO bt. Tim Henman GBR (6) 7–5, 6–7, 0–6, 7–6, 6–3

Patrick Rafter AUS (3) bt. Andre Agassi USA (2) 2–6, 6–3, 3–6, 6–2, 8–6

Men's Singles Final

Goran Ivanisevic CRO bt. Patrick Rafter AUS (3) 6–3, 3–6, 6–3, 2–6, 9–7

Women's Singles Semi-finals

Justine Henin BEL (8) bt. Jennifer Capriati USA (4) 2–6, 6–4, 6–2

Venus Williams USA (2) bt. Lindsay Davenport USA (3) 6–2, 6–7, 6–1

Women's Singles Final

Venus Williams USA (2) bt. Justine Henin BEL (8) 6–1, 3–6, 6–0

Men's Doubles Semi-finals

Jiri Novak CZE (3) and David Rikl CZE (3) bt. Bob Bryan USA (15) and Mike Bryan USA (15) 6–4, 7–6, 4–6, 6–1

Donald Johnson USA (4) and Jared Palmer USA (4) bt. Max Mirnyi BLR and Vladimir Voltchkov BLR

Men's Doubles Final

Donald Johnson USA (4) and Jared Palmer USA (4) bt. Jiri Novak CZE (3) and David Rikl CZE (3) 6–4, 4–6, 6–3, 7–6

Women's Doubles Semi-finals

Lisa Raymond USA (1) and Rennae Stubbs AUS (1) bt. Kimberly Po-Messerli USA (5) and Nathalie Tauziat FRA (5) 6–3, 7–5

Kim Clijsters BEL (9) and Ai Sugiyama JPN (9) bt. Virginia Ruano Pascual ESP (2) and Paola Suarez ARG (2) 6–4, 6–4

Women's Doubles Final

Lisa Raymond USA (1) and Rennae Stubbs AUS (1) bt. Kim Clijsters BEL (9) and Ai Sugiyama JPN (9) 6–4, 6–3

Mixed Doubles Semi-finals

Leos Friedl CZE and Daniela Hantuchova SVK bt. David
Rikl CZE (15) and Karina Habsudova SVK (15) 6–2,
5–7, 6–3

Mike Bryan USA and Liezel Huber RSA bt. Mahesh
Bhupathi IND (4) and Elena Likhovtseva RUS (4)
6–2, 6–2

Mixed Doubles Finals

Leos Friedl CZE and Daniela Hantuchova SVK bt. Mike
Bryan USA and Liezel Huber RSA 4–6, 6–3, 6–2

US OPEN, 27 August–9 September

Men's Singles Semi-final

Lleyton Hewitt AUS (4) bt. Yevgeny Kafelnikov RUS (7)
6–1, 6–2, 6–1

Pete Sampras USA (10) bt. Marat Safin RUS (3) 6–3,
7–6, 6–3

Men's Singles Final

Lleyton Hewitt AUS (4) bt. Pete Sampras USA (10)
7–6, 6–1, 6–1

Women's Singles Semi-finals

Serena Williams USA (10) bt. Martina Hingis SUI (1)
6–3, 6–2

Venus Williams USA (4) bt. Jennifer Capriati USA (2)
6–4, 6–2

Women's Singles Final

Venus Williams USA (4) bt. Serena Williams USA (10)
6–2, 6–4

Men's Doubles Semi-finals

Wayne Black ZIM (14) and Kevin Ullyett ZIM (14) bt.
Paul Haarhuis NED (15) and Sjeng
Schalken NED (15) 6–3, 6–4

Donald Johnson USA (2) and Jared Palmer USA bt. Max
Mirnyi BLR (4) and Sandon Stolle AUS (4) 6–4, 3–6,
6–3

Men's Doubles Final

Wayne Black ZIM (14) and Kevin Ullyett ZIM (14) bt.
Donald Johnson USA (2) Jared Palmer USA (2) 7–6,
2–6, 6–3

Women's Doubles Semi-finals

Lisa Raymond USA (1) and Rennae Stubbs AUS (1) bt.
Cara Black ZIM (3) and Elena Likhovtseva RUS (3)
6–3, 6–4

Kimberly Po-Messerli USA (4) and Nathalie
Tauziat FRA (4) bt. Sandrine Testud FRA and Roberta
Vinci ITA 4–6, 7–5, 6–0

Women's Doubles Final

Lisa Raymond USA (1) and Rennae Stubbs AUS (1) bt.
Kimberly Po-Messerli USA (4) and Nathalie
Tauziat FRA (4) 6–2, 5–7, 7–5

Mixed Doubles Semi-finals

Rennae Stubbs AUS (1) and Todd Woodbridge AUS (1)
bt. Ai Sugiyama JPN (5) and Ellis Ferreira RSA (5)
6–3, 6–4

Lisa Raymond USA (2) and Leander Paes IND (2) bt.
Kimberly Po-Messerli USA (3) and Donald
Johnson USA (3) 7–6, 6–4

Mixed Doubles Finals

Rennae Stubbs AUS (1) and Todd Woodbridge AUS (1)
bt. Lisa Raymond USA (2) and Leander Paes IND (2)
6–4, 5–7, 7–6

QUOTES OF THE YEAR

January

'The old bloody nonsense of burying their heads in the sand.'
Kildare manager Mick O'Dwyer being forthright in his opinion of the GAA's attitude to the Gaelic Players' Association.

'I got fed up wriggling around in my shorts looking for my balls.'
Andre Agassi explains why he has switched from baggy shorts, which he pioneered, to the more classic tight variety.

'Rather than making any comment I'd like to talk to the player first, but he let us down badly.'
Bray Wanderers manager Pat Devlin after Wesley Charles was sent off in a game against St Patrick's Athletic.

'Myself, Michael Galwey, Paddy Johns, Peter Clohessy, we're a dying breed. We all went to the school of hard knocks and the university of getting the s*** kicked out of us. I used to go to Paris and I was bricking it. I was crapping myself when we played the All Blacks as well.'
Gary Halpin describes how he felt playing international rugby when Ireland were ostensibly amateur against some great sides who had already moved well into professionalism.

February

'International rugby is incredibly clean because it is so fast and there is no time to get embroiled in anything off the ball.'
Perhaps stretching credibility itself, Martin Johnson returns from a five-week suspension all gung-ho about clean play.

'There are no rules.'
Former Phalangist and out going IOC president Juan Samaranch to the candidates campaigning to replace him.

'The sport is so corrupt now, I wouldn't want my children doing it.'
Drug banned Linford Christie on the current state of athletics.

'It is hard to perceive the incredible disruption these events cause to the lives of locals, with people urinating and vomiting in our gardens, the constant knocking and tapping on doors and peering through the windows of terraced houses.'
The Croke Park Residents Alliance, for obvious reasons, object to the playing of other sports in the stadium.

March

'Last year balls came out of trees and in Canada I hit a guy on the fly and made birdie.'
Tiger Woods explaining that even golfers with his natural talent occasionally have to rely on a little luck to win tournaments.

'Completing the championship next season would be a last resort.'
Six Nations chief executive Roger Pickering on the continuing problems which face rugby due to the foot-and-mouth outbreak.

'... we cannot afford to allow the bedrock of the game to be undermined. This will happen if the chronic shortage of games is not addressed as a matter of urgency ...'

GAA director Liam Mulvihill on the association's problems over the same issue.

'The atmosphere around the place was terrible when he was about. It was just his presence — he didn't have any.'

Gerry Taggart reflects fondly on Lawrie McMenemy's days as Norn Iron manager.

April

'If Ronald Koeman had been sent off before he scored in that infamous defeat in Holland, we would have qualified and who knows what we might have achieved.'

And there was you thinking former England player David Platt had no sense of humour.

'Barrera must be prepared mentally for being hit harder than he ever thought possible. Hamed's power has the effect of a shock or electric current passing through your body.'

Wayne McCullough graphically illustrates why Hamed is rated the world's top featherweight boxer.

'Anybody who can do anything at Leicester, apart from make a jumper, has got to be a genius.'

Brian Clough pays tribute to Martin O'Neill.

'God is the righteous one and, because of him, losing by so many goals does not matter.'

American Samoa coach Tunoa Lui after his team's World Cup qualifier against Australia (0–31).

'Donal [Lenihan] tried to ring me this morning but I had the phone diverted so I didn't get the call initially. I was in bed.'

Malcolm O'Kelly showing a refreshingly laid-back attitude to the Lions selection on Wednesday morning.

'Statistics are like mini-skirts — they give you good ideas but hide the important things.'

Aberdeen manager Ebbe Skovdahl on lies, damned lies and ... mini-skirts?

'When we had our recent depressing run and did not win for seven matches, five of them were away from home. And we actually lost the two home games against Middlesbrough and Manchester City. So while things were bleak, they looked a lot bleaker than they really were.'

Earth to Bobby Robson?

June

'Lanny doesn't have to worry about offending his friends out here on tour, because he doesn't have any.'

Hal Sutton's bitter reaction to news that former Ryder Cup colleague Lanny Wadkins will be commenting for CBS television at the Memorial Tournament.

'You can keep talking about how you can be hungry. But what did this team win? One All-Ireland final. If any serious player is going to be happy to win one All-Ireland final, he probably wouldn't have won one in the first place... Winning is the be-all and end-all of serious sport, so hunger should be an automatic thing.'

Brian Cody, Kilkenny manager after winning the Leinster Senior Hurling Championship semi-final (Kilkenny 3–21, Offaly 0–18).

'My colleagues in the press ten don't like the way Mark Brooks conducts interviews. They say he's cranky, condescending and always complaining. Sounds to me like he's got the three attributes it takes to be a sports writer.'

Tim Rosaforte of Golf Digest, during the US Open.

'We gave it to them. The Lions will be sore boys tomorrow. I hope the Wallabies now give them a thrashing.'

New South Wales captain Phil Waugh in an on-pitch interview after being beaten 41–24 by the Lions. Ronan O'Gara was left needing eight stitches to two lacerations below his left eye.

'My initial aim was to clear the ruck, and I thought I did that quite effectively. I cleared the full-back but from then on I don't really know what happened. I got a bit of a hammering.'

Ronan O'Gara explains his version of the incident when he was punched 11 times by New South Wales full-back Duncan McRae, while still smarting from a ghastly red swelling which almost completely closed his left eye.

July

'Going to the start he had seen the band and coming back he picked them out again but the ground could have swallowed up this horse and he would still have won.'

Michael Kinane explains that steering Galileo past the band was his only anxious moment during the Derby at the Curragh.

'You know I've had a lot of experiences like that with the crowd. It doesn't seem that often that I'm the player the crowd wants to win. Who knows maybe there will be a day they'll root for me. But for me it's not an issue. I don't function this way where I have to have approval.'

Venus Williams comments on the crowd's lack of enthusiasm for her second consecutive Wimbledon title.

'It is the biggest mistake he will make in his life. He won't do it again. He will have a severe bollocking when I get in, but I am not going to sack him. He's a good lad, he just has to watch what he's doing.'

Ian Woosnam on caddy Myles Byrne after the Welshman was penalised two shots for having an extra club in his bag.

August

'I think it's absolutely a coincidence. We have no members from Hungary either, and none from Lithuania and Estonia.'

Sound, reasoned argument from a Texas lawyer, reacting to a report that four of the most expensive golf clubs in Dallas have no so-called minority players.

'No thought or comments on the referee. There was one outrageous decision. I'd said during the week that I was fearful about one decision going against us, but...'

Dublin manager, Tom Carr's comment on the referee, whose performance brought on a fit of bench rage in Carr during the second half of the draw in the Kerry–Dublin All-Ireland SFC quarter-final.

'Us Kerry people don't speak about referees.'

Kerry's Páidí Ó Sé is even more tight-lipped when asked to comment on the same referee's performance.

'I like them, other people seem to like them and I can fit into them. Honestly, there's even enough room for a spare ball and my score-card in the back pocket.'

Catrin Nilsmark on the hot-pants in which she caused quite a stir during the Women's British Open.

'I've heard some of Victoria's new album and it's frightening.'

David Beckham on Posh Spice's latest musical offering.

'When they put Clinton Morrison's name on an Irish team-sheet, they may as well have engraved RIP on Irish soccer's gravestone.'

St Patrick's Athletic manager Pat Dolan issues a hearty 'Cead Míle Fáilte' to the Crystal Palace man.

September

'If he can't find a club I'll bare my backside in Burton's window.'

Mick McCarthy on Jason McAteer's transfer prospects after scoring the only goal in the Republic of Ireland v Holland World Cup Group Two qualifier at Lansdowne Road.

'We have a group of players who could have gone very far in a World Cup, but we got knocked out.'

Louis van Gaal does a damn good Graham Taylor impression.

'Personally, this is the realisation of a dream. It means everything. You give your life to playing hurling. The ambition for everybody is to win an All-Ireland medal. I've been hurling with Tipp eight years and won nothing except a couple of national leagues. Winning a Munster championship and All-Ireland makes everything worthwhile, all the training, all the sacrifices.'

An emotional Tommy Dunne, Tipperary's captain, has finally fulfilled his goal and won an All-Ireland senior medal.

'I keep asking myself if I am letting my youth slip away because of football. I don't have fun. I don't go to the cinema or the theatre and never visit bars or discos. I'm always thinking ahead to the next training session or the next match. I suffer from stress, and I am permanently under pressure.'

So said Liverpool's Stephane '£30,00-a-week' Henchoz last week. Honest, we haven't made it up.

'One doctor told me that drink was like a tap that you could switch on or off. I was really pleased to hear that from a doctor, although I know now that once I turn on the tap, I leave it running.'

George Best on his battle with the booze.

'Look lads there are no excuses. Sometimes these things go for you. Days like today, they didn't.'

Seán Boylan, Meath manager, makes no excuse for his team's defeat by Galway in the All-Ireland Football final.

'Every player in our team lifted themselves today. To watch it was unbelievable. At the end, with the crowd cheering, the passes and us so far ahead, well, I don't know. You could never write a script for a game like that.'

Galway captain Gary Fahey, after leading his team to becoming All-Ireland Senior Football Champions 2001.

INDEX OF AUTHORS AND ARTICLES